NOKIA – The Inside Story

NOKIA

The Inside Story

MARTTI HÄIKIÖ

An imprint of Pearson Education

London Boston Indianapolis New York Mexico City Toronto Tokyo Singapore
Hong Kong Cape Town New Delhi Madrid Paris Amsterdam Munich Milan Stockholm

First published in 2001 in Finnish by Edita Plc as *Nokia Oyj:n historia*
English translation © Nokia and Edita Plc, 2002
First published in Great Britain by Pearson Education by arrangement with
Nokia and Edita Plc, in 2002.

The right of Martti Häikiö to be identified as the Author of this
Work has been asserted by him in accordance with the Copyright, Designs
and Patents Act 1988.

ISBN 0-273-65983-9

British Library Cataloguing in Publication Data
A CIP catalogue record for this book can be obtained from
the British Library.

Library of Congress Cataloging in Publication Data
Applied for.

10 9 8 7 6 5 4 3 2 1

Design: Edita Publishing Ltd./Petteri Kivekäs, Mika Huovinen
Translated by Olli V. Virtanen
Adapted for the English language edition by Michael Johnson
Typeset in Finland by Edita Publishing Ltd.
Printed and bound by Rotolito Lombarda, Italy.
The Publishers' policy is to use paper manufactured from sustainable forests.

Table of contents

Foreword

Throughout its long and colorful life, Nokia has featured prominently in Finnish history and more recently in global business history. The company has transformed itself and expanded so rapidly that even people who are close to it sometimes have difficulty grasping the whole picture. Therefore the Board of Directors decided in January 1997 to commission a corporate history that would tell the full story from the beginning – from the 1860s – to the 21st century. The complete history was published in the Finnish language at the end of 2001, comprising three volumes: *The Merger*, covering the evolution of early businesses into a Finnish conglomerate from 1865 to 1982; *Sturm und Drang*, covering major acquisitions and the building of a European electronics company from 1983 to 1991; and *Globalization*, the story of Nokia's emergence as a global telecommunications company from 1992 to 2001.

This book is drawn from the three volumes and adapted for the international audience. Both the full history and this book were authored by Martti Häikiö, senior lecturer at Helsinki University, to whom I extend my warmest thanks. Dr. Häikiö was given free access to Nokia personnel and documents for his research, and was assured of editorial independence. He was supported by a History Committee that included Professor Edward Andersson as chairman, Casimir Ehrnrooth and Sakari Salminen as members and Harry Collin as secretary. Edward Andersson was a member of the Board of Nokia from 1973–2000, Casimir Ehrnrooth was a member of the Board from 1989–1999 and served as chairman of the Board from 1992–1999, Sakari Salminen was a member of the Executive Board in charge of Telecommunications from 1986–1993 and Harry Collin was secretary of the Board of Directors and Executive Board from 1974–1996. I also took part in the work of the History Committee.

The purpose of the book is to provide well-researched and reliable information about the company in its various stages of development. It is written for the general reader interested in the company's history as well as for Nokia's personnel, investors and other stakeholders.

Jorma Ollila
Nokia Chairman and CEO

Acknowledgements

I wish to extend my warmest thanks to Nokia's History Committee as well as to the company's management and personnel. It has been a pleasure to work in such an open and encouraging environment.

For his contributions to the historical accuracy of the cables and rubber businesses, I reserve a special thanks to Dr. Juhana Aunesluoma. I am also grateful to the numerous people who have read parts of the manuscript and helped me with their detailed and useful comments.

At the production stage I have been grateful to teams led by Lauri Kivinen, Nokia's senior vice president of Corporate Communications, Dr. Jukka-Pekka Pietiäinen, publication manager at Edita, and Michael Strang of Pearson Education, the English-language publisher of this book.

Olli V. Virtanen translated this condensed version of the book. And I would like to extend a special thanks to Michael Johnson, who edited it, for his close and inspirational cooperation.

Responsibility for any shortcomings in this book is mine alone. But luckily I have not been alone in writing it; thank you Tytti, Onni and Toivo.

Martti Häikiö
Helsinki, January 2002

Understanding Nokia's explosive growth

Nokia is nothing less than a national institution in Finland because of its contribution to the national economy and its long history, but the keen interest in the company today stems more from its recent success as Finland's first real world-class corporation.

Yet this global role has been achieved so quickly and so quietly that the story of Nokia's rise to world prominence is little understood. Outsiders are fascinated by the Nokia story, as am I, and I shall tell it from my historian's perch in a way that provides a clear and complete record, focussing especially on the past 25 years.

In the opening three chapters I attempt to answer some of the most frequently asked questions about the company, with a more detailed account to follow in later chapters. Links are indicated in the text for quick reference to the detailed story.

Unlike many other published articles, books and studies of Nokia, this history was made possible in large part by unlimited access to documents in Nokia's files, most of them confidential until now. As a historian and researcher, I have applied academic rigor to these and all other sources of information.

I was offered the opportunity by Nokia to write an honest, complete and credible history of the company, and was able to operate without interference from any quarter. I had a free hand to pick and choose the areas I would examine. Over five years, I tracked down and interviewed numerous past and present executives and other players around the Nokia story, and had their personal files at my disposal. Based on this largely untapped wealth of material, I published at the end of 2001 a 975-page, fully documented Finnish-language history of Nokia, covering the period from 1865 to the end of 2000. The volume at hand is an abridged English-language edition of that book.

The logos of three original companies that formed Nokia Corporation, in 1967. The oldest was Nokia Ab (est. 1865) in the forest industry and power production. Suomen Gummitehdas Oy (Finnish Rubber Works, est. 1898) was manufacturing galoshes and other rubber products, and Suomen Kaapelitehdas Oy (Finnish Cable Works, est. 1912) was producing telephone and power cables. The current Nokia logo dates from 1992. The arrows were later dropped.

To be credible and have sustainable value, a good history must cover all relevant aspects of its subject, including the bad judgments and wrong turns. Nokia has had its moments of glory but also has seen times of grave crisis, at times facing the dangers of hostile takeover or financial ruin. All the major ups and downs are in this book. Painful events such as the death of Chief Executive Kari Kairamo by his own hand, the confusing corporate governance situation in 1986–1992, and the massive losses of the Consumer Electronics division are described as accurately as present documents and sources allow.

Secrets of success

● Of course one question soars above all others: What explains Nokia's phenomenal rise to the status of a global giant in the 1990s? Even as I described the company's earlier stages, I could feel that the story was overshadowed by that all-embracing question.

It is a long and complex story. From its early years, Nokia was an important part of Finnish industrial history. Beginning in the late 1980s, it was among the leaders in Europe's industrial development, and in the 1990s became a major player on the global stage. The issue of moving away from Finland closer to customers and sources of international money has arisen over and over but management has always come down in favor of staying home. Nokia is a Finnish company and proud of it. The gleaming new "Nokia House" corporate headquarters at Keilalahti in the seaside town of Espoo on the outskirts of Helsinki is an architectural landmark.

Nokia's dynamic evolution is a story of how visionary industrial thinking and courageous decisions have enabled a company on the edge of Western Europe to grow rapidly into a truly global force. Investors, customers and business partners throughout the world have been touched by the Nokia story and undoubtedly will continue to be. For Nokia is the kind of company that thinks of, plans for, and influences the future of its industry.

Nokia is the first Finnish brand to be recognized by the general public throughout the world. In its home market, Nokia and its antecedent companies have ranked among the biggest for decades. So perhaps the question should be: How did a large Finnish company grow first into a European force, then rise to the status of global giant? A key part of the answer is the management's business acumen and its ability to reinvent the company continuously around sectors that seemed the most promising at the time – even if this meant divesting businesses that once formed the very core of the firm.

A second theme in this book is the interaction between technological and organizational innovations, as well as between profit-oriented business operations and the regulatory measures of public authorities.

Accumulation of knowledge is a characteristic feature in the history of technology. New inventions borrow from older ones and eventually replace them. Yet industrial success is also about people and organizations. Their knowledge does not accumulate the same way. I have become convinced that a political system cannot produce technological innovation, but it can do a great deal to prohibit, slow down and create obstacles to it. The process of adoption of innovations is a fruitful area for further research.

Business economics forms a third theme, a kind of gray area between technology and people. It is a mix of science and emotion. On the one hand it represents security, clarity and sustainability. On the other hand it encompasses human weaknesses such as inexperience, prejudice and dreams.

Business and politics

● The development of new technologies depends not only on technical features and commercial opportunities but also on political decisions. Cellular telephone technology offers a prime example of how to operate in this labyrinth. While digitalization of voice is based on technological progress, the allocation of radio frequencies and deregulation is pure politics. Any company's performance in this sector depends upon a mix of those two forces.

In this book I am examining Nokia's strategy primarily from the point of view of the owners and management. One of the key issues deals with the question of the conglomerate: How best to choose the business areas in which it ought to invest? Secondly the book aims to shed light on the internal business logic and major events taking place in the various business areas. Corporate governance, the functions of top management and large shareowners, are also covered extensively. This includes the ownership structure, shareholders' impact on Nokia's management, roles and responsibilities of the various governing bodies, as well as the organization and functioning of top management. All of these have had a profound impact on the company's history.

In these pages I also describe those circumstances, external decisions and realities that have influenced Nokia's operating environment. Nokia had to adapt to changing circumstances, but it has also been able and willing to shape the external environment.

It is important that all decisions made during Nokia's extensive history be examined against a framework of Finnish, global and political circumstances prevailing at the time. The 137-year history of Nokia spans world wars and revolutions. There have been closed and regulated economies, and also periods of deregulation. At times galloping inflation and sky-high interest rates played havoc with financing strategies, which were then followed by deflation and low interest rates. Deep recessions and overheated economies have by turns kept businesses on their toes. Finland has looked toward the East at the time of the Cold War, then turned to the West as it became a member of the European Union. And finally, Nokia is equally familiar with protectionism and the economic freedom of globalization.

If this book has a message for others seeking success, it would be a plea for flexibility and open-mindedness. Only with those qualities can a company in today's volatile global environment hope to prosper.

To simplify this story for the non-European reader I often use the name 'Nokia' rather freely to describe the company in its past incarnations, its present structure, and for some of its joint ventures and divisions.

And to make financial discussions simpler to follow, all euro conversions are calculated on average 2000 exchange rates unless otherwise specified.

Nokia and its predecessor companies

THREE INDEPENDENT COMPANIES

1865	1898	1912
Nokia Forest and Power 1865–1966	Finnish Rubber Works 1898–1966 (Suomen Gummitehdas Osakeyhtiö, Suomen Kumitehdas Osakeyhtiö)	Finnish Cable Works Suomen Punomoteh- das Osakeyhtiö 1912–1916 Suomen Kaapelitehdas Osakeyhtiö 1917–1966

THE DE FACTO GROUP OWNED BY RUBBER WORKS

Nokia Forest and Power	1918	Finnish Rubber Works	1922	Finnish Cable Works

OFFICIAL MERGER 1967

Nokia Corporation
(Oy Nokia Ab
1966–1997
Nokia Oyj 1.9.1997–)

NOKIA CORPORATION IN 2002

Nokia Mobile Phones (NMP)

Nokia Networks (NET)

Nokia Ventures Organization (NVO)

Nokia Research Center (NRC)

Nokia Mobile Phones 1989– Nokia-Mobira 1986–1989 Mobira 1979–1986	Nokia Networks 1999– Nokia Telecommunications 1992–1999 Telenokia 1981–1992 Televa 1976–1981

CHAPTER 1

The fading of
time and place?

I n my view, the third industrial revolution, the breakthrough of computers and telecommunications in which Nokia played a part, has been
somewhat oversold as 'the fading of time and place'. Curiously, the very
same words were used to explain the impact of the expansion of railway
networks in the 19th century. Faster land transport led people to believe
that the fundamentals of the economy had somehow changed, and that
time and place would never be the same.

In discussing the 1990s we face the same question about whether fundamental change has taken place, and the answer is 'yes and no'. It is true
that telecommunications has become vitally important, it has widespread
influence on the economy and on personal life, and indeed it has turned
into one of the world's leading industries. Yet there is a difference compared to the advances of the 19th century. Although the mobile telephone and Internet connections can reach the remotest parts of the globe,
they have hardly 'faded time and place', let alone altered the fundamentals of the industrial world.

Nokia's operating environment brought major changes in the 1990s, but
not nearly as great as those ten years earlier, not to mention the changes in the
second decade of the 20th century or in the 1940s when the world wars
redrew the map of Europe and Asia. In many respects, this is a story of
continuity. Three companies – Suomen Gummitehdas Oy (Finnish Rubber
Works), Nokia Ab, and Suomen Kaapelitehdas Oy (Finnish Cable Works) –
formed the roots of Nokia (see Chapter 4). They were all industrial companies, as is Nokia today. The modern Nokia manufactures and sells industrial
products that require substantial expertise, as did the antecedent companies.

The computer emerged as the primary industrial engine in the 1980s.
It launched the 'third industrial revolution' much like the first revolution
was powered by the steam engine at the beginning of the 19th century,

The Snake Game is a prime example of how the use of industrial products assumes unpredictable forms. Other features in mobile phones include (among many others) the clock, a calendar, short message facility, wake-up calls and a calculator. The Snake Game is the most popular; competitions are organized with rankings of the best scores.

and the second revolution was driven by electricity at the beginning of 20th. The fundamentals of the economy still remain. Structural changes are brought about by inventions, tremendous growth figures in new business areas, variations in obstacles to world trade and national regulatory measures – and, of course, speculation on the stock markets.

The rise to global prominence

● My primary interest in this book is Nokia's industrial activity, how its businesses have evolved and changed, how its operational results have developed at various junctures, how research and development have been carried out and how the company has been managed.

Nokia became a world-class corporation during the second half of the 1990s, riding mainly on the back of the growth of telecommunications. Three factors have contributed to the development:

- Deregulation of operators opened competition in the field of telecommunications equipment, previously controlled by national telecom monopolies.
- Analog communications technology gradually gave way to digital technology, enabling operators to offer a host of new services and creating a steadily expanding market.
- The pan-European GSM (Global System for Mobile Communications) cellular phone standard networks first introduced in 1991 grew rapidly both in geographical scope and in functions offered.

Thus the Nokia phenomenon can be somewhat simplistically explained in one sentence: Nokia became successful in the 1990s because telecom operators in several countries needed network equipment and phones based on the new GSM technology and they needed it fast.

Nokia's timing at this transition point was ideal. In the 1990s, the company managed to capitalize on rising demand in Europe, then repeat this success globally. It achieved a trailblazing position in technology, production efficiency, design and marketing. This can partly be explained by the experience Nokia and its wireless communications acquisition Mobira had in the cellular phone markets dating from the beginning of the 1980s. In addition Nokia could tap into its experience of building telephone networks and exchanges since the 1970s.

Also, in the 1980s, the deregulatory political winds out of the United States and the United Kingdom introduced competition to the telecom operator sector that previously had been controlled by national monopolies. New operators quickly adopted the latest technology, forcing

The opening ceremony of the new factory of Beijing Capitel Nokia Mobile Telecommunications Company (BNMT) and Xingwang (International) Industrial Park in December 2001. From right to left Mr. Antti Wäre, general manager of BNMT, Urpo Karjalainen, president of Nokia (China) Investment Co. Ltd., Veli Sundbäck, member of Nokia Executive Board, Ouyang Zhongmou, president of China Putian Corporation, Sauli Niinistö, minister of finance, Finland, Nokia CEO Jorma Ollila, Li Rongrong, minister of the State Economic and Trade Commission, Zhang Mao, vice mayor of Beijing, Wei Jianguo, vice minister of Foreign Trade Economic Commission, Susan Fan, executive vice chairman of Nokia (China) Investment Co. Ltd.

Jenni Hannula working on Nokia's 100 millionth mobile phone at the Salo plant in Finland.

established operators to react by updating their networks and systems. Combined with the introduction of GSM, this provided equipment manufacturers with a growing market.

With hindsight, we can date the beginning of the modern Nokia success story rather precisely. Nokia received its first GSM network order in Finland in the spring of 1989 from Radiolinja Oy, the network operator established in the previous autumn by the country's private regional telephone companies. Inaugurated on July 1, 1991, Radiolinja was able to create the world's first GSM network – thanks in large part to Nokia and its equipment. Soon Nokia received large network orders from the United Kingdom, Europe, and subsequently throughout the world.

Meeting the management challenges

● But these are external factors. Another element of the success was the strength of Nokia's internal operations, and here we have seen the company confront a series of management challenges. Three crises dogged Nokia's operations in the 1990s, and recovery from each of them improved the company's competitiveness. The management team that led

Nokia through the 1990s and into the 21st century had weathered major storms.

The most important lessons were drawn from the company crisis of 1987–1992. The roles of share ownership and executive management became mingled for several reasons, distorting the corporate governance mechanism. In addition both Telecommunications and Mobile Phones, the core business groups of Nokia in the 1990s, suffered unrelated crises, but each bounced back with improved efficiency.

The Telecommunications division faced the moment of truth in 1991. Profitable trade with the Soviet Union collapsed while Finland dived into a deep domestic recession that was worsened by the downturn in western markets. As a result, the Telecommunications division had to re-evaluate and redirect its operations. This enabled it to transfer experienced telecom people to the emerging GSM markets and thus strengthen resources in that area. The Mobile Phones division suffered its own severe crisis in logistics in the mid-1990s. This led to a similar re-evaluation and reorganization of production, sourcing, internal communications, inventory, financial management and several other critical functions.

Another key element in maintaining growth in the 1990s was the constant and vigorous investment in research and development. Strong R&D is essential in a field of technology where product lifespans are ever shorter (see Chapter 8). A further significant factor was Nokia's design and adoption of the common platform principle, which provides a basis for a growing and changing the product portfolio by simplifying the technology and allowing economies of scale in production.

Nokia's focus on two key industries – handsets and network equipment – is based on both internal decisions and external circumstances.

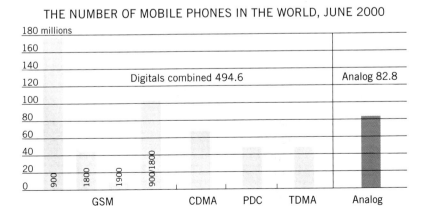

THE NUMBER OF MOBILE PHONES IN THE WORLD, JUNE 2000

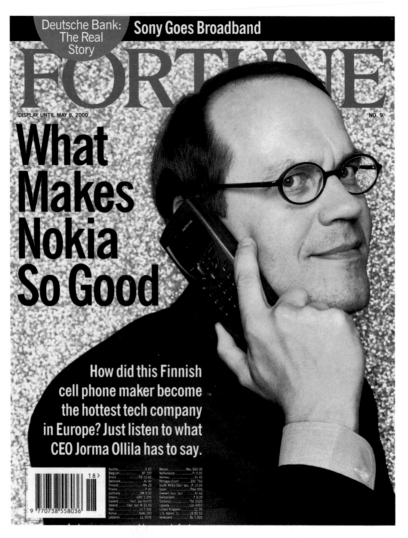

On the magazine cover:

Deutsche Bank: The Real Story

Sony Goes Broadband

FORTUNE

DISPLAY UNTIL MAY 8, 2000   NO. 9

What Makes Nokia So Good

How did this Finnish cell phone maker become the hottest tech company in Europe? Just listen to what CEO Jorma Ollila has to say.

Nokia's rapid rise on the stock markets since 1997 has made Jorma Ollila a familiar name in the international press. Yet, he has strictly limited his interviews and other appearances for the industry and corporate affairs.

Burgeoning demand in the liberalized telecommunications markets helped guide strategy. And throwing off the conglomerate structure that had prevailed since 1966 required a rethink about where the company was going and how it would get there.

Mobile phone sales had gradually assumed a key position among Nokia's businesses. With sales growing at 30–50 percent per year throughout the 1980s and well into the 1990s, profits had risen impressively in the early 1990s, and within a few years mobile phones had become one of the group's two main business areas.

By the mid-1990s, handsets were small enough and inexpensive enough to advance from the category of business tools to consumer goods with much larger market potential. With its successful market segmentation and a popular product portfolio, Nokia became the world's leading mobile phone manufacturer in 1998. Since then, each year Nokia has increased its lead.

Changes in the ownership structure helped pave the way for growth. The Finnish banks that had been for so long the dominant owners of Nokia often disagreed on key issues, including the company's financial needs. Gradually the share ownership became much more diversified. Foreign, and particularly US, institutional and retail investors today make up a sizable majority of the Nokia shareholder base.

The Ollila touch

● Nokia's success in the 1990s cannot be explained without evaluating the role of management. Overcoming strong external pressures and internal conflicts, the current team succeeded in building a strategy, a corporate culture and modus operandi that provided a structure for successful R&D as well as efficient production and sales. Under the direction of President and Chief Executive Officer Jorma Ollila, this was accomplished in a highly cost-conscious environment.

Ollila, a trained engineer and economist, focussed on profitable growth areas and management of the elements of growth. He stabilized the company's ownership by creating fluent and open relations with shareholders, and built a productive top management team while also inspiring employees. All the while, he kept the levers of change firmly under his control.

Nokia's future was now in the hands of a self-effacing but firm executive who was well prepared for the job. People who know him better regard Ollila as a very social person. He likes to run his affairs through personal contact on the phone, not on paper. He has extensive political contacts, as well as an active network of top business colleagues around the world. His ideas are often generated in informal gatherings, and he keeps in contact with colleagues by telephone, small pieces of paper and by e-mail.

Ollila did not regard Kari Kairamo, his predecessor and a highly charismatic figure, as a role model. In public appearances and speeches

Ollila prefers carefully constructed arguments. He shies away from social events, and the outside world knows little about his private life. For distraction, Ollila plays tennis, but not golf, the customary activity for his corporate peers. He has also become a keen hunter in the Finnish forests, much like the old-time Nordic patriarchs.

As a leader of people, Ollila combines the roles of orchestra conductor and solo violinist. He is the one who determines the tempo and leads the music, but at the same time he has devolved considerable freedom and responsibility to lower levels.

As opposed to a number of other executives, Ollila has been selective in accepting board memberships in other companies. His current board positions include Ford Motor Company, UPM-Kymmene (the Finnish forest products group) and Otava Books and Magazines Ltd. (the Finnish publishing house).

Learning from the past

● It was perhaps the trying experiences of the 1980s and 1990s that explain Ollila's no-nonsense corporate culture. Nokia is known as a desirable place to work but one that makes heavy demands on each employee's performance. Management communicates early on and openly with employees and investors to avoid misunderstandings when problems arise. Part of the Nokia culture is efficient implementation, and management strives to ensure that decisions are followed through. In the same vein, Ollila aims to reduce the gap between corporate vision and market reality. This does not mean lowering targets, but rather ensuring the viability of objectives.

The company seems to have acted wisely in the 1990s, refraining from costly acquisitions of the type it had made in the 1980s. Instead, the company built up its own knowhow by investing in R&D both in mobile phones and telecommunications. Thus Nokia was ready for the wave of deregulation that created global telecom markets. But it was digital technology that opened the floodgates for new services, and the emergence of mobile phones as a mass-market product.

Comparison of Nokia's rise with the lessons found in the classics of economics is striking in the case of *Capitalism, Socialism and Democracy* (1942) by Joseph Schumpeter. The Schumpeter book lists the same core elements of capitalism that can be found behind Nokia's success more than half a century later: production of consumer goods at constantly lower production costs to increasingly larger markets; continuous innovation of products and organization – not price – as the key element of profitability, and even creative destruction (in Nokia's case in 1988–1991) which forms the basis for renewal.

As a world-class industrial company, Nokia has followed in the footsteps of two great models in the previous industrial revolution. First, the invention of the mass-market automobile which saw Henry Ford simplify the production line to achieve lower costs. Second is the talent of Alfred Sloan, the mastermind of General Motors' complex organization. He diversified and controlled the company systematically through key performance figures and credible argumentation.

Alfred Sloan is as good a model for Jorma Ollila as anybody. Mobile phones became a consumer goods industry during Ollila's tenure and new models were brought to market annually to suit various consumer segments. Marketing and branding were key elements while the organization was refined and restructured constantly to match changing circumstances. Driving all this was the explosive growth of a new product – the mobile phone – as was the case with the automobile in the 1920s–1950s.

When one competitor succeeds in fierce competition and others lag behind, the reasons lie not only with the winner's strategy but also with that of its competitors. I must emphasize that this is not a comparative study. Nevertheless the picture of the mobile phone markets in the 1990s would not be complete without a detailed comparison. It must one day include the decline of Motorola, the market leader in the early 1990s, and the difficulties of Ericsson, the dominant telecommunications company for several decades. To tell that story fully, however, we must await their respective documented histories.

Finland's information technology culture

● To find the answer to Nokia's success, one cannot avoid the question of Finland's role in it. How much has the country of origin contributed to this miracle? True, today Nokia has distanced itself from the mother country in terms of sales and share ownership. In both categories, Finland accounts for just a few percentage points. On the other hand Nokia's top management and technological expertise are predominantly homegrown. Nokia's Executive Board comprises only Finns, creating a homogenous working culture.

More than one-third of the total Nokia workforce is in R&D, and two-thirds of these are based in Finland. Nokia's management capability, telecommunications research and training are therefore deeply rooted in Finland.

Toward the end of 1990s, Nokia assumed a pivotal role in the program to develop Finland's higher education resources in information technology, and in the donation of equipment for the program. This initiative grew rapidly, and its scale soon equaled that of a mid-sized university. This partly explains why Nokia has remained true to its heritage and stayed in Finland (see page 116).

Nokia's home turf has also provided a receptive marketplace for the company's pioneering products. Finland is one of the world's leading countries in mobile phone penetration and computer usage. The country's high penetration figures have attracted as much international interest as does Finland's Winter War with Russia (1939–1940) and *Kalevala*, the national epic on emerging nationalism. Nokia's rise in the business world is perhaps the economic equivalent of these in terms of survivalism and mythology.

I have deliberately tried to avoid terms such as 'information society' and 'new economy', although the Nokia name is often attached to both. In fact neither can be defined in a universally accepted way. In this book I use the term 'information society' merely to describe the proliferation of computers as well as telecommunications networks and the Internet. A broader definition of the telecommunications sector would include data communication networks, or infrastructure, and terminals, software and the transfer of content. Combined, these make up the world's fastest-growing industry.

'Information society' is perhaps best described by negation, explaining what it is not. The rise in the level of education, and the obscure definition of knowledge, has often been raised in this context. I don't think they are particularly relevant to the information society. Instead education and knowledge continue a process begun centuries ago. Likewise the volume and speed in production and delivery of information do not describe this era adequately. Quantitative measurement of information does not provide a key to the mystery of information society.

Exports of electric and electronic products as percentage of Finland's industrial exports and the total exports in FIM billion
(euros in parentheses, deflated to 2000 value)

1960	1 %	2.9	(0.05)
1970	2 %	9.2	(10.4)
1980	4 %	51.3	(19.8)
1990	12 %	100.0	(20.2)
2000	32 %	288.0	(48.4)

The electric and electronics products industry created 24,000 new jobs in 1994–97

Nokia Networks' Sonera Business Team in September 2001. From left: Jari Toivo, Timo Uusimäki, Satu Pöntinen, Pekka Poutanen, Yvonne Sterman, Esa Kesänen, Elina Herttonen and Kristina Glushkova.

As in my previous research on such subjects as data transfer, the liberalization of energy markets and the emergence of GSM mobile phone operator business, it is the interdependence of three elements – technological innovation, commercial enterprise and political regulation – that form the nucleus of the history of Nokia. Each development has been analyzed against these questions: Was it due to technological innovation, change in the business enterprise, or action by public authorities?

Traditionally all countries had kept a tight rein on telecommunications for two reasons. First, control of communications is a strategic defense issue. Second, radio frequencies are a limited resource that are allocated by an established international procedure. Finland broke free because it became one of the first countries in the 1980s to open competition in all areas of telecommunications. Indeed, my main thesis is that Finland became a leader and an innovator in the global information arena due to the early deregulation of its home market and breakthroughs in the digital era. Competition then drove its rapid development and adaptation of advanced technology products and services.

A legacy of open competition

● Competition came naturally to Finland. Early on, there were two major operator groupings: the state-run Post and Telegraph Administration (renamed Tele, then Sonera), and private regional telephone cooperatives. The former had a monopoly in telegraph, trunk and international calls, mobile phone calls as well as local calls in its operating area. The latter enjoyed a monopoly in local calls in their respective operating areas. Furthermore, Finnish industry enjoyed a competitive edge as each grouping procured its equipment through open tenders. In other words Finland has always been an open market: domestic and foreign suppliers have competed for contracts with both camps.

Finnish public authorities including the cabinet, Parliament and the Ministry of Communications managed to open the markets in a controlled manner. Consequently they never had to scale back the process. At the end of the 1990s, Finnish officials still found themselves having to defend liberalization at the level of the European Union when other more restrictive countries wanted to rein in the process.

Deregulation nevertheless gathered speed in Finland with the advent of innovations such as telefax and data communications. These required new legislation, which came into effect as early as 1987. That year marks a turning point. The same year, political decisions launched competition in the fastest growing business, mobile telephony, as well as in international calls, trunk calls and local calls.

Granting licenses to competing operators prompted these players to embark on innovations, and eventually new businesses. The Helsinki Telephone Association (currently Elisa Communications) was refused a license to operate in the Nordic Mobile Telephone (NMT) network, the analog first generation wireless telephone technology. However, together with other regional telephone companies and corporate users of new services, it established Radiolinja in 1988, which won a license for the new mobile phone network based on GSM technology. A fierce political fight preceded the decision, and hectic competition followed.

Impetus for investment

● In many cases new operators seemed to be more prepared to adopt the latest technology than the established ones because existing operators were focussed on earning back their original investment. Thus Radiolinja

NOKIA'S SHARE OF FINLAND'S EXPORTS AND GDP

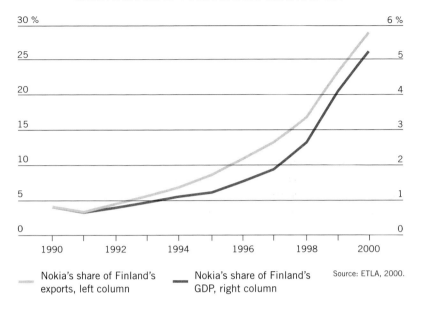

Nokia's share of Finland's exports, left column

Nokia's share of Finland's GDP, right column

Source: ETLA, 2000.

embarked on the construction of the digital GSM network while the state-owned Tele was stuck with its monopoly in the analog NMT network. NMT was a significant innovation involving all the Nordic state telecom monopolies. This concept later helped untangle several key questions in the field of international radio telecommunications. NMT operated at two frequencies, first at 450 MHz, and later at 900 MHz. When inaugurated in 1981 the NMT capacity was expected to match demand until the mid-1990s. However, without the introduction of GSM, demand for mobile phones would have exceeded network capacity in just a few years.

One of the biggest events in Finland's recent industrial history took place in April 1989 when Radiolinja placed its first order with Nokia for a GSM network. This order provided Nokia with an important reference case attracting considerable international attention when GSM rapidly gained ground, largely thanks to its versatility. It can accommodate a constantly increasing number of users as well as technical innovations and new products and services (see Chapter 11).

In the context of the zeitgeist (the spirit of the times), it is worth noting that the most significant breakthrough in the world of information societies took place in 1989–1991 when at the same time as the two Germanys merged, the Cold War came to an end, centralized economies were buried and the European Union emerged as the most cohesive European force.

The mobile phone revolution, as the second major phase in the industry was called, started in the mid-1990s. While up until then the construction of networks and handsets continued to grow at a steady pace, the market was still largely a domain for business users. But the handsets were becoming smaller and smaller. The fixed carphone model became portable, then fitted into a briefcase, and soon into a pocket. At the same time, prices dropped and network coverage expanded, making the cellphone a mass-market product all over the world in the second half of the 1990s. Nokia already had one foot in this new era.

Meanwhile, the telecommunications sector was in constant flux with revolutionary innovations sprouting up in quick succession. Communication between computers through modems gave birth to data communications and the network became the arteries of modern society. The invention of fiber-optic cables increased network capacity thousands of times over and simultaneously brought prices down dramatically.

The increased capacity and cheaper price also paved the way for the latest development in telecommunications, the Internet. With the addition of mobility, telephones become as popular as wristwatches, and the combination of the two opens the way for access to the Internet anywhere, any time. We are clearly talking about a new era.

Deregulation spreads across Europe

● As a result of deregulation, a constant stream of new operators entered the markets. One of the most challenging questions of the research for this book was how deregulation spread so rapidly. What forces drove authorities to remove obstacles in the 1980s, facilitating the explosive growth of the industry in the 1990s, is a fascinating and difficult topic, but one that is beyond the scope of this book.

The field of telecommunications includes three groupings – operators, equipment manufacturers and regulators. The most important grouping is the operators, who aim to attract paying customers to services on their networks. Operators offer services by building networks on which they carry voice and data. For this purpose operators purchase infrastructure, i.e. networks and systems developed by equipment manufacturers. The equipment includes digital switching, radio base stations and base station controllers as well as handsets. Consumers only purchase handsets.

The fixed copper wire or fiber-optic networks that traditionally have carried voice have expanded to carry data and other information services.

The new mobile and digital era brought about new services – a prime example is the Short Message Services (SMS), which annually amounts to billions of messages in Finland – a country of five million people.

It is easier to describe the expansion of deregulation than to explain its birth. Anti-trust legislation in the United States goes back to the beginning of the 20th century and the court cases against John D. Rockefeller's oil interests. The slicing up of AT&T into 'Baby Bells' by the US authorities in the mid-1980s directly follows from the first anti-trust cases. Another root of deregulation originates in Britain where Conservative Prime Minister Margaret Thatcher adopted the principles of the Milton Friedman 'Chicago school' of monetarism. As per her strong political convictions, competition and market forces were to be introduced into as many areas of the public sector as possible.

The European Community (later European Union) began to awaken from its 'Eurosclerosis' in the early 1980s, marking another key phase in deregulation. The EU gradually moved toward uniformity and true common markets, making a great impact on telecommunications. The GSM mobile phone standard was arguably one of the EU's most successful achievements, but globally the problem is more complex. Currently, the most pressing battles in communications concern the creation of international standards, and the technical architecture of the third generation mobile phones. Global telecom companies are in constant turf fights all over the world.

The more I have studied the present change and the more research I have accumulated, the better I like the definition the 'third industrial revolution' – emphasis on the traditional word 'industrial'. The air is dense with hyperbole – superlatives and phenomena without precise content. This is why the history of Nokia is best regarded as a straightforward industrial history, an analysis of the development, production and sale of industrial products.

Products made by Nokia have enjoyed very strong demand in recent years, and they have played a part in the transformation of Finnish society, and even the world. Yet before comparing Nokia's impact on any society, cellphones should be compared with two earlier industrial revolutions. Inventions such as the steam engine, electricity, the automobile, television, the jet engine – and the fixed line telephone – have transformed human life even more than the mobile phone.

From an individual citizen's perspective, I would be inclined to brush all these aside and elevate television above the rest as it truly shrank the globe and changed the nature of local communities by opening their windows onto the global village.

CHAPTER 2

Managing change in a dynamic market

The history of Nokia includes a range of management styles brought in by executives whose backgrounds and operating methods reflect the gradual change from owner-dominated management to more professional managers. Each generation had its own approach to business and each managed change in its own way.

- Fredrik Idestam, founder of Nokia Ab and its forest products industry, was a typical patriarchal owner-entrepreneur in the last decades of the 19th century. He was not shy about pulling strings in society to develop the industry and safeguard its growth.
- Eduard Polón, the long-serving head of the rubber industry, was an equally adroit influence-peddler, but he was first an entrepreneur and later became an owner. Polón can be credited with building the Nokia group when his rubber company, Suomen Gummitehdas Oy (the Rubber Works), bought a majority of Nokia Ab and Suomen Kaapelitehdas Oy (the Cable Works).
- Torsten Westerlund, the well-educated chief executive of the Rubber Works, was a typical manager representing owners in the 1930s–1950s.
- Björn Westerlund, son of Torsten, also represented owners as chief executive of the Cable Works and later Nokia Corporation, but in addition, he introduced management professionalism in the early days of the merged group in the 1960s and 1970s. During his tenure Nokia's four main business areas – cables, rubber, paper and electronics – operated independently while he took charge of profitability, investment allocation and making sure that inventory did not grow excessively and tie up capital.
- Kari Kairamo had no shares in Nokia Corporation but his

heritage, which included several leading Finnish industrialists, was surely instrumental in his rise to top positions. Kairamo's great-grand-father, Alfred Kihlman, was one of the icons of Finnish industry.

Kairamo's tenure at the helm of Nokia went through two phases. During the first part, from his appointment as president in 1977 until 1983, he continued on the path laid out by his predecessor. In those years Kairamo did not initiate major change, nor did he challenge the grip of the main owner, Union Bank of Finland. In the latter part of Kairamo's tenure (in 1983–1988) things were different. He began with a major internal reor-ganization and aggressive acquisitions. The aim was to internationalize the group, shift the focus to electronics, and strengthen the position of the operational management by the appointment of an internal Board of Directors in 1986.

Objectives of growth and international expansion were placed on all business areas, and none of them were shed from the group. The over-riding business idea was to build a giant conglomerate. Nokia became a kind of a holding group whose top management periodically embarked on aggressive interventions in selected business areas without observing cohesive management systems.

Although Kairamo's era included deep difficulties for the group, his inspirational and uncomplicated management style attracted young, competent and internationally minded staff. He set the company on a course toward the great multinational companies, and modern Nokia has continued to take long strides down that road. Sadly, Kairamo com-mitted suicide in 1988 amid circumstances that remain somewhat mysterious.

Seeking diversity

● Nokia's commitment to things electric and electronic goes back many years, well before the recent focus on wireless networks and handsets. As early as 1900, Nokia Ab, then predominantly a forest products company, expanded its power-generation facilities beyond its own requirements and entered the energy market. The roots of cable manufacturing, Nokia's largest business area until the end of 1980s, reach back to 1912 when a company called Suomen Punomotehdas (later to be called Suomen Kaapelitehdas, or Finnish Cable Works) was established. This business was integral to the transfer of electricity, voice and data.

Prior to the Kairamo era, Björn Westerlund as head of the Cable Works aspired to diversify its operations and established an electronics presence in 1960. Preparations for this were made by Olli Lehto, then a mathematician at the Cable Works. The main businesses of the department were the importation of large-scale computers, a computation center based on those computers and manufacture of its own electronic equipment. The manufacturing activity was considerably smaller than the others, particularly in profitability.

With the merger of the cable business with the forest and rubber industries in 1966, Westerlund became president and CEO of the group, and electronics was elevated and separated into a new division. It was still rather modest in size, accounting for less than 4 percent of group sales in 1967 – and that was mainly generated by computer imports.

Equipment production developed gradually in the 1960s, complemented by the massive project of building a control system for a nuclear power station, the first tentative steps in building computers, as well as the creation of an information system for banks. The first telecom infrastructure products were in transmission equipment. In the mid-1970s Nokia took the visionary decision to commence production of telephone exchanges, in direct competition with Ericsson and Siemens, the dominant players in the field. In retrospect this proved to be an important decision since mastering the total mobile telecommunication systems – including base stations, exchanges and handsets – was to become the company's crucial competitive advantage.

Nokia's growth in electronics took two separate routes. Telecommunications and handset manufacturing grew mainly organically, and to a lesser extent through acquisitions such as Televa in 1981 and Mobira in 1983. Consumer electronics was primarily built through acquisitions (Salora-Luxor in 1983, Oceanic in 1987 and SEL in 1988). The same applies to computers and data processing (Ericsson-Data in 1988). Two men deserve a mention here: Kurt Wikstedt built Nokia Electronics as its first head during the first two decades while Sakari Salminen, head of the Telecommunications division, exerted a strong influence on the development of the telecommunications activity.

Troubled waters ahead

● Nokia management has not always been so capable of controlling events. The tenure of Simo Vuorilehto as Nokia's president and CEO in 1988–1992 is perhaps the most difficult period in the company's recent

British Prime Minister John Major, Simo Vuorilehto (right) and Jorma Ollila (left) at the Nokia Telecommucations Official Opening in April 1992 in London. Second from left: Michael Phillips of Nokia.

history. It saw the collapse of Finland's trade with the Soviet Union in 1991, the beginning of a deep recession in Finland, retrenchment in many of the key export markets, and finally the realization that huge losses were building up in Consumer Electronics. Vuorilehto had the delicate task of cutting out the excess personnel and capacity left behind from the massive acquisitions in the second half of the 1980s.

At the same time Nokia was hit with a governance crisis when the Union Bank of Finland (UBF) and Kansallis-Osake-Pankki (National Bank, KOP), the country's two leading commercial banks, drifted into direct conflict. UBF was close to jumping ship, and KOP actually did – at a time when Nokia needed all the help it could get. In 1991 KOP's willingness to sell its holding led UBF and other shareholders allied with UBF into negotiations with Ericsson. These negotiations did not result in a deal but they left Nokia management with a bitter reminder of the owners' lack of commitment to the company's independence.

A solution to the ownership question was reached in December 1991 when Ahti Hirvonen, CEO of UBF, and Yrjö Niskanen, CEO of the Pohjola insurance company (which had been closely allied to KOP), agreed that the UBF-led group would purchase the shares held by KOP, and Pohjola would remain a shareholder in Nokia.

The two chief executives, together with Casimir Ehrnrooth who became Nokia's chairman of the Board in 1992, resolved another conflict between Nokia's CEO and president. In April 1990, Kalle Isokallio was appointed president, and was dismissed just 18 months later, in January 1992. Meanwhile Simo Vuorilehto retired, as planned, in June 1992. As a result, all operational authority became concentrated in the hands of the president.

The new generation arrives

● The crisis and the departure of top executives had the positive effect of clearing the way for a talented and well-educated generation of young managers who would build Nokia into a global force.

Enter Jorma Ollila, head of the Mobile Phones division in Salo in 1990–1992 and previously Nokia Group senior vice president, Finance, in 1985–1990. He was appointed president and this arrangement eased the tension among the top management.

World events had created a challenging environment as one era swiftly merged into another in 1988–1992. The Berlin Wall, the symbol of the threat of another world war, came down and the two Germanys united. Likewise the Iron Curtain, which divided Europe into two camps, disappeared. The countries under the influence of the Soviet Union became independent and gradually redirected their command economy structures toward capitalism. The European order as we had known it since World War II had modified fundamentally, and the new free markets were suddenly open for business. A new federation of states was born peacefully in Western Europe under the aegis of the expanding European Union.

Change was sweeping through Finland, too. Deregulation of the financial markets resulted in an overheating of the economy, which abruptly plunged into the deepest peacetime recession the country had ever encountered in the early 1990s. The national economy and its institutions were subjected to fundamental structural changes. It was in the midst of this turmoil that a new generation took over at Nokia.

Twists and turns on the way to success

● Achieving global success at Nokia has been a journey with more than its share of twists and turns. The acquisition of manufacturers of television sets in central Europe in 1987 turned out to produce the biggest losses in Nokia's history, and the company learned hard lessons that even today result in a cautious management style and a bias toward organic growth.

When the dust settled, three questions remained: Why were the companies bought in the first place, why was Nokia unable to turn them into profitable businesses, and how did Nokia finally get rid of them?

Nokia made its first moves toward entering the television set business in the early 1980s when the division between professional and consumer electronics was softened. Prior to that Nokia had been careful to keep its distance from consumer electronics, which inside the company was given the derogatory nickname of 'amusement electronics'. At that time Nokia was waging a virtual war against the political trend of centralizing the whole electronics industry under state control. This was a major factor in Nokia's acquisition of Salora Oy, a leading Finnish television manufacturer. With a limited domestic market, Nokia then looked abroad for expansion and soon acquired Luxor Ab, the Swedish television set and electronics company. Nokia's involvement in Salora was a precondition for that purchase. Yet another reason for the purchase of the mobile telephone company Mobira was its interest in Salora's rapidly developing mobile phone production. Unbeknownst to the strategists, the seeds of the successful 21st century Nokia were already being planted.

But Nokia's corporate strategy in the 1980s was based on a strong belief in growth, internationalization, acquisitions, expansion and diversification, and, not to put too fine a point on it, a management team that believed it couldn't fail. Far from trying to narrow its focus, Nokia was expanding in several directions.

The various business groups and members of the internal Board came forward with their own suggestions for acquisitions. Antti Lagerroos proposed new acquisitions in television set production. Meanwhile, CEO Kari Kairamo wanted to purchase computer makers. Both of these were realized in massive acquisitions at the end of 1987 and the beginning of 1988. It is now clear that neither deal was based on a clear vision of the industry's future profitability or growth prospects, but rather on Nokia's ambition to grow and become more international.

Nokia's management soon realized that computer markets did not offer prospects for profitable growth. Consequently Nokia Data was restructured quickly by a team led by Kalle Isokallio, and sold off at a reasonable price to ICL-Fujitsu in the late spring of 1991.

Carrying the television burden

● In contrast, television set production of Standard Elektrik Lorenz (SEL) in Germany became a major burden that was difficult to unload. The restructuring process got well under way in the spring 1988 but came to an abrupt end after six months. Why this happened is one of the crucial but most difficult enigmas of this study (see pages 102–103).

Extensive restructuring plans that called for drastic headcount reductions and other measures were drawn up by May. At this point, group management sidetracked Antti Lagerroos, a member of the internal Board and the man in charge of the acquisition and the subsequent restructuring. He was replaced at the instigation of outside consultants by Jacques Noels, a Frenchman from Groupe Thomson, who became head of the business area. It is difficult to say whether this was done out of fear of public outcry caused by the major restructuring, power politics and personal relationships in top management, excessive optimism in the future of the television business or personal ambition for international status.

In any case the lines of command in top management became entangled, and effective restructuring measures were delayed by several years. Losses accumulated, and by the end of 1988 management faced very serious questions.

Several rounds of negotiation were conducted with major international companies for the sale of the division but failed to produce results. The business remained burdensome, and it was only in 1996, after extensive restructuring, that Nokia managed to part with it, selling the Finnish television set production and the European sales network to Semi-Tech (Global) of Hong Kong.

The bottom line: negative

● But did the adventure in the world of television set production benefit Nokia in any way? The answer appears to be negative. Synergies between business areas were never found. It is difficult to find any direct evidence that the cellular phone business would have learned anything major from television production in terms of brand creation, marketing, production or management.

It is always problematic to define a uniform corporate culture in a multi-brand conglomerate organized as Nokia was at the time. Different business areas and their respective cultures inside Nokia have varied, sometimes extensively. When corporate management placed the emphasis on international acquisitions in the 1980s, for example, the Telecommunications division shied away and confined itself to organic growth. An exception was Technophone, acquired in 1991 and made part of the Mobile Phones division but this was primarily an acquisition of technical expertise and quickly boosted Nokia's mobile phone research and development effort.

Not that the Telecommunications division didn't explore opportunities as well. One project code named 'Sunrise' studied the possibility of acquiring the PRM (Private Mobile Group) of General Electric. After concluding that instead of competitive edge and growth potential the company would have brought old technology and cautious customers, Nokia abandoned the idea. The third major study on potential acquisition targets was made in the mid-1990s, when a number of larger data transmission companies changed hands. Yet Nokia confined itself mainly to acquiring smaller companies such as Ipsilon, the router technology expert, which strengthened selected areas of knowhow.

CHAPTER 3

The mobile phone: a good fit with the Nokia outlook

H ow does the mobile phone rank compared to changes created by other inventions? Throughout history, people have felt they lived in the middle of a revolutionary era. Historians sometimes feel obliged, almost apologetically, to point out that earlier inventions and developments just might have been greater and brought even faster change than the current ones.

Neither Nokia nor any of its predecessors played a part in the first industrial revolution, which began in the 1760s. The main inventions – the efficient steam engine and the iron foundry – totally changed the shape of production machinery and land-based transport. The advent of new technology required a well-educated workforce, which gradually led to a widening of income gaps among the population.

Nokia's history is however linked to the second industrial revolution commencing in the 1860s. Those changes were based on chemicals, the internal combustion engine and electricity as the new source of power for industry. Both the wood industry and electricity generation, which started in 1900, were the main business areas of the early Nokia Ab, the current Nokia's oldest antecedent. In those fields Nokia's technology was on a par with any global competitor.

Nokia never gained a leading position, however, with any of the main products of the second industrial revolution. Nokia's cable production grew with the electricity and telephone markets, and it was a player in the triumph of the automobile but only by producing tires for cars and bicycles.

The third industrial revolution in the 1970s, the world of computers, telecommunications and mobile phones, finally moved Nokia to center stage.

A comparison of technological innovations should be made from two angles. First, their impact on human life and second their proliferation and impact on the growth of their industry. The greatest impact on

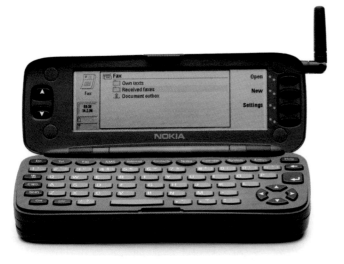

Launched in 1996, the Nokia Communicator 9000 was a totally new mobile phone concept. In addition to voice it included extensive data and telecommunications features making it a real 'pocket computer'. Other new products launched the same year included the Nokia 8100 GSM phone, the Nokia 1610 GSM phone and the Nokia 2160, the world's first dual band AMPS/TDMA phone.

human life in terms of communications was undoubtedly made by the television. In Finland, television reached most homes within about 10 years beginning in the 1960s. Nokia tried to join the television revolution but entered the market at a very late stage – too late.

Computerizing Finland

● Nokia played a pivotal role in computerizing Finland, initially as an importer of large computers in the 1960s, then in the 1980s as a significant manufacturer of microcomputers. But its role in the international markets was modest. The most profitable sector in the forest and power industries of Nokia was electricity production from hydroelectric installations.

From Nokia's point of view the difference between mobile phones and networks on the one hand, and television and computers on the other, is that with the former Nokia hit the markets just as they were beginning explosive growth. Another difference is that digital technology and other innovations facilitated the constant introduction of new properties without compromising high yields.

A history of looking outward

● Seeking international markets has always been part of the Nokia ethos, and the mobile phone phenomenon fits in naturally. Looking abroad for markets has been key to Nokia strategy since the beginning of its early activities in wood processing. As early as the 1860s Nokia Ab sold most of its woodworking products outside of Finland. Exports to Western European markets have traditionally constituted the largest part of the sales of Finland's timber industry. Nokia's other early industries, rubber and cables, were equally international in terms of knowhow and raw material procurement.

The post-war years in the 1940s provided Nokia with new lessons in internationalization. Having been judged to be on the losing side of the war in 1944, Finland was forced to pay massive war reparations to the Soviet Union during 1944–1952, largely in industrial products. The Cable Works played an important role in manufacturing goods to meet reparations obligations. This business continued with normal commercial trade with the Soviet Union, making cable manufacturing the industrial backbone of the Nokia Group. Cable exports also provided Nokia with an umbrella under which electronics exports found a foothold in Moscow, mainly with telephone exchanges. Nokia's rubber business also exported goods at a growing pace.

The third wave of internationalization is linked to trends of the 1980s, the decade of deregulation. Global markets were liberalized and Nokia had a strong desire to participate. The fastest way was through acquisitions. As mentioned in Chapter 1 and detailed in Chapter 7, the bridgehead was established by the purchase of Luxor, the Swedish television maker, in 1984 and the related acquisition of Salora of Finland. In cellphones Nokia had traditionally exported most of its production and had gained significant market share in the international markets, but overall volumes remained rather small until the end of 1980s. At the same time Nokia's cable machinery also made headway in the global markets.

Protectionist economic policies established during and after World War II were then cast off. In telecommunications this meant the breakup of national monopolies of operators and the advent of open competition. Later in the 1990s one of the most significant developments was the Internet, which enabled on-line trading and a multitude of new ways to communicate.

From the second half of the 1980s onward, an increasing proportion of Nokia's production and markets were relocated outside Finland. The shift accelerated throughout the 1990s, and the character of the company

The Radio Shack retail chain provided Nokia with a vital tool in penetrating the market in the United States. It had some 7,000 outlets by the time Nokia made an agreement with Tandy, Radio Shack's parent company, in 1983. In 1993, Nokia acquired Tandy's stake in the joint venture mobile phone plants in Ft. Worth and in Korea. Radio Shack's CEO Leonhard Roberts (on the right) and Kari-Pekka Wilska, president of Nokia Americas, in January 2000. In the background to the left is Jaakko Laajava, Finland's ambassador to the United States.

changed fundamentally. Since 1993 Nokia's ownership has been international in every respect. One milestone was the 1994 listing of Nokia on the New York Stock Exchange and the related share issue of which two-thirds was sold to investors in the United States. About the same time, Nokia's role in China strengthened considerably.

It is no exaggeration to say that Nokia was reared on the international markets.

The Finnish base – a burden or advantage?

● Finnish soil has nurtured Nokia's roots well since the beginning. Being managed from a small and remote country has always forced Finnish companies to think internationally and become internationally competitive early on. Straddling the fence between East and West has taught Finns how to market in all directions. Finally, several crises have given Finns the survival skills they need in a competitive world. International expansion and language and cross-cultural skills therefore come naturally. The historical Finnish spirit called 'sisu', which loosely translates as 'guts' or 'tenacity', has served the firm well.

Nokia's homogenous top management culture holds together in part because many of the managers have similar backgrounds. Their early years were spent in an era of Finnish schooling where talent, hard work, language skills, internationalism and equality were celebrated, all spiced with an element of collegiate humor. The resulting network is similar to those in US, French, German and other cultures where bonds are created during formative years and graduates depend upon these old contacts throughout their professional lives.

At Nokia today, a modern, international youth culture thrives, a kind of 'Venice Beach' attitude that shares youthful values and leisure pursuits such as snowboarding. A uniform dress code and lifestyle has emerged that to this author's generation seems rather superficial. But it works.

Nokia also has made it a point to work with the Finnish authorities on various levels. In the post-war decades until 1991, Nokia's extensive and politically regulated trade with the Soviet Union required close contact with politicians and civil servants. The company benefited from the government's domestic decentralization policy at the time it established its production unit in Oulu, in Northern Finland.

Features of the GSM mobile phone standard increased constantly throughout the 1990s. The next stage was the GPRS standard for which Nokia introduced the Nokia 8310 mobile phones in September 2001. They featured considerably faster data connection, as well as an FM radio.

Building a brand name requires participation in major events. Nokia's largest campaign in the United States is to sponsor the Sugar Bowl, the college football final. In 2000, Nokia built an extensive array of sponsorship and marketing events around the Nokia Sugar Bowl from the Internet pages to the actual event marketing.

On the other hand, Nokia faced the danger of the state as a competitor. Nokia has often found itself in opposition to its government on questions of energy as well as the electronics industry. In broader terms, however, large companies are usually loyal to democratically elected public authorities that provide the environment for long-term development, and Nokia is no exception.

Pointing Nokia toward the future

● But stepping back, it is clear that Nokia's success has often relied upon its willingness and ability to grasp and capitalize on major changes in the marketplace. The first change was the introduction and rapid development of the analog mobile phone in the 1980s. Secondly Nokia took advantage of the switch to the digital world, and the simultaneous deregulation of the operators. The introduction of multimedia communications at the end of the 1990s and early 21st century marks the third major change for which Nokia seems fully prepared.

The history of Nokia contains a number of lessons, primary among them a respect for past generations' wisdom, industriousness, and patience, and the agility to adapt to dramatically changing circumstances. Perseverance and good luck have also helped carry Nokia over numerous obstacles. The company has survived two world wars, the Cold War between two global alliances, revolution on its home turf and on its doorstep, depression, recession, inflation, devaluation and, most recently, membership of the European Union and adoption of the euro as Finland's new currency.

This history does not reveal a magic formula for Nokia's success, nor was that the purpose of the telling. What I have set out to demonstrate is that changing circumstances call for changing strategies. Therein lies the common denominator – the need and the ability to renew and adapt.

Emblem of the city of Nokia. The Nokia name comes from the river Nokia, which in turn apparently took its name from a dark, furry rodent called the nokia (in English, the mustelid), a member of the weasel family.

CHAPTER 4

Tracing Nokia's family tree

I t was the second industrial revolution in the late 19th century that opened the way for the birth of Nokia and propelled its growth into the 20th century. The year 1865 marks the establishment of Nokia's original antecedent company, when a stone groundwood plant planned by Fredrik Idestam, a 25-year-old mining engineer and a Finn who had been studying abroad, received a license to operate a business. In Saxony, Idestam had familiarized himself with groundwood techniques, a new process for the paper industry. He brought it to Finland, a country blessed with ample forests and water-power resources, and his plant came onstream the following year in the Finnish town of Tampere. A few years later he moved it 15 kilometres to the west, along the river Nokia.

Idestam's company was named Nokia Aktiebolag (literally 'Nokia Limited Liability' in Swedish, then the language of commerce). The Nokia name comes from the river Nokia, which in turn apparently took its name from a dark, furry rodent called the nokia (in English, the mustelid), a member of the weasel family.

Consolidation under the Rubber Works

● The company became a cohesive group in the years 1918–1922. During this time, Suomen Gummitehdas Oy (Finnish Rubber Works) acquired a majority of Nokia Ab and Suomen Kaapelitehdas Oy (Finnish Cable Works), a company that was established in 1912 by Arvid Wikström under the name Suomen Punomotehdas Oy. Although they operated under one umbrella organization, these three firms were not officially merged until 1966, leading to the establishment of the current Nokia Group the following year.

Hence it is Eduard Polón, Master of Law and primary owner and chief executive of the Rubber Works, who can be considered the real founding father of the company we know as Nokia today. Established in 1898, his firm manufactured rubber footwear. The company lost money every year until 1914, struggling in markets dominated by large international manufacturers. World War I, however, reduced foreign competition and created new demand. At the same time, unprecedented inflation in Finland wiped out most of his heavy debt. The Rubber Works had begun to prosper.

Finland was an autonomous Grand Duchy of the Russian Empire from 1809 to 1917, and launched its own currency in 1860. The first Finnish Parliament was elected at the same time, with its own domestic legislation. But Russia sought to unify the Empire's legal system, prompting a split among the Finns into two political camps – the more conciliatory ones and those opposed to Russia's plans. Eduard Polón belonged to the opponents and as a consequence was exiled deep into Russia with his son in 1916–1917.

The founding fathers of Nokia. From top: Fredrik Idestam, Eduard Polón and Arvid Wikström. Polón was the real founding father of the Nokia Group when his Rubber Works bought the majority of the two other companies in 1918–1922. Polón was exiled in Russia in 1916–1917 because of his staunch opposition to Russian rule in Finland. Paintings by: Werner Thomén, Eero Järnefelt and Hanna Appelberg.

The pretext for the exile was that Polón's second son had traveled to Germany, a country then at war with Russia, to undergo military training for the purpose of separating Finland from Russia. During his exile, however, Polón remained de facto chief executive of the Rubber Works and invested wisely in the new Helsinki Stock Exchange that had been established during World War I.

Finland had managed to stay out of the war, but became involved financially and in fact flourished as the Russian military relied on Finnish industry for part of its war materiel. In the process, Polón amassed great wealth, paving the way for the establishment of the Nokia Group.

Meanwhile, other Finns related to the history of Nokia made distinguished careers in the service of the Russian Empire. The most notable was General C.G. Mannerheim, a Board member of Nokia Ab from 1903 to 1906. He was commander-in-chief of government forces in Finland's war of independence in 1917 in which the Russian troops were finally expelled and the socialist revolution was defeated in 1918. He was also commander-in-chief of Finland's armed forces during World War II. During these periods he also served twice as head of the state of Finland.

Another Finn who served in Russia was Verner Weckman, technical director and managing director of Finnish Cable Works from 1921 to 1956. Among other things, he ran an asbestos mine in the Ural mountains for 12 years but he is best known for winning Finland's first Olympic gold medal in the heavy middleweight class in wrestling at the Athens Olympics in 1906. Two years later he brought another gold medal home from the London Olympics.

There was an effort in the 1930s to bring the loose grouping of the three companies owned by the Rubber Works closer together by appointing a common chief executive. This failed, however, because Torsten Westerlund, chief executive of the Rubber Works, didn't want to have what he called 'an overcoat' for himself. Instead, coordination took place mostly through the representatives of the Rubber Works who sat on the boards of the other two companies.

The Merger in 1966

● The formal merger binding the three companies was executed in 1966. The company was now called Oy Nokia Ab and the new CEO was Björn Westerlund, son of Torsten and managing director of the Cable Works, now the largest of the three companies. Technically, the other companies

It is here that Fredrik Idestam started his stone groundwood plant in the 1860s. The river gave the necessary power, and there were plenty of forests around. At the turn of the century also, Finnish Rubber Works found their way here. Nokia divested the forest industry and rubber industry in the 1990s and is no longer present at her birth place.

were acquired by the smallest, Nokia Ab. The reason was that under Finnish law at the time a forest products company could not be merged into another company but could make acquisitions of its own. The new name of the Group, Nokia, was chosen because it was already the well-known brand name of the rubber company.

Ownership of the three companies had remained largely unchanged for decades. At the beginning the biggest investors were private individuals but as has been typical for Finnish companies, commercial banks gradually increased their share of ownership. During the 1960s, the official merging of the three businesses to form a conglomerate was finalized, heavily influenced by the Union Bank of Finland, the country's largest commercial bank at the time. The reasoning for the restructuring of the company was typical of 1960s strategy: a conglomerate could better ride out business cycles in its various sectors. Secondly, the merger created critical mass, which would help in future financing.

In retrospect, it is difficult to assess the impact of the merger of the three businesses. Coordination was, at least initially, detrimental since no value was added by changing from one smooth-functioning system to another. Rather the process consumed a great deal of management time and operational energy. On the other hand, the credibility and image created by the increased size probably helped win several new and larger deals. As expected, the Group's critical mass also was instrumental in obtaining financing.

Another consideration was that strategic planning could be handled efficiently at the Group level. Yet it is difficult to pinpoint any concrete benefit that the businesses themselves could not have achieved alone. It is apparent in hindsight that the cable business, the Group's cash cow, could have managed the required investments in electronics by itself; in fact it could have invested more than the Group did. Perhaps the problematic and capital-intensive wood products industry was resuscitated and kept alive longer than it might have lasted without the merger. Finally, the rubber business might not have overcome its difficulties in realizing its investment program in car tires by itself, which would have forced the Group to focus

Two eminent Finns who made distinguished careers in Russia before Finland became independent. Marshal C.G. Mannerheim, twice the Finnish head of state in 1918–1919 and 1944–1946, and commander-in-chief in 1918 and in 1939–1945, was member of the Nokia Board 1903–1906. Verner Weckman was the first Finnish Olympic champion, in wrestling in 1906 and in 1908, and served as head of Cable Works from 1937–1955.

on its strongest product lines. It is somewhat ironic that wood products and the rubber business benefited more from the merger than cables and electronics.

Getting a foothold in electronics

● Interest in Nokia's early business history is naturally focussed on the electronics industry in the 1960s, but this should not be over-emphasized in the Group context. Electronics became a significant contributor to net sales only in the late 1980s and Nokia did not really focus on electronics until the 1990s. Equipment remained an insignificant activity, as measured in sales figures, for a number of years but it led down an interesting, albeit winding, road to later mass production.

Nevertheless, the roots of Nokia's telecommunications strengths of the 1990s are in electronics and cables, an area in which Nokia had accumulated extensive experience since the beginning of the century. The groundwork for digitalization, the foundation for Nokia's modern-day success, was laid as early as the 1960s.

The main business of electronics in the early days consisted of sales and marketing of other manufacturers' computers. The second line of business was the Computing Center, a data-processing service center that enabled leading Finnish companies to get a start in their computing function in the Center, which was part of the Electronics Department of the Cable Works. This service business in turn created a ready-made base for later computer sales.

The key person in the establishment of the electronics activity was Björn Westerlund, an engineer and president of the Cable Works. He believed Cable should diversify into to the fast-growing electronics industry, particularly the design and production of computers. A turning point was December 10, 1958, when the Cable Works Board decided to take the plunge, but only via imports as a first step in order to gain knowhow. A central figure in the preparations was Olli Lehto, a mathematician at the Cable Works who later became professor of mathematics, rector and chancellor of Helsinki University, and president of the International Mathematical Union.

The computer business took off in 1960 as the English-made Elliot 803 and the German-made Siemens 2002 briskly achieved strong sales figures. Nokia recruited a number of bright young men, many of whom became computer science pioneers at Finnish universities. Customers

Dr. Olli Lehto wrote the first plans of the Electronic Department of the Finnish Cable Works at the end of the 1950s. Later he became head of the department, but made another career in the university, becoming rector and chancellor of the University of Helsinki, and the president of the International Mathematical Union.

were known to remark: 'IBM has better computers but you have better people.'

In addition to its imported computer sales and the Computing Center, the Electronics Department of the Cable Works began to manufacture equipment. The first product was designed for nuclear power research just as Finland was preparing to enter the nuclear era. First produced in 1962, the pulse analyzer was used to measure transit times of low-temperature neutrons in the sub-critical nuclear reactor at the Technical University of Helsinki.

The computer business remained in the black, and its profits were invested in the development and manufacture of original products. Some of these were designed for the defense forces, notably measurement systems for artillery projectiles, and fire control systems for coastal artillery and gunboats. Volumes were small and these defense contracts were minimal, in keeping with Finland's modest defense industry, which was only about one-tenth as large as Sweden's in the 1970s. The department also developed products to measure the operating speed of paper-making machines and the control systems for the Loviisa nuclear power plant on the south coast of Finland.

Westerlund was succeeded as the head of the Cable Works by Einar Mattsson, a strong personality with a pronounced dislike of the electronics activity. Westerlund moved the Electronics Department into a separate unit within the newly established group, Oy Nokia Ab, in 1967. At that point sales of electronics amounted to a mere 3 percent of the group's total sales.

Building computers and digital telephone exchanges

● Finally in 1971, Nokia began to develop its own computers. Erkki Rajulin, then a young engineer at Nokia Electronics, recalls that he came up with a catchy name for the first machine, the Mikko, an acronym of

Pulse analyzer, the first electronics product manufactured by Nokia in 1962.

the Finnish for Micro Computer. The young engineers set themselves the objective of printing out their first message as 'Merry Christmas' but the project was delayed. Instead, they managed 'Happy New Year' a short time later, in January 1972. Mikko 2 was first adopted by the Finnish banking systems and as the electronic processor for the cash registers at state-owned alcohol retail stores.

Production of computers expanded on a larger scale when Nokia developed Mikro Mikko, an office computer, which became a major division for Nokia in the 1980s. Ericsson Information Systems was acquired in 1988 but the numbers were still too small, and Nokia decided to pull out. The business was sold to Britain's ICL-Fujitsu in 1991.

Nokia's most far-reaching decision in the 1970s was to commence the production of digital telephone exchanges. Computer sales volumes in the 1960s and the early 1970s had driven up Nokia's domestic market share to 80 percent. The business was profitable enough to create a base from which Nokia could take the next technological leap – to digital telephone exchanges.

Markets for telephone exchanges were considerably larger than markets for transmission equipment. The new integrated telephone network facilitated by the digital technology provided opportunities, but also created pressure to expand quickly into digital exchanges. Research in this field began in the early 1970s and led to the acquisition of a technology license from CIT-Alcatel of France, which was then Europe's leading company in digital exchange technology. The agreement was signed in 1976.

The exploitation of the technological transition at the right time enabled Nokia to gain a substantial share of these growing markets. Several factors justified Nokia's move into telephone exchanges: they were becoming computer-controlled and fully electronic, using time-division technology. Nokia had 15 years' experience in computer technology and was a pioneer in time division. In the future, exchanges and transmission networks were sure to integrate, requiring the capability to supply total systems. Investment in exchange equipment was very significant for the national economy.

There were also risks and potential rewards on the international scene. Nokia was aware that it was challenging L.M. Ericsson in its core business. Nevertheless the step was taken because 'to a large extent it was the question of whether Nokia wanted to be in the telecommunications business in the long run', as Kari Kairamo, then Nokia's CEO, put it to a board member who had doubts about the bold move. Vice chairman of the Board Mika Tiivola, who also served as chief executive of the Union Bank

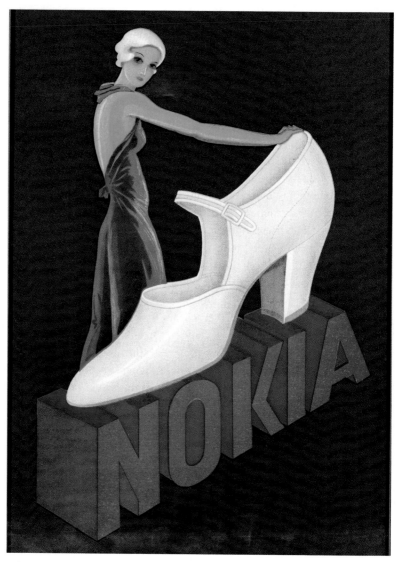

Women's rubber shoe ad in 1933. The name 'Nokia' has been used as a brand for over 100 years in various products from paper to galoshes, computers to mobile phones.

of Finland, added: 'The plan went well with Nokia's business strategy in this field which was largely dominated by foreign companies.'

By that remark, Tiivola meant that in telecommunications, Finland was an open market. There were two competing operator groupings in the country. One was the state-run Post and Telegraph Administration, which had a monopoly in trunk calls and international calls as well as in mobile telephony. The other camp consisted of private local telephone companies led by the Helsinki area that had monopolies in local calls in their areas. Both camps invited competing tenders from several domestic and international suppliers for all their equipment.

A significant move in telephone exchanges took place in 1978 when two domestic manufacturers joined forces. The state-owned Televa Oy and Nokia established a 50-50 joint venture called Telefenno Oy to develop and market telephone exchanges. Nokia acquired a majority stake in Televa three years later, and bought the state out altogether in 1987.

The mobile phone business first saw daylight in the early 1960s when Finland's defense forces requested bids for military radiophones. As it turned out, the state's appropriations were insufficient to place an order, but various manufacturers, including Nokia, began their own research and launched their first phones in the mid-1960s. The initial market was closed public services such as fire brigades, the police and railways. This business then expanded to the open market via the analog ARP (a Finnish acronym for 'car radio-telephone'), which was switched on in 1971. At its peak it reached some 35,000 subscribers.

As in other fields, Nokia aimed to proceed through business partnerships with other companies. In 1975, Nokia signed a cooperation agreement with Salora, Finland's leading radio and television producer, and two people behind the agreement were destined to become key figures in the field. Jorma Nieminen of Salora became head of Nokia Mobile Phones division and was later founder of Benefon Oy, a mobile phone manufacturer; and Kari-Pekka Wilska of Nokia, who would head the company's operations in the United States. Under the terms of the initial agreement, Salora would supply multi-channel car telephones and their support structures to Nokia while Nokia would supply Salora with base stations and links.

Against state dominance

● Nokia had a delicate relationship with the Finnish government during the rise of the electronics industry. Although Finland was a stable Western democracy, left-wing voices, particularly from the Social Democratic Party, the largest party in the coalition government, grew louder in the 1970s. Industrial circles felt the political pressure to increase state involvement in the national economy.

Finnish Rubber Works ad from 1916. Under heavy international competition Rubber Works had been deeply in the red for its first 16 years of existence, but the First World War changed everything: inflation wiped out the debt, war closed the borders and dispelled the competitors and the company became so profitable that after the war it could purchase a majority of shares in Nokia Ab the paper company, and the Finnish Cable Works.

The Social Democrats worked out a plan in the mid-1970s to establish a state-owned electronics company. The idea was to build an electronics industry alongside energy (oil and electricity) which was also state-dominated. The most visible result of the plan was the establishment of Valco Oy, the television picture tube manufacturer. Nokia felt it was in mortal danger, and soon became a leader in the industrial policy counter-strike organized by private industrial companies.

This political impetus was partly behind Nokia's decision at the beginning of the 1980s to buy a majority of the state-owned Televa and the privately owned Salora, which was known to be poorly managed. Although its television business was sound, diversification had taken Salora into oil tankers, manufacturing in Africa, and even television sales in various black markets. Overall performance suffered, making the company vulnerable to acquisition by Ericsson.

So it can be concluded that the growth of Nokia's electronics business was both due to internal visionary business objectives and to the peculiar industrial policy situation in Finland, which called for defensive action. This dual strategic outlook must be borne in mind when, as we shall see in Chapter 6, Nokia sets about establishing electronics as the Group's primary business.

CHAPTER 5

In the shadow of Russia

Finland has over 1,000 kilometers of common border with Russia, and this has meant one long dance of survival – economically, politically and militarily. The uneasy relationship between the two countries is also an integral part of the Nokia story. The company has ridden the triumphs and tragedies with Russia, the Soviet Union, and now Russia again, for 137 years.

The initial business plan for Fredrik Idestam's stone groundwood company in the 1860s was aimed at markets in St. Petersburg, the capital of Imperial Russia. World trade was relatively unrestricted before World War I and Finland found excellent markets next door when Russia was struggling to fulfill the needs of her war economy. Virtually all of Finland's exports went to Russia towards the end of the war, but the near-exclusive relationship came to an abrupt end in 1917, the year of the Bolshevik Revolution in Russia and Finland's independence. As a result, Finland turned toward Western Europe for new markets.

Finland's foreign trade policy has traditionally succeeded in securing access to Western markets irrespective of its relations with Russia. Finland's position was largely determined by the country's successful defense against the Soviets in both the Winter War of 1939–1940 and then in the Karelian peninsula offensive in 1944. But Finland was never occupied by the Soviets. The democratically elected governing bodies continued to function, and communists never penetrated the key civil service positions. Constitutional principles and practices survived.

Allied forces established a Control Commission in Finland in 1944, which continued to operate up to the signing of the final peace treaty in Paris in 1947. In the following year Finland and the Soviet Union signed a treaty of friendship, cooperation and mutual assistance, which included articles on military cooperation. This was no mini-Warsaw Pact alliance, however. Finland drew up its own peculiar neutrality policy which combined the security interests of the Soviet Union with Finland's cherished democratic principles and the vital economic and trading relations with the Western democracies.

Finland re-established an extensive Nordic and Western cooperation network in the early years of the Cold War and joined the European Free Trade Agreement (EFTA) at the beginning of the 1960s. A decade later the country signed an agreement with the European Economic Community (EEC) and, proving its Western credentials once and for all, became a full member of the European Union in 1995. Finland decided to join the founding members of the European Monetary Union (EMU) and adopted the euro as its currency as of the beginning of 2002.

Finland's fine balance between East and West often affected economic relations, too. One of the more momentous battles was fought over nuclear energy. In the 1960s, Imatran Voima, the state-owned power company, planned to build a nuclear power plant in Finland. Under political pressure, the company opted to commission the plant from the Soviet Union, and it was built in Loviisa, on Finland's south coast – but the safety features were redesigned by Finns along western lines. At the same time Teollisuuden Voima Oy, a consortium of large privately owned

Finland's international position

Until 1809	Part of the Kingdom of Sweden
1809–1917	Autonomous Grand Duchy of Russia
1914–1918	World War I
1917	Independent Republic
1918	Finland's War of Liberation and socialist revolution
1939–1945	World War II, Finland not occupied by the Soviet Union
1945–1952	War reparations to Russia
1948	Finland and the Soviet Union sign a pact on friendship, cooperation and mutual assistance
1955	Finland joins the Nordic Council and the United Nations
1961	Agreement with the European Free Trade Association (EFTA)
1973	Agreement with the European Economic Community (EEC), later the EU
1995–	Member of the European Union (EU)
1999–	Member of the European Monetary Union (EMU)

Finnish companies, managed to build another nuclear power plant on the west coast, based on a reactor supplied by ASEA-ATOM of Sweden. Both of these plants added second reactors, so the country currently has two nuclear power plants with a total of four reactors. As a result, Finland has been able to maintain a high level of self-sufficiency in the production of cheap energy while also balancing the political realities.

The success of the privately owned nuclear power plant was largely down to the skillful diplomacy of Björn Westerlund, then chief executive of Nokia. The company's cable exports had helped him to create a close personal relationship with Moscow decision-makers with whom Westerlund managed to find a solution involving intricate political and economic considerations. As Westerlund memorably put it: 'Finland is a free country, but one must not offend Russia.'

Open competition on home turf

● The rapid rise of Nokia's electronics industry was largely due to Finland's commitment to open market policies, which forced the company to face open competition on its home turf. This was a time when many other countries in Europe and elsewhere strongly protected their home markets. For example in 1980 imports of electronic goods averaged below 10 percent in most countries. The most protected markets included France (imports 3 percent) and West Germany (4 percent). At the opposite end of the spectrum were Denmark (66 percent) and Finland (42 percent).

Protectionism in Finland affected individual products and components, particularly in communications network equipment, including telephone exchanges, transmission systems and cables. In contrast, equipment for the more private sector such as switchboards, telephones, modems and radiotelephones, was less restricted. These, however, amounted to a mere 10–15 percent of the total investment in a basic communications network.

Protectionism in some sectors was not illegal in those days. The original GATT agreement, although designed for the promotion of free trade, did not cover telecommunications equipment because it was considered strategically important to each nation. Buyers such as the national post and telecommunications administrations routinely protected domestic industries by manipulating procurement standards. Prime examples were found in West Germany, France and Britain. Another way to safeguard domestic production was the establishment of joint ventures between

Urho Kekkonen, president of Finland, and Leonid Brezhnev, president of Soviet Union, visiting Cable Works in 1961. Björn Westerlund, CEO of Cable Works, presenting the products. Nokia's cable and later electronics exports to Soviet Union were a profitable business until 1991.

buyers and sellers. Examples of this included companies from Sweden and France. A third way was to commission major new investments from national industries (as was done for broadband networks) or from a consortium involving a few countries (as with satellite systems and cellular networks).

Nokia also received public subsidies for research and development, but only up to 10 percent of total investment in research and development. It also received a share of public procurement, and benefited from the unique technical specifications that were chosen to give an advantage to Finnish companies.

As Finland was never occupied, it was able to avoid becoming a satellite of Moscow. Finland's genuinely competitive western-style economy safeguarded it from sliding into Moscow's centrally-controlled economic

Nokia 35 kV cables for the Caspian Sea oilfields leaving the port of Helsinki in 1985. Each roll contained 25 kilometers of cable.

empire as had the countries of eastern and central Europe. Thriving exports were led by the forest industry, which sold most of its product to western markets.

Nokia was highly dependent on the international raw material markets until 1991. The cable industry required copper while the rubber industry had to import raw rubber. Since then, Nokia has focussed on telecommunications, where the role of raw materials is minuscule compared to brainpower, and research and development.

Until World War II, Nokia's primary export was paper, while the rubber and cable industries largely relied on domestic markets. Only in the 1950s did the rubber industry expand to international markets, mainly with winter tires for cars. Around the same time, the Nokia Cable Works began exporting its products to the Soviet Union. In value terms, cable products amounted to 5.7 percent of the country's total war reparations to Russia. It consisted of copper wire and power cables worth $13 million in 1938 currency – the conversion date the Russians insisted upon in order to gain a large increase in the value of reparations.

Pros and cons of Soviet trade ties

● The cable quota in reparations was fulfilled in 1948, after which Nokia's Cable Works continued shipments as part of normal commercial trade with the Soviet Union. At this time, western cable markets were tightly closed by cartels. One quarter of Nokia's total cable production, mainly power and relay cables, was exported to the Soviet Union in the 1950s and 1960s, making it a highly profitable activity.

Trade between Nokia and the Soviet Union included some special features that had their roots in the Soviet system. Moscow insisted that its way of conducting trade was the only way. The Soviet system was based on central planning in which all means of production was state-owned. This naturally led to multi-layered bureaucracy, and it was up to Nokia to learn how to function within it.

The system had its advantages, too. The Soviet Union paid reliably and promptly, ordered long lines of products and was predictable in its order volumes. The profits were quite high as the prices were linked to international market prices that were often dictated by monopolies within closed western markets. The Soviets received good products and the Finns did well financially. A key to Nokia's success in these markets was direct, continuous and trustworthy relations with the people who were instrumental in preparing the orders. Nokia also benefited from the European cable cartel, which restricted the access of other cable producers to Russia and Finland. Cable became the mainstay of Nokia's exports to the Soviet Union.

Due to the oil price hikes of the early 1970s, the Soviet Union, a large oil producer, was able to double its imports from Finland. Under the terms of the bilateral trade agreement, Finland paid for its Soviet oil imports with an equal value of exports. When the oil price rose, so did the total value of Finnish exports. In addition to cables, Nokia exported cable machinery. Nokia's exports to the Soviet Union in 1977 totaled €126 million, of which the Cables division accounted for €104 million.

More to the point, Nokia's electronic exports to the Soviet Union got under way in the 1960s. Among the first products were multi-channel analyzers, which remained in the trade protocol for two decades. Other products included communications links for gas pipelines, pulse code modulation (PCM) equipment for telephone networks, an electronic scoreboard and result service for Lenin Stadium in Moscow, and mobile phones. The most important electronics export product was the DX200 telephone exchange in the 1980s. Trade with the Soviet Union played a great role in the development of these exchanges. It paved the way for Nokia's success in winning orders for complete communications systems in the West when the markets opened up at the end of the 1980s.

It is no exaggeration to say that without its substantial contracts with the Soviet Union Nokia might well have discontinued its production of telephone exchanges. Officially the trade in telephone exchanges was called co-production, but in fact the Soviet role amounted to that of a subcontractor. Nokia maintained tight control over all key components.

Nokia also watched its home markets carefully, doing its best to keep competitors out of this profitable territory. Nokia was active on the sidelines in 1981 when Finland's License Administration refused to grant the Finnish subsidiary of L.M. Ericsson of Sweden an export license for the sale of products to the Soviet Union. The reason given was that the products' non-Finnish manufactured components exceeded the 20 percent limit. Nokia also managed to block Ericsson's second attempt when the Swedish company tried to acquire the state-owned Televa Oy, which already manufactured exchanges and exported them to the Soviet Union. Instead the state sold the company to Nokia at the beginning of the 1980s.

Under Mikhail Gorbachev's leadership of the Soviet Union in the 1980s, glasnost and perestroika also affected trade with Finland. In order to maintain its Soviet trade, Nokia had to adapt once again. This time, the way forward was to be joint ventures with entrepreneurial Russian partners.

Nokia's biggest ever publicity coup took place on April 9, 1987, when Mikhail Gor-
bachev made a call on a Nokia mobile phone in Helsinki. The 'spontaneous' phone call
attracted global publicity for Nokia's newest handset. In fact, the move was well orches-
trated by Nokia. Stefan Widomski, director of Nokia's trade with the Soviet Union, had
two handsets, one of which was a backup, and a special link was set up nearby. As it hap-
pened, one of the phones lost its connection just before it was handed over to Gorbachev,
but the other worked fine. Gorbachev spoke with Soviet Communications Minister Glin-
ka in Moscow. In the photo, Nokia's representatives to the right of Gorbachev are Wid-
omski and President Simo Vuorilehto. The world's smallest portable mobile phone, the
Mobira Cityman 900, weighed 800 grams, and had a price tag of FIM 24,000 (€4,560).

The US export embargo and Nokia's trade
with the Soviet Union

● Being dependent on trade with the Soviet Union, Nokia walked a fine
line in international politics. In a larger context, Finland faced a similar
challenge, to strengthen ties with Western trading partners without losing
the profitable trade with Moscow, or compromising her political independence. In other words, Finland was nurturing relations with equal care
in both directions. This was not easy, particularly when US President

Ronald Reagan began an effort to strengthen COCOM, the organization that was set up to restrict Western exports of high technology to the Soviet Union and other communist-led countries.

The virtual embargo by Reagan put the brakes on the export of electronic products to the Soviet Union and its client states in East Europe. This was of vital concern to Nokia, whose exports to the Soviets contained American-made components. The threat of restrictions also extended to cable machinery.

In a presentation to the Executive Committee of the Nokia Board in January 1982, Kari Kairamo explained his position on the COCOM embargo:

> Nokia acted as if nothing had happened. It is not likely that the US would place sanctions against Finland. Nokia is not involved in so-called high technology exports.

Kairamo wanted to deal with potential doubts about the embargo as early as possible by establishing a permanent and open network of contacts

US Senator Richard G. Lugar (second from left) visiting Nokia in Finland. To the left Jan Klenberg, later commander-in-chief of the Finnish Armed Forces. To the far right Jaakko Pöyry, prominent consultant of global forest industries.

between Nokia and the United States. These contacts went beyond Nokia's interests; the aim was to include as many Finnish companies on the 'Gold Card List' as possible – in other words to allow free exports.

The embargo was a double-edged sword for the United States. On the political side, the United States had a clear interest in weakening the Soviet Union in the battle of the great powers, especially on products that could benefit the Soviet military. On the other hand, American companies would naturally benefit from free trade. These conflicting interests often worked to Nokia's advantage, as it was also apparent that the United States aimed to keep Finland technologically well ahead of the Soviet Union, and prevent the country from sliding closer to Moscow.

But did Nokia actually export electronics that were banned by the embargo? There is no simple answer. As people close to the deals tell it, the source codes of products were not given to the Soviets, even though the trade protocols stipulated they must be provided until the next generation of the product was developed. Hence a technological advantage was maintained. (Source codes enable the user to change the product's original application or use.)

The Finns also had to reassure the Americans that modernization of their defense forces did not somehow pose a threat by strengthening the Soviet military. Nokia was a major supplier of electronics to the Finnish military and worked closely with Finland's top foreign policy authorities to underscore the country's commitment to neutrality.

Eventually a positive solution was reached at the highest political level. President of Finland, Mauno Koivisto, spared no effort, as is made clear in Kairamo's letter to Koivisto in August 1987:

> As the technology relations between Finland and the United States have now reached a satisfactory level, please allow me as a close observer to express gratitude on behalf of Finnish industry. The State of Finland has rapidly and skillfully, more skillfully than any other European country, we understand, brought this matter to a conclusion.
>
> First of all the fact that the Gulf of Bothnia [between Finland and Sweden] did not become a technology border is of vital importance to Finnish industry today, and particularly in the future.
>
> Our industry's ability to obtain technology and receive equal handling of applications with other Western industrial countries is already today a key for maintaining our competitiveness.

Zeitgeist – digitalization, deregulation, opening of borders, 'casino economy'

● Zeitgeist is difficult to describe in a few words, but it's easy to sense when you are in the middle of it. Likewise, a person's charisma can easily be felt, but it is much more difficult to define. Both of these phenomena also belong to the history of economics as explored by Joseph Schumpeter, perhaps the most significant economist of the 20th century, in his outstanding book *Capitalism, Socialism and Democracy*, published in 1942. The most notable feature of capitalism, says Schumpeter, is innovation and renewal – 'creative destruction'.

As recently as the 1970s the world order was considered solidly established. The post-World War II division of Europe, the coexistence of two economic systems with their own distinct rules and operating principles seemed permanent. The division of Europe into two military camps was ratified in 1975 at the European Conference on Security and Cooperation in Helsinki. The Finns adapted to this period of détente by continuing to balance their interests between East and West. In practice, détente meant accepting a Europe in the shadow of the Soviet Union, and increasing adaptation to the values and policies of the socialist system. Nokia had to take this into consideration when it looked for new international markets.

In the early 1980s, however, the world felt both economic and political tremors. Ripples were felt in Finland, too. The question today is how to differentiate between cause and effect. The Soviet Union attempted to expand its empire by marching into Afghanistan in December 1979. In the United States, President Jimmy Carter began to distance himself from détente, but the real change in politics was brought about by his successor, Ronald Reagan, who became president in 1981. Reagan not only aimed to stop Soviet expansion but also to prove the superiority of the capitalist system.

Furthermore, Reagan changed the basic premise of his country's economics by opening the way to more liberal fiscal and monetary policies, and an even less restricted model of capitalism. This included a fight against monopolies, which culminated in the splitting up of AT&T into smaller companies. A few years earlier British Prime Minister, Margaret Thatcher, had embarked on a similar crusade for free competition. The principles of deregulation gradually found their way to many other countries.

From Nokia's perspective, four trends highlighted the final years of the 1980s. The most important was technological development, and

'Open the windows to Europe!' Nokia's CEO was active in lobbying for Finland's closer ties to the integrating Western Europe. Kairamo opens a window on Europe. Cartoon by Terho Ovaska, Helsinki daily Uusi Suomi.

particularly digitalization, which now prevailed in electronics. Secondly, deregulation opened competition in the previously protected national markets. Thirdly, national borders opened as the European Economic Community evolved into the European Union and obstacles to free trade were gradually removed. The fourth trend is a kind of 'black sheep' of the era. The Finnish economy overheated badly, qualifying as a 'casino economy'. Pressure built up on Finnish companies to make acquisitions and expand internationally.

It is clear that much of Nokia's global success is due to having Finland as its home base. Not that the state over-supported Nokia's development, particularly compared with other countries' support for their industries. Rather, it was a question of deregulation of the markets. Finland opened its markets earlier and more consistently than most other countries. This forced Nokia to adapt early to the mechanisms and dynamics of competition. As Finland was such a small market, Nokia and other companies needed to expand internationally to grow.

In the autumn of 1981, a change in zeitgeist occurred when an ailing president of Finland, Urho Kekkonen, stepped down after two and-a-half decades in office. His overpowering influence on society had extended well beyond politics. In his era, state-owned companies had occupied a prominent position while trade and joint projects with the Soviet Union expanded steadily. At the same time, he carefully nurtured Finland's rela-

As a striking symbol of changing times the rock band Leningrad Cowboys performed together with the Red Army Choir in Berlin on the very day of the Allied Forces leaving the city. Nokia sponsored the event, bringing phones closer to consciousness. Painting by Markus Forss.

tions with western Europe. Kekkonen's successor was Mauno Koivisto, former prime minister and governor of the Bank of Finland, a man much more restrained in his use of political power. He quickly gave new leeway to Parliament and majority governments. Since 1983, coalition governments, representing a majority of members of Parliament, have consistently lasted the full four-year election term. Until then the average lifespan of the government was only about one year.

The rapid deregulation of the financial markets opened the floodgates and resulted in an unprecedented economic boom in the 1980s. This, in turn, was followed by in Finland's deepest recession in post-war history – an event of the type that Schumpeter called 'creative destruction'.

The first steps in deregulation in Finland were taken among telecom operators when authorities allowed free transfer of telefax pages. This was followed by unrestricted competition in data transfer in 1988. A fierce battle over liberalization of cellular networks ensued, leading to a decision to allow competition in all telephone services. The emergence of new operators ushered in a new era in the manufacture of telecom equipment.

At the same time, Western Europe was awakening from 'Euro-sclerosis', a period during which economic growth and the European integration process had slowed to a halt. The year 1985 marked a watershed for Finnish industry in general, and for Nokia in particular. Focus shifted from east to west. As chairman of the Confederation of Finnish Industries from 1985–1987, Kari Kairamo, then chief executive of Nokia, vigorosly promoted Finland's integration with western Europe. In his capacity as chairman of Finland's Foreign Trade Association, Kairamo said in May 1987:

> For the past three decades Finland has belonged to the European economic family, which consists of the European Economic Community and the countries of the European Free Trade Association. So it is only natural that we aim to stay involved in the development that takes place among these countries. Stepping aside or lagging behind would lead to a fatal reversal of our position.

'Now we don't assume anything'
– a shift from East to West in 1991

● One of the most dramatic events in Nokia's recent history took place in 1991 when the lucrative trade with the Soviet Union came to an abrupt end. It hit the cable industry and telecommunications particularly hard. Nokia's telecommunications business survived, however, by replacing the loss of its largest market with new exports to the West, as well as by cost-cutting – one of the most impressive turnarounds in Nokia's history. It was helped by deregulation and the emergence of new operators. The Telecommunications division had already managed to build bridgeheads in the western markets at the end of the 1980s.

Sakari Salminen, president of the Telecommunications division, warned his No. 2 man, Matti Alahuhta, of problems in the trade with the Soviet Union in April 1990. Salminen had trained Alahuhta as his successor and encouraged him to undertake further studies. Salminen wanted to make sure that Alahuhta would stay at Nokia Telecommunications (NTC) instead of taking the No. 2 job at the Mobile Phones division, as had been privately decided.

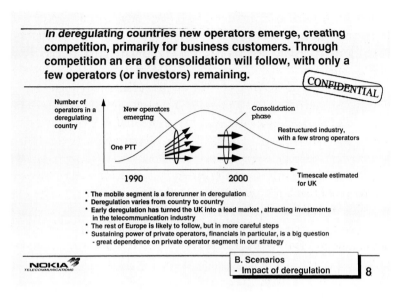

In deregulating countries new operators emerge, creating competition, primarily for business customers. Through competition an era of consolidation will follow, with only a few operators (or investors) remaining.

Number of operators in a deregulating country

New operators emerging

One PTT

Consolidation phase

Restructured industry, with a few strong operators

1990

2000

Timescale estimated for UK

* The mobile segment is a forerunner in deregulation
* Deregulation varies from country to country
* Early deregulation has turned the UK into a lead market , attracting investments in the telecommunication industry
* The rest of Europe is likely to follow, but in more careful steps
* Sustaining power of private operators, financials in particular, is a big question
  - great dependence on private operator segment in our strategy

NOKIA
TELECOMMUNICATIONS

B. Scenarios
- Impact of deregulation

8

A forecast slide by the Telecommunications division in April 1992 was prophetic in seeing the window of opportunity for Nokia.

At that time Alahuhta was studying at the International Institute of Management Development (IMEDE, now merged into IMD) in Switzerland while holding his position as a director at Nokia. In August 1990 he completed his doctoral dissertation on global growth strategies of competitor companies in high technology. Alahuhta took the view that high-technology companies would succeed globally if they managed an early entry into markets where changes in technology and consumer patterns were evident. A further requirement, he noted, was a strong emphasis on research and development. This could hardly have been a more suitable study for the era Nokia was entering.

The Telecommunications division's forecasts for 1991 remained optimistic about the lucrative Soviet exports, but in April a strategy meeting of the business group faced the cold facts. Sales to Eastern Europe in January-February totaled just FIM 2 million (€384,000) compared with 121 million Finnmarks (€23 million) expected in the division's budget. In March–April 1991 the top management came to the conclusion: 'Now we don't assume anything.' Strategy was completely recast and the division ceased to rely on Soviet trade.

Over the next few months, the Telecommunications division struggled to survive. At the end of April 1991 a new strategy underlined overall cost cutting and focussed on key countries including Finland, Sweden, Germany, Britain, France, Thailand, Malaysia and Australia. On the more positive side, the division had already realized that the 'challenger operators', the new telecom companies that would challenge existing monopolies, offered opportunities in new market segments. In June 1991 the division's sales figures for January–May revealed a budget shortfall of FIM 335 million (€65 million). Profit for the period was a disturbing FIM 158 million (€31 million) below budget.

The turnaround came good in the summer of 1991. August brought further proof that Soviet exports were collapsing, while western markets were full of good news. Exports to Western Europe outside of Scandinavia increased by 65 percent from budgeted figures in the January–July period amounting to FIM 234 million (€45 million). Exports beyond Europe grew by 25 percent. By October it was clear that the Soviet markets were lost, and that virtually no business was to be expected from them for the foreseeable future.

At the same time a cost reduction campaign was launched. Some employees recall that the effort resulted mainly in increased cash flow to consultants and savings of just a few million Finnmarks whereas the problems amounted to hundreds of millions. Top management saw things differently. Savings did amount to about FIM 100 million (€19 million) that that was redirected into research and development as well as marketing.

The Telecommunications division was largely saved by the surge in cellular networks. The division was forced to reduce personnel in fixed network production, but these employees could conveniently be transferred to the development of mobile networks. The drive to penetrate international telecommunications markets bore fruit just as it was desperately needed.

Nokia also succeeded in restructuring itself and putting together teams for the development, production and sale of cellular networks. The division had not engaged in costly acquisitions, nor did the management panic. The situation was, in the end, handled in a cool, controlled manner.

The new strategy proved successful. Thanks to the penetration of new markets, the division's result for 1991 remained above the waterline, even though it lost about FIM 1 billion (€190 million) in sales. In comparison, the sales had been FIM 2.5 billion (€500 million) the year before.

CHAPTER 6

Getting to grips with corporate governance

I n March 1986, Nokia's Board of Directors received a proposal from CEO Kari Kairamo. The proposal had a familiar ring to it. As Kairamo had previously suggested to Mika Tiivola, chairman of the Nokia Board and chief executive officer of Union Bank of Finland (UBF), he was saying once again – and this time formally – that Nokia needed a Supervisory Board positioned between the main Board and the shareholders.

Tiivola and Jaakko Lassila, vice chairman of the board and CEO of the bank Kansallis-Osake-Pankki (KOP), were not enthusiastic about the idea but to avoid open confrontation with Kairamo they agreed. Lassila thought that non-executive directors should not meddle with operational matters unless they felt the business was clearly heading in the wrong direction.

In practice, the Kairamo plan increased the distance between the company's largest share owners, UBF and KOP, and senior management. At the same time another proposal concerning top management was presented to the Board: to create a dual leadership structure with the chairman of the internal Board acting as CEO, and a separate president to be appointed as second-in-command, a de facto chief operating officer (COO). This suggestion was also accepted, and proved to be the most significant change in Nokia's management structure in the 1980s.

Most importantly, the move strengthened the formal position of Kairamo, who had already served as president for nine years. Nokia's management had also gained more operational freedom due to the recurring rifts between UBF and KOP. The traditional gentlemanly and cartel-like coexistence in Finnish banking was giving way to open competition and gradually increasing hostility in the mid-1980s.

In addition, the deregulation of the Finnish money markets increased Nokia's freedom to deal with foreign financial institutions while also loosening its ties with domestic banks – its largest owners at this stage. The grouping headed by UBF owned about 30 percent of Nokia while companies and institutions close to KOP held 21 percent. The chief executive of UBF wielded great power as chairman of the Board of Nokia.

Kairamo explained the reasoning behind his plan in a memo to the Board:

> The structure of the group, its fast growth and international expansion have led Nokia to a situation in which the tasks and duties of the management have increased and become more complex. This has led to problems in allocating time for customers and other external relations as well as in internal responsibilities, motivation and recruitment.

The changes were finalized at the annual general meeting in spring 1986. As a result Nokia ended up with a complex dual management structure that functioned on three levels. First, the new Supervisory Board, headed by Mika Tiivola, retained all the duties of the previous Board of Directors and was manned by the same people. Second, the new internal Board of Directors handled roughly the same matters as the Supervisory Board but was headed by Chairman and CEO Kairamo and manned by executives who were nominally in charge of business areas but in practice had no real responsibility for the divisions. The top management was divided between chairman and CEO and the president and COO, whose respective responsibilities were confused from the beginning. Third, the Executive Board was headed by President Simo Vuorilehto, Kairamo's closest colleague since 1983, and included most heads of division.

While the aim of the new Board was to distance Nokia's largest shareholders from operations, the top management itself also became somewhat removed from the running of the business. The members of the internal Board had no hands-on role in the business areas. Actual control of the business areas thus became the responsibility of the president, but even his role was compromised by the full-time Board members, and especially the chairman and CEO.

The role of the internal Board, as stated in its first meeting, was to 'actively develop the corporation without unnecessary formalities'. Nokia's objective since the beginning of the decade had been rapid growth, particularly in electronics. This goal could only be achieved through major acquisitions.

The new organization kept Kairamo further away from day-to-day business. He focused instead on lobbying as chairman of the

Confederation of Finnish Industries, working to bring Finland closer to the European integration process. He was also an active member in the European Round Table of Industrialists where he promoted international education policies.

Simo Vuorilehto took a firm grip on operational management as the newly elected president and ran Nokia operations from his office while the roles of chairman and CEO were left in the void. Meanwhile, full-time Board members Timo H.A. Koski and Antti Lagerroos developed grand ideas for acquisitions to expand the electronics business.

Nokia has seen a number of corporate governance models during its history. The first stage involved the founding fathers or owner-entrepreneurs such as Fredrik Idestam, Eduard Polón and Arvid Wikström. In that era the organization of the company was based on personal ownership, and manned by the owner's relatives and acquaintances. In the second phase ownership fragmented, but actual control was externalized by commercial banks, which provided finance in capital-poor Finland. The banks established their spheres of influence, particularly around the forest industry, the primary source of the country's export income. This system lasted for decades, and began to crumble only in

Nokia's organization as of March 1986

Supervisory Board
• Mika Tiivola, *Chairman* • Jaakko Lassila, *Vice Chairman*
• Edward Andersson • Carl-Olaf Homén • Pentti Kouri • Kurt Swanljung • Pentti Talonen

Executive Committee of the Supervisory Board
• Mika Tiivola • Jaakko Lassila • Kari Kairamo

Board of Directors
• Kari Kairamo, *Chairman, CEO* • Simo Vuorilehto, *president*
• Timo H. A. Koski • Antti Lagerroos • Harry Mildh • Matti Nuutila (until Annual General Meeting in spring 1987)

Executive (Operating) Board
• Simo Vuorilehto, *chairman, COO* • Kari Haavisto, *controller* • Kaarlo (Kalle) Isokallio, *Nokia Information Systems* • Heikki Koskinen, *Salora-Luxor* • Sven Laakso, *Nokia Cables* • Jorma Nieminen, *Nokia-Mobira (Mobile Phones)* • Jorma Ollila, *Finance* • Sakari Salminen, *Nokia Telecommunications* • Janne Simelius, *Nokia Paper*

In 1986 Nokia created a dual management structure: Kari Kairamo became chairman of the internal Board and Simo Vuorilehto, president and chairman of the Executive Board. The owners were in the Supervisory Board. The dual management structure was dismantled in 1992.

the mid-1980s, together with the old world order that had long divided East and West.

The organization created in 1986 seemed to work rather well for two years, until the spring of 1988, but the weaknesses of the model became apparent when the company ran into difficulties. This lesson had a great impact on how Nokia's management was to be organized in the 1990s. All of Nokia's current key directors also featured in the organizational chart of 1986.

Kairamo wanted to create more room to maneuver through ownership arrangements. One milestone was reached in the spring of 1986, at about the same time as the new organization was created. Nokia arranged a private placement of shares to George Soros, the US-based investor. Preparation for the issue was handled by Jorma Ollila, head of international operations, who had moved over from Citibank a year earlier. Another, more ambitious, attempt was to establish cross-ownership between Nokia and Volvo. This idea, developed by Kairamo with Volvo Chairman Pehr Gyllenhammar, failed, and neither of these moves helped loosen the banks' grip on Nokia.

Management complexity leads to errors

● The acquisition of two television set manufacturers in central Europe in 1987 marks the beginning of the greatest odyssey in the history of Nokia, and the story is closely tied in with the confusion in the structure of top management. Besides television, Nokia was making several other acquisitions, including a majority of Maillefer, the cable machinery manufacturer, the remainder of Telenokia's shares from the Finnish government, and Ericsson Information Services. It is fair to ask whether these moves were the outcome of a thoroughly planned strategy or a response to the pressure of circumstance.

Nokia had made its first major international acquisition in 1983 by purchasing a majority of Luxor Ab, the Swedish consumer electronics company owned by the Swedish government. Luxor was a television set manufacturer but it also made a range of other electronic products. At about the same time Nokia bought a majority of Salora, the Finnish television set maker. Overnight, these two deals made television sets the biggest business area for Nokia.

As both acquired companies were reorganized into reasonably good shape, the outlook for the business seemed bright. The vision behind the moves was that the television/monitor activity would form the nucleus of a strong electronics business. A prevailing pan-European belief at the end of the 1980s placed consumer electronics at the vanguard of industrial development. High-definition television (HDTV) was one of the major ventures in Europe at that time.

The primary spark for the acquisitions came from Nokia's strategy and its strong financial position. It aimed to grow and expand internationally through major acquisitions. In May 1987, Nokia was listed on the London Stock Exchange, a move that increased pressure to expand.

In the summer of 1987, Nokia signed a deal to acquire the French-based television set manufacturer Océanic and two related companies,

Sonolor and Televisso from Electrolux of Sweden. The shopping spree continued later in the autumn when Nokia bought the German-based television production business of Standard Elektrik Lorenz (SEL) from Alcatel. Simultaneously Nokia management was busy negotiating the purchase of Ericsson Information Systems, which was successfully concluded at the end of the year.

The acquisitions transformed Nokia into Europe's third-largest manufacturer of color television sets, in the same league as Philips and Thomson. The purchase of Ericsson's Information Systems division made Nokia the largest information technology company in the Nordic countries, and in desktop computers it was neck-and-neck with IBM.

Annus horribilis – how the big picture went dark

● In January 1988 Kari Kairamo told members of the internal Board:

> It goes without saying that the integration and restructuring of the acquired companies, and how quickly and skillfully we will execute this integration, will decisively affect the future of Nokia.

The integration of the television business became the responsibility of Antti Lagerroos, who had prepared the deals. In information technology, a similar task was given to Kalle Isokallio.

It appears that group strategy worked as expected until the spring of 1988. Then things started to go wrong and the year turned into an *annus horribilis* for Nokia. Why? That is one of the biggest mysteries in the history of the company. Three assumptions help us to grasp the situation:

- Nokia became a victim of circumstances. According to this scenario Nokia just went with the tide of events, and nobody could foresee the drastic changes in the global economy and politics. Overheating of the economy and the subsequent crash were universal developments, albeit deeper in Finland than in most other countries.
- High speed led to 'engine failure'. The massive deals exhausted management resources, and the strain began to show in misjudgments and increasingly costly mistakes. This applied particularly to Kairamo who was personally overextending himself.
- It was a conspiracy. Nokia Chief Executive Kari Kairamo had become a larger-than-life figure in Finland, prompting resentment in some quarters. An unspoken consensus emerged for holding

Kairamo on a shorter leash. For example, the Nokia Supervisory Board gradually changed its role from one of supporting new ideas and the management to that of brakeman. Members of top management became impatient with the chief executive who spent much of his time in the public arena. Personal relations in the management team became strained as 'crown princes' jockeyed for position.

The first visible setback took place at the beginning of April 1988 when Timo H.A. Koski, member of the internal Board in charge of reorganization of electronics and international negotiations, died suddenly of cerebral hemorrhage at the age of 40. The next to be set aside was Antti Lagerroos, another young Board member who had prepared the massive television set deals and started their reorganization. Kairamo relieved Lagerroos of his duties in the integration of consumer electronics, but he kept his position on the internal Board.

The integration process of the television set manufacturing companies had come to a halt in May, partly due to Nokia's large share issue campaign that was marketed under the slogan 'Become an owner of Europe'. Kairamo felt that major restructuring, which would have included a reduction of the workforce at production plants, clashed with the dynamic image he had cultivated for Nokia.

In August, Nokia appointed a Frenchman Jacques Noels of Thomson, to head the Consumer Electronics division. Noels initially based his headquarters in Paris, and later in Geneva, well away from the head office and production sites, which were primarily located in Germany. Lagerroos was strongly opposed to the appointment of Noels and the measures he took.

Kairamo also had a problem with the division of labor between himself and President Simo Vuorilehto. Kairamo had spent three active years lobbying in Finland, the Nordic countries and Europe as chairman of the Confederation of Finnish Industries. He even played a role in the formulation of Finnish government policies in the aftermath of the Parliamentary elections in spring 1987. His return to the smaller pond of day-to-day operations at Nokia in the spring of 1988 didn't seem to suit him or to succeed very well. Power had drifted to Vuorilehto and the internal Board. Kairamo even tried to establish the division of labor between himself and Vuorilehto in a formal memo, but without effect.

The company's financial performance gave even more cause for concern. The situation was particularly grave in the consumer electronics business in August, and got worse by the week. The chief executive's assurances to the Supervisory Board did not materialize. Instead, losses accumulated faster than ever. It appeared that television set production, bought with such high hopes and inevitably creating large headlines in the domestic and international press, had turned out to be a serious miscalculation.

A devastating blow

● A stark message from President Simo Vuorilehto was delivered to all Nokia personnel on Monday December 11, 1988:

> Our Chairman and Chief Executive Kari Kairamo died last Saturday night of sudden illness. Despite the heavy loss we will continue to work as normal.

The secret could not be held back for long, however. Finland's leading daily newspaper *Helsingin Sanomat* told readers that Kairamo had committed suicide. The business world was shocked. 'It is always a puzzle when a person takes his life,' said Pehr Gyllenhammar, a close friend and Volvo chairman and CEO, when asked about his death.

The reasons behind Kairamo's death remain one of the most puzzling issues in the history of Nokia. One often-cited explanation goes to his personality – he suffered from manic depression. There is ample evidence of his tremendous energy and operational efficiency but he managed to hide the depressive periods of his mental roller coaster so well that even his closest colleagues failed to notice them. His death came as a complete surprise. Treatment and medication were available for him but he didn't accept them. Several people had suggested he take a few weeks' leave, but to no avail.

Another equally plausible explanation is simple burnout. Overwork often leads to mental and physical fatigue or to complete collapse. For years, Kairamo had lived life in the fast lane with extremely tight schedules and punishing travel itineraries. He had changed Nokia's structure and the way it operated throughout the 1980s. This had culminated in the two major acquisitions, television set manufacturing and information technology, in December 1987. But in the spring of 1988 Kairamo's grip seemed to loosen. Integration of the acquisitions slowed, ownership and management arrangements became tangled and internal appointments often lacked logic – all symptoms of an overstretched chief executive.

A third perspective involves the company. To a large extent, Nokia was Kairamo's entire world. The company's situation in the autumn of 1988 was not catastrophic but its outlook, perhaps best understood by the chief executive, was rapidly deteriorating. In fact the situation was beyond Kairamo's control, and he probably believed there was no way to get it back on track.

The acquisitions made a year earlier had not turned out to be winners. On the contrary, operations in central Europe were deeply in the red, and their restructuring had never really begun. Operational performance had been practically in free-fall since June 1988. Figures in November were appalling. Management's credibility for stopping the rot was disappearing.

The situation was not helped by the fact that Kairamo's relations with the largest shareholders and his closest colleagues had become strained in 1988. The internal Board, established two years earlier, failed to operate as a team. Cracks emerged in the relationship between Kairamo and the president. Kairamo became increasingly distant from the CEOs of the main shareholders, UBF and KOP. He felt withdrawn but could not communicate his feelings, and apparently lacked the strength to take a firm grip on the helm. The company was slipping away from him.

The impression of this author is that the rapidly deteriorating profitability that followed the major acquisitions created huge pressures on the chief executive who had ridden from one success to another for two decades. The collapse of the share price was also a severe blow to him, a man who carefully nurtured his public image. He may also have felt that he didn't get enough support at a time when the pressure from the acquisitions was most severe.

Kairamo's legacy

● Posterity has left a dual image of Kari Kairamo. He led Nokia into its biggest mistake, the adventure in the world of television set manufacturing. On the other hand, his inspiration, focus on international electronics and striving for critical mass laid the foundation for Nokia's build-up in the 1990s and beyond.

Kairamo's career intersected a number of trends and developments in society. It is linked with long lines of family careers in the service of Finnish industry, the events that led to the end of the Cold War and changes in Finland's international position in the 1980s, as well as the fundamental

Kari Kairamo explaining the nuances of a crayfish party to Jacques Delors, president of the European Commission, at Nokia in Summer, 1988.

changes in the structure of the industry, which were created by break-throughs in research and education.

Although he headed Finland's largest industrial group, Kairamo was not a steamroller in terms of management style. Rather, he was a very amicable and inspiring teacher. He took after his great grandfather, a teacher of religion and personification of the protestant ethic, who was one of the key figures in the establishment of Finland's industrial companies and the two commercial banks – the banks that Kairamo later attempted to rein in.

Kairamo had been a leading figure in Finland since his student days. During his mandatory military service, he was elected chairman of the prestigious Student Corps of the Reserve Officers' School. Before joining Nokia, he had acquired wide experience elsewhere. A civil engineer specializing in the forest industries, he landed his first job in Poland, moving on to São Paolo, Brazil, for two years. Later he was based in New York where he spent five years selling paper machines as head of the local sales office. With such broad international experience, Kairamo's background resembled that of his grandfather A. Oswald Kairamo, a scientist who made adventurous expeditions to the Kola Peninsula and Lapland before settling down and exerting a major influence on the country's economy and society.

Kari Kairamo joined Nokia in 1970. His tasks were initially concerned with exports to western markets, and from 1972 to 1977 he was responsible for the group's energy and forest products exports to the West. The forest industry was then the backbone of Finland's exports and the country's national wealth. But Nokia's forestry business was rather modest even compared with domestic competitors. The banks, which controlled Nokia, opposed Kairamo's initial plans – to grow Nokia's forest industry.

Nokia then focused on electronics, which was a new industry and as such was not part of the territorial fights between rival banks. Instead Nokia ended up in a dispute with the government, which had wanted a state-owned electronics industry, along the lines it had followed in the energy sector (see Chapter 2).

But instead Nokia became a showcase for private business in its battle against state domination of industry. Nokia bought majority stakes in Salora, the privately owned television set manufacturer, and the state-run Televa. When Sweden's Luxor became available Nokia made a quick decision to purchase it. Subsequently it organized all the units making electronics into its biggest business area.

Kairamo's vision for Nokia did not stop at electronics. He envisaged a Japanese-type conglomerate in which all sectors were encouraged to grow and expand internationally through acquisition. In the mid-1980s Nokia was involved in some 180 businesses, from rifles to flooring materials, from aluminum products to rubber boots, from toilet paper to cables, and, of course, from computers to telephone exchanges.

During the second half of the 1980s Finland was in search of new directions. The Cold War was coming to an end and protectionist mechanisms in international trade were gradually being dismantled. Finland's position on the world map came under review. Kari Kairamo spent much

CEO Kari Kairamo and future CEO Jorma Ollila, then in charge of finance, introducing Nokia in the London Stock Exchange in May 1987. On the left Matti Saarinen, vice president of corporate communications.

time and energy promoting Nokia and the traditional and profitable Finnish trade with the Soviet Union. Yet his most significant achievements in foreign trade were in the removal of obstacles to the integration process between Finland and Western Europe. His main partner here was Volvo's Gyllenhammar. Kairamo was an active member of the European Round Table of Industrialists, which was set up by Gyllenhammar. Kairamo vigorously chaired its Education Committee.

Several colleagues regard Kairamo as a unique personality and the most inspirational boss they ever had. He was always on the lookout for young, well-educated people with international backgrounds, and one of those he hired was Jorma Ollila, his eventual successor.

Kairamo was also a sociable person. He was equally hospitable to Soviet ministers and US senators. Crayfish parties – a Finnish specialty – often led to international small talk at the company's seaside resort near Helsinki. There were spectacular performances at the Savonlinna Opera Festival and hunting trips for elk, deer and pheasant. Kairamo had a knack for entertaining at social gatherings with appropriate humor, ranging from discreet to rowdy. He seemed comfortable with everybody, irrespective of political hue. He was as effective with up-and-coming politicians as with heavyweight union bosses or top government leaders. Whether on helicopter rides or yacht trips with guests, if Kairamo was there it was always bound to be showy and impressive.

Kairamo prepared his public appearances meticulously. Speeches were drafted with care by his colleagues or outside specialists. Kairamo had a habit of picking out ideas from newspapers and sending clippings and publications to his large circle of friends. Several friends received *Peter the Great*, the book by Robert K. Massie, from him. This apparently reflects Kairamo's self-image: armed with mere willpower, he saw himself building a western bridgehead alone in the middle of a vast eastern swamp. However, Kairamo lacked Peter the Great's despotic brutality, the ability to remove and destroy all obstacles by violence. Kairamo was not a man to cut back the headcount or chop up his company.

Although his reach exceeded his grasp, Kairamo laid the foundations for Nokia as we know it: a highly specialized electronics group present in all corners of the world. His legacy in modernizing Nokia and Finland, underlining the importance of knowledge and education and opening markets to the West in the heady days of the 1980s, is indisputably important.

Dismantling dual management

● Soon after Kairamo's death, Simo Vuorilehto was appointed chairman and CEO. He fought to keep all the reins in his hands, but he failed to win unanimous support from the internal Board. Nevertheless he aimed to systematize top management by various means such as the clarification of roles and responsibilities. He also embarked on the rationalization of administration, a round of heavy-handed cost cutting and looking after such details as speeding up the approvals of meeting protocols.

Vuorilehto abolished the internal Board by merging it with the Executive Board. Overall management was streamlined by placing each member of the new internal Board in charge of a business division. The six business areas and their managers were:

- Telecommunications, Sakari Salminen
- Mobile Phones, Antti Lagerroos

- Nokia Data, Kalle Isokallio
- Cables and Machinery, Seppo Ahonen
- Basic Industries, Harry Mildh
- Consumer Electronics, Jacques Noels

Vuorilehto's most trusted allies during the implementation of his strategy seemed to be Kalle Isokallio who was active in organizing Nokia Data, and notably Jorma Ollila, who received special duties in the divestiture of forest products and increasingly in the build-up of the mobile phone sector. Also on the trusted team were Seppo Ahonen, who prepared the reorganization at Cables and Hannu Bergholm, who was in charge of financial oversight.

Having suddenly landed the top job, Vuorilehto's biggest challenge was to consolidate his position. This worked better for the largest shareholders than for his subordinates, as there was an element of the military in his management style. He compared the role of a head of a business unit to that of an orchestral conductor, while he preferred to think of the chief executive (himself) as head of a concert bureau. He did not consider himself to be personally in charge of operations.

In April 1990, the Supervisiory Board again became the internal Board of Directors. As the directors took a tighter grip on the company, Vuorilehto's position weakened. Some of his subordinates began to bypass him and deal directly with Board members. It was apparent that Nokia still did not have clear lines of reporting following Kairamo's death. At the same time, some investment bankers close to Nokia were drafting their own radical plans for Nokia's new ownership structure.

Nokia's corporate governance became an issue again when two key positions, chairmanship of the Board of Directors (formerly the Supervisory Board) and the issue of Vuorilehto's succession were placed on the agenda. The situation became more Byzantine when Kalle Isokallio, son-in-law of Mika Tiivola, chairman of the Board, was appointed president of Nokia in April 1990. Vuorilehto had promoted Isokallio as his deputy in February, mainly to bypass and force out Antti Lagerroos, another powerful personality in the top team. Vuorilehto wanted Isokallio to sell Nokia Data, but did not want to have him as president.

So when Isokallio became president, severe strain at the top surfaced almost immediately. The relationship between the chief executive and chairman of the Board suffered, and similar tensions prevailed between the chief executive and the fast-moving and blunt president. Top managers did not trust each other and failed to exchange information freely. The president began to develop his own agenda without informing his superior. This resulted in conflicts over major moves such as the sale of consumer electronics and the reorganization of the cable business.

More complications arose when Tiivola announced that he would resign as chairman of the Board of Nokia in the spring of 1991. Tiivola had retired as chairman and CEO of the Union Bank of Finland a year earlier. The grouping headed by UBF had to find a solution to this problem. Ahti Hirvonen, Tiivola's successor at UBF, and Casimir Ehrnrooth, a Board member of Nokia and Chairman of Kymmene, the forest products company and one of Nokia's larger shareholders, teamed up with Vuorilehto to seek solutions to Nokia's most urgent problems.

This again created a dual management structure. One camp consisted of Tiivola and his trusted son-in-law Isokallio. But the real power brokers at Nokia were Hirvonen and Ehrnrooth who felt Isokallio would be unsuitable as Nokia's next chief executive, whereas Tiivola was pushing him toward the position.

A further complication appeared in spring 1991 when KOP decided to sell its holding in Nokia. UBF and KOP were rivals on the banking scene, and KOP was tired of holding a minority position in Nokia. First KOP offered the shares to Ericsson of Sweden. At that point Ericsson was interested in a 20–25 percent holding in Nokia but on the condition that Nokia get rid of the information technology and consumer electronics businesses prior to the deal. Nokia Data was finally sold to ICL-Fujitsu of Britain in May 1991.

Negotiations between UBF and Ericsson, (with the aim of including Ericsson in the camp of owners headed by UBF) continued during the spring and summer. In September, UBF learned the price KOP had managed to negotiate with Ericsson for the Nokia shares, and considered selling its stake to the Swedes, too.

But the fate of the failing Consumer Electronics division remained an insurmountable obstacle. While Ericsson wanted to keep it out of the deal, the sellers insisted that they would not assume responsibility for the division. The difference of opinion prevented any real negotiations between the two parties.

The talks culminated on October 10, 1991, when Ericsson representative Carl Wilhelm Ros called his Finnish negotiating counterparts in Helsinki. He conveyed as 'final' the decision by the Board of Ericsson that the company was prepared to accept the deal at the discussed price provided that Consumer Electronics remained the seller's responsibility. The Finns still would not accept these terms and the talks collapsed.

Thereafter, the owners continued to search for domestic solutions to the ownership question.

The day was dramatic for other reasons. Jaakko Lassila, KOP's chairman and CEO, announced his resignation. This was significant for Nokia's ownership structure because it marked the end of the pact between KOP and the insurance company Pohjola. Together with Mika Tiivola's departure as chairman of the Board, this paved the way for new ownership alliances at Nokia. The new grouping, including UBF, Pohjola and Kymmene, abandoned their traditional trenches. Led by their respective strongmen Ahti Hirvonen, Yrjö Niskanen and Casimir Ehrnrooth, the group found a solution to both the ownership and management problems at Nokia. Hirvonen, representing the largest shareholder, was the driving force behind the arrangements.

Under terms of the agreement, KOP's stake in Nokia was first bought by a group of companies headed by UBF, which immediately sold it to Nokia's subsidiary in Holland. Pohjola held on to its stake until 2000 – by which time it was worth 400 times the price in 1991.

Next, the group working outside the Board tackled the issue of Nokia's operational management. In the autumn, Hirvonen and Vuorilehto had discussed the succession issue. Jorma Ollila's name had frequently cropped up in these and other talks. Having headed the Mobile Phones division since the beginning of 1990, Ollila had managed to stay clear of the disputes at head office.

The agreement on Ollila's move to the Nokia chief executiveship was made in December. The formal decision was taken at the Board meeting on January 16, 1992. The same meeting decided that Vuorilehto would stay on as chairman of the Executive Board until his retirement at the end of May. Since then Nokia has had just one top man: Jorma Ollila.

However, the departures of Mika Tiivola and Kalle Isokallio were more dramatic. Tiivola felt sidelined by his colleagues. He agreed to 'ask to be relieved of his duties' only after the rest of the Board threatened to resign at the Annual General Meeting. Tiivola resigned with an exceptional flourish, dictating his differences of opinion on ownership arrangements into the Board meeting protocol, thereby formally disowning the Board decisions.

Discussion of Isokallio's departure revealed an agreement under which Isokallio was guaranteed a lifetime pension if he resigned. It was signed by Vice Chairman Lassila and Carl-Olaf Homén, but had never been brought to the Board's attention. With Isokallio only in his early 40s, the agreement amounted to a golden handshake. Nevertheless the Board honored the agreement, and Isokallio relinquished his position immediately.

In the spring of 1992, Nokia's Annual General Meeting elected Casimir Ehrnrooth as chairman of the Board, as planned. Yrjö Niskanen became vice chairman while Ahti Hirvonen declined consideration for either position and remained a rank-and-file Board member.

Nokia was now handed over to Jorma Ollila.

CHAPTER 7

The most costly odyssey ever: television production

Behind all of Nokia's major expansion moves – from wood processing to paper and energy production, from rubber galoshes to car tires, and cables to computers, telephone exchanges and mobiles phones – decision-makers have included both doubters and believers. Likewise, differences of opinion have accompanied decisions to restructure the company through the divestiture of key business areas such as forest products and cables, which had once been the company's core businesses.

Throughout its history Nokia tried to build its future on a range of business areas that seemed promising but sometimes turned out to be less so. These include plastics, office machinery and television sets.

This chapter covers the most significant of the odysseys: the buildup of television set production as Nokia's largest business at the end of the 1980s. Why did Nokia endeavor to become one of Europe's top three manufacturers of televisions? Why did it fail to make the business profitable? Why and how did it get out of the business? In addition we examine the disposal of Nokia's traditional business areas, forest products, cables and rubber.

The early 1980s marked a major change in strategic thinking in Nokia's top management both for internal and external reasons. Internally, a younger generation took over when two powerful figures of the 'Old Nokia' finally departed in 1982. First Björn Westerlund, who had been chief executive from 1966 to 1977 and chairman of the Board the following two years, relinquished his position as a regular Board member. Westerlund was followed by Bengt Widing, who retired as senior vice president and chief financial officer the same year. This paved the way for CEO Kari Kairamo to adapt his management style and bring in new blood.

The new managers contributed new thinking at the top. Kurt Wikstedt, as former head of Electronics division, had held the view that Nokia should stick to professional electronics and not venture into the world of

Industrial production in Bochum, Germany, has transformed from coal and steel to consumer electronics and then to mobile phones. Former television engineer Wilfried Piecha (above) was one of the first dozen employees to start the new mobile phone production line. At the start it took one day to produce two mobile phones. Here he is with colleagues in 2001.

consumer electronics. At the time, however, the distinction between the two began to blur as new visions about technologies based on the convergence between computers and television sets emerged. Two people were instrumental in this change and the later development of the group.

One was Timo H.A. Koski, Lic. Sc. (Tech.), who had lived in France and Germany, and was becoming a technology visionary for Nokia in electronics. In Koski's view, Salora's knowhow in the mass production of television sets ideally complemented Nokia's knowhow in computers. In a 1983 memo, Koski wrote:

> The liberalization of telecommunications together with the integration of computers and telecommunications will lead to the increasing importance of end user marketing, particularly as technological differences between professional and consumer electronics are vanishing.

The second force behind changes was Antti Lagerroos, a corporate lawyer who was chief executive of Salora when Nokia acquired the company. Lagerroos moved over to Nokia with the acquisition and later played a key role when Nokia expanded its television set production.

Actually, the Salora acquisition was the first sign that Nokia was taking an interest in consumer electronics. Salora made television sets and other consumer electronics products, but Nokia's main interest at the time was Salora's mobile phone manufacturing. Following lengthy and complex negotiations, Nokia ended up buying a majority share of Salora. As Salora's chief executive, Lagerroos had also targeted Luxor, the Swedish state-owned television and electronics manufacturer, for acquisition. However, the Swedes declined Salora's offer and insisted that the buyer should be Nokia. Thus Nokia not only bought Luxor but also Salora in order to gain further synergy.

CEO Kairamo's corporate strategy was built on three pillars: growth, international expansion and profitability – apparently in that order. As late as the early 1980s, Nokia suffered from a shortage of managers with international background. With the acquisition of Luxor came visions of both internationalization and growth, largely designed by Koski, who had joined Nokia directly from Siemens. At the same time a battle between young lions ensued, each attempting to propose larger international growth projects. This created a spin that resulted in the huge acquisitions in television production capacity in the second half of the 1980s.

Nokia acquired a majority holding in Luxor and Salora in December 1983. Key numbers for the three companies in 1982 were:

- Nokia Electronics, sales FIM 1,100 million (€348 million), personnel 4,996
- Salora, sales FIM 570 million (€180 million), personnel 1,526
- Luxor, sales SEK 730 (€178 million), personnel 1,522

Although Nokia invested heavily in television production capacity, Kairamo had a larger vision – to create a global conglomerate. According to an internal analysis prepared in 1984, Nokia had as many as 37 strategic business units, each of which was composed of three to five strategic business areas. Over the next two years, the number of strategic business areas grew from 150 to 180.

Following the huge Salora-Luxor deals, Nokia put together a new strategic plan. It covered all the existing business areas and their outlook. According to the plan: 'The production of monitors, representing industrial electronics, offers particular growth prospects. *It is likely that the share of consumer electronics at Salora-Luxor will decline.*' (Author's emphasis.)

It is appropriate to note that grand strategies and real-world outcomes do not always match. That was certainly the case here.

The simultaneous preparation of several large acquisitions revealed a management weakness at Nokia. Despite the powers of the newly established internal Board, the group's management resources were stretched too thin for so many major overlapping projects. Another weakness was discord at the top in critical ventures. Finally, insufficient emphasis was put on the analysis of the real health of the acquisition targets.

The television set acquisitions were based on the vision that the television/monitor business would be a driving force behind the development of electronics. Here Nokia was not alone. The expectation in Europe in the late 1980s was that consumer electronics, particularly television and its new features, would exceed military electronics as the drivers of industrial development.

Nokia's strong financial position was obviously one factor that led to its ambitious expansion plans. In 1987 Nokia made its largest profit ever. The target ceiling for new acquisitions was set at FIM 3 billion (€720 million). To prepare for that, Nokia examined prospective acquisition targets worth ten times more, FIM 30 billion (€7.2 billion). Nokia's strong position coupled with its listing on the London Stock Exchange in 1987 increased the pressure to grow, particularly in international markets. Each of the three growth sectors, Mobira, the mobile phones division, Salora-Luxor, the television set division, and Nokia Data, the computer division, could have made acquisitions equal to their own size.

Against this background, internal Board member Antti Lagerroos proposed acquisitions in consumer electronics. In April 1987 Nokia bought the French television set producer Océanic SA and the associated companies Sonolor SA and Televisso SA from Electrolux of Sweden. This was not an isolated case. Around the same time, Nokia bought 61 percent of Maillefer Holding SA, the Swiss-based cable machinery manufacturer. It also bought the remaining stake held by the Finnish government in Telenokia Oy, the company that had been formed when Nokia bought the majority of state-owned Televa.

At the end of the same year Nokia acquired the television set production of Standard Elektrik Lorenz (SEL), from Alcatel. The deal increased sales of Nokia's television set business from FIM 3 billion to FIM 7.3 billion (€720 million to €1,760 million), and the number of personnel shot up from 4,900 to 11,000.

Big as that was, the purchase of SEL was not the end of the acquisitions. At the end of 1987 Nokia bought Ericsson Information Systems,

'Last year our share price rose by 109%. Which company?' The massive posters campaign all around Sweden in the spring of 1987 started building the Nokia image in Sweden.

which was huge compared with Nokia's existing IT operation. The combined price tag on the SEL and Ericsson deals amounted to FIM 3.750 million (€900 million), which compares with Nokia's profit before taxes and minority items in 1987 of FIM 1,225 million (€295million).

As a result of the purchases in 1987, Nokia's annual net sales rocketed to FIM 21.5 billion (€5 billion), of which electronics accounted for 63 percent.

Nokia was now a 'truly European company', Kairamo declared with satisfaction. More than 70 percent of sales accrued from exports and production outside Finland while less than 50 percent of the workforce was located in Finland. Several product families were now genuinely competitive in the European marketplace. Among these, Kairamo named mobile phones, mobile phone networks, color television sets, tissue paper products, cable machines as well as workstations and personal computers.

Why the integration process failed

● Early steps in the integration process were promising. Post-acquisition teams worked actively on improvements in production efficiency and profitability. Then something surprising happened. The restructuring of television set production came to a halt in late spring 1988. The reasons behind this are among the most puzzling turning points in Nokia's history. Let us try to unravel the mystery.

Nokia's share issue in the spring of 1988 might partially explain it. Kairamo might have been reluctant to engage in restructuring and face workforce reductions at a time when a positive image was important to the success of the share issue. In Germany, Kairamo had promised that no employees would be laid off, and undoubtedly felt unable to go back on that commitment.

Meanwhile cracks began to emerge in the solidarity of the top management team. Some people were impatient toward the CEO, who was spending a great deal of time on activities outside Nokia.

'Timo H.A. Koski passed away last Friday night (April 8, 1988) in London as a result of brain haemorrhage.' So began Kari Kairamo's letter to members of the Supervisory Board on the major tragedy that hit the company. Koski had been a member of the Board in charge of restructuring of the electronics business, and had headed important negotiations on international cooperation as well as numerous internal projects.

At board level, things were more complicated. The relationship between Kairamo and Koski had gone sour in the early spring of 1988. Kairamo was displeased with Koski and trust between the two had almost dissolved. It is difficult to say why, but Kairamo probably disliked Koski's tendency to exaggerate his Nokia role in public.

Following Koski's unexpected death, the Nokia Board was left with four members, CEO Kari Kairamo, President Simo Vuorilehto, Antti Lagerroos and Harry Mildh. Kairamo also seemed unhappy with Lagerroos, the other strategist behind the reorganization of the electronics business. This can be inferred by Kairamo's wish to replace Lagerroos as the man in charge of Electronics at the critical point when the restructuring of the television set production in central Europe was beginning.

Figures in mid-May of 1988 showed that one of the recently acquired companies, Nokia Graetz, the consumer electronics firm in Germany, was much more deeply in the red than had been budgeted. This called for more drastic reworking of the figures than planned, and prompted Lagerroos to bombard the head office with grim memos. An example:

After the completion of reorganization at Nokia Graetz in April 1988 it became evident that excess staff in traditional consumer electronics will initially total 1,500, excluding the tube production plant at Essling and the speaker plant in Straubing.

Lagerroos backed up his message on production efficiency with figures:

The most recently reorganized Luxor plant produces 1,422 units per employee, while the same figure at Nokia Graetz is 792 units. In other words Luxor is about twice as efficient in production. The corresponding figure at Salora is 1,409 units. Efficiency figures in marketing are similar.

Nevertheless Kairamo was unwilling to continue Lagerroos' mandate at Electronics, even though Lagerroos was prepared to move to Düsseldorf to run the newly acquired unit. The restructuring process virtually stopped. Without a doubt, this decision led to the greatest losses in the history of Nokia.

In early June 1988 Kairamo made the following proposal to the executive committee of the Supervisory Board:

It is necessary, not only for international credibility but also for more effective management, that our Board in the future include non-Finnish members. We aim to find such a person to head the newly established Nokia Consumer Electronics whose background would enable us to appoint him also as a Board member.

Kairamo saw such qualities in the Frenchman Jacques Noels of Groupe Thomson in Paris, and Noels was soon appointed. But the choice did not go down well with Lagerroos who rightly felt sidestepped and undermined. He strongly opposed the appointment but abstained from the Board meeting that made the decision – thus avoiding the notation of this difference of opinion in the minutes. Lagerroos shared his views in no uncertain terms with Kairamo and Vuorilehto, however. He put his concerns in an internal memo:

Why would Nokia let a foreigner run one-third of the group's business? Compare this with other international companies. Why was there no internal appointment? Language skills: more than half of the business is in Scandinavia and German-speaking Europe. Why was Noels good enough for Nokia but not for Thomson? He held no key position in Thomson's new organization. To whom will Noels report? What is the division of labor between Noels and Lagerroos? Interfering with the operational affairs of a board member without externally informed clear division of labor weakens the effectiveness and credibility of the organization.

It is difficult to say why Lagerroos was passed over. First, top management was probably aghast at the magnitude of the restructuring and pruning necessary in Germany and the reactions that might cause. Power politics may also have been involved. Kairamo and Vuorilehto may have felt apprehensive toward a man who as head of the largest division could have been a strong candidate to rise to the top at Nokia. The third alternative is that Lagerroos was regarded as unfit for the position, but there is little evidence of this. On the contrary, if this was the case, why was the restructuring process stopped without restarting it under someone else's supervision? In any event the strong-willed head of the largest business area was shelved, and he continued strong his criticism of Noels from the sidelines.

A painful exit

● Jacques Noels was appointed at the beginning of June of 1988 and he took up the position in August. Initially he wanted to establish the head office of Consumer Electronics in Paris where he was based throughout that autumn. When Nokia's top management considered Paris an unsuitable base, Noels moved the office to French-speaking Geneva, still far removed from the production plants in Germany and the corporate head office in Helsinki. So he remained distant from production and top management.

Thereafter, Nokia's consumer electronics business lost its rudder, and by early August reports turned ever darker. As Nokia group controller Hannu Bergholm reported in his figures for July to Kairamo:

> Consumer Electronics will perform considerably worse than forecast. Salora, Luxor and Océanic were profitable, although below budget, while Nokia Graetz was FIM 174 million (€40 million) in the red. Lagerroos continued to complain, sending frustrated messages about unsolved problems at Consumer Electronics to Kairamo and Vuorilehto.

Pressure on Kairamo was compounded by events. He had a number of external engagements, including the time-consuming chairmanship of the Confederation of the Finnish Industries, which he held until the end of 1987. When he reduced his external activities in the spring of 1988 and focussed again on Nokia, Kairamo showed signs of fatigue. In the autumn he tried but failed to establish a workable division of labor with Vuorilehto. At the same time, performance of Consumer Electronics was in free-fall, and getting worse by the month.

The executive committee of the Supervisory Board convened on December 9, 1988, at 10 a.m. to deal with figures for the first 10 months of the year. Results were FIM 417 million (€95 million) below the budget and FIM 690 million (€158 million) lower than a year earlier. Minutes show that other than the grim figures, the committee did not discuss

A state visit to Nokia Electronics in Kilo, Finland in July 1987. From left: President of France, François Miterrand, President of Finland, Mauno Koivisto, Timo H.A. Koski, Nokia CEO Kari Kairamo, Harry Mildh, Jyrki Jalasto and J.T. Bergqvist.

anything extraordinary. It appears that Kairamo left the meeting with a nagging feeling that his position was in danger. He indicated this to a colleague after the meeting but there was no evidence of plans for the Supervisory Board to remove him. His suicide the following weekend came as a shock to his superiors and even his closest colleagues.

At the beginning of the following week, Simo Vuorilehto, Kairamo's right-hand man since 1983, took the helm as chief executive officer. His first task was restructuring of the Nokia group. Oddly, he chose not to touch the position of Jacques Noels, head of Consumer Electronics. This was perhaps due to the fact that critics of Vuorilehto also wanted to re-place Noels.

In February 1990 Vuorilehto sacked Antti Lagerroos, the most senior figure who had been highly critical of Noels. Then disagreements emerged between Vuorilehto and Kalle Isokallio, who had been appointed president in April 1990, over the restructuring measures required at Consumer Electronics. Isokallio also wanted Noels removed from his position, but in the power struggle Vuorilehto felt obliged to defend the Frenchman.

Vuorilehto's tenure in the top position was relatively short-lived, and Jorma Ollila replaced him in the spring of 1992. Ollila wasted little time in sacking Jacques Noels and appointing Hannu Bergholm, group con-troller, as his successor. Another key appointment was Heikki Koskinen,

This ad was preceded by one where the Nokia 2110 could be seen. That picture was used so much that even when the phone was removed the audience knew which phone was being talked about. The 2110 became an icon.

Bergholm's right-hand man and an executive with extensive experience at the Salora-Luxor division. Bergholm presented his first budget for Consumer Electronics in June 1992. Its targets were revised downward by FIM 267 million (€51 million), but the actual result for the year fell half a billion Finnmarks (€95 million) short of even the previous forecast.

Consumer Electronics was obviously Nokia's main problem and the alternatives were not attractive. First, the business area could have ceased operations immediately, but this would have caused huge losses. A second alternative was to improve the division's profitability through drastic restructuring measures and sell it as one entity or make other industrial arrangements. Nokia's dilemma was that its balance sheet could not assume the massive losses resulting from a complete stoppage of Consumer Electronics operations. Hence the only remaining alternative was to reduce losses by trimming operations. Paradoxically, this led to massive investments in the loss-making business area.

There were two main problems: the multitude of television set models and the unprofitability of tube production. Nokia's capacity was 2 million tubes a year, whereas the minimum for a profitable operation was considered to be 3 million tubes.

In October 1993, Nokia's Board decided that its primary objective would be to get rid of the Consumer Electronics operations. The first public action was to close down the Esslingen tube manufacturing plant in March of 1994. The company succeeded in negotiating an amicable agreement with the workforce by agreeing to the continuation of operations up to the date of closure. For instance employees were given a bonus for each tube manufactured – against the wishes of the local trade union.

With the strong profitability of Telecommunications and Mobile Phones, the corporate balance sheet had strengthened considerably, and Nokia was prepared to shoulder the costs accruing from the discontinuation of television set production. Meanwhile the Mobile Phones division was growing briskly, and it took over part of the former television set production facilities at Bochum, Germany. Tapio Hintikka, the new head of Consumer Electronics, who had been in charge of Nokia's Basic Industries division and corporate planning, estimated that a loss provision of FIM 2.3 billion (€420 million) in the Group results for 1995 would suffice for Nokia to be free of Consumer Electronics completely.

In the end, Nokia sold the television set production facilities in Finland and the related sales organization in Europe to Semi-Tech (Global) Limited of Hong Kong in the summer of 1996. The deal included everything except production at the Bochum plant in Germany, which was gradually closed down. Under terms of the agreement, Semi-Tech received the right to use the Nokia brand in sets based on Nokia technology, and other variations approved by Nokia, until the end of 1999. Furthermore the buyer received rights to the Luxor, Salora, Finlux, Schaub-Lorenz, Océanic and Guestlink trademarks with only minor restrictions.

The acquisition of the television set manufacturing units in central Europe was Nokia's equivalent of Napoleon's campaign into Russia. It was a grand strategic play but in the end it resulted in the biggest losses in Nokia's history. Without the tremendous growth of Telecommunications and Mobile Phones, Nokia's very existence as an independent company could have been jeopardized. Cumulative losses from television set production totalled FIM 7.1 billion (€1.3 billion).

In retrospect, it is clear that two major mistakes were made:

- First, the acquisitions of the television production plants were not based on sufficient research on the outlook for profitability and growth. Instead the decisions were made according to more general strategy of growth in the electronics sector. The units themselves were not studied with care.
- Second, the decision to stop the restructuring halfway through prevented any hope of recovery. The company failed to tackle rampant losses with sufficient force. Management problems at Consumer Electronics dragged on for several years. Behind it all was Nokia's long-standing over-confidence in its own capabilities; the belief that somehow Nokia management would succeed against all odds.

Selling off forest products, rubber and cables

● As the profitable electronics divisions continued to grow rapidly, Nokia wanted to rethink its position on some of the old business operations. These included the forest products industry, which reached back to the birth of the company in the 1860s, and the rubber and cable industries, which commenced operations in the early 20th century.

Nokia's paper industry was tiny in the international markets and even in Finland it ranked only as a mid-sized company. But, for a forest products company it produced a lot of electricity. The first questions about the viability of the forest products industry were raised as early as the late

Hakkapeliitta snow tires were one of the success stories of Nokia Rubber. The first models had been introduced in the 1930s.

1960s, at the time of the merger of the three businesses: forest products, rubber and cables. The subject was debated through the next decade. Seizing upon a ruling by Finland's Supreme Court on wastewater contents as a pretext, pulp production was halted and Nokia's paper business focussed on tissue paper production.

There were two somewhat conflicting views on how to develop the paper industry. Janne Simelius, head of Nokia's Paper division, believed that Nokia could succeed by creating strategic alliances with other companies while retaining majority control. Chief Executive Simo Vuorilehto, who had headed the division before, also saw alliances as a solution – as a vehicle for gradually getting rid of the business area altogether.

Emotionally, dumping forestry was comparable to selling the small cottage in the countryside where your grandmother had lived all her life. It was too difficult for Kairamo the paper engineer but not for his unsentimental successor Vuorilehto. Since Simelius wanted to retain his domain, Vuorilehto assigned Nokia Group CFO Jorma Ollila to preparate for the sale of forest products.

The Board moved decisively in the spring of 1989. At that point Nokia sold 50 percent of the division to James River of the United States. The

Nokia 66 kV cables on the Nile in Egypt in 1993. Cables was the largest and most profitable business unit of Nokia until 1991.

deal included an option for the remaining half. The tissue paper industry's net sales then amounted to €511 million. Its operating profit amounted to €44 million, which made it the third-best performing business area in absolute terms, trailing only Telecommunications and Cables.

At the beginning of 1990, Nokia's tissue paper production became part of a joint venture with James River and Montedison of Italy. Nokia sold its stake in the venture the following year to JA/MONT N.V., the tissue manufacturer. Although the timing of the deal coincided with the need to raise funds for covering losses at Consumer Electronics, the decision was made a good while earlier. Ultimately the decision was based on Vuorilehto's view that Nokia could not make capital-intensive forest products into an internationally competitive business.

The Rubber division grappled with similar issues. It was divided in two business areas: footwear and tires. The latter aimed to expand internationally in the late 1980s. The first step was the incorporation of the business into Nokian Renkaat Oy (Nokian Tires Oy), of which Sumitomo, the Japanese tire manufacturer, owned 20 percent. Next the company sold off various specialty rubber production units, such as flooring materials. The company was listed on the Helsinki Stock Exchange in 1995, when Nokia reduced its holding to a minority stake. As late as 2000, Nokia still owned 19 percent of Nokian Tires. Throughout the 1990s the company was the most profitable tire maker in the world.

One significant deal within the Rubber division was the management buyout of rubber footwear in spring 1990. This was previously the main business in Nokia's rubber industry, but continuing was considered risky due to sinking prices and demand as well as the growth of cheap imports.

The Cables division was in a different situation. Nokia considered it one of the key future industries, and it was the group's most profitable business area until 1991. Cables held a dominant position in its home market and had profitable trade agreements with Russia. In 1989, Nokia Cables' net sales totaled FIM 2,544 million (€540 million), which was about 10 percent of Nokia's consolidated sales. Some 40 percent of the revenues were generated by exports. Employees totaled 4,800.

Nokia's cable business was keen to penetrate Western markets. In 1987 a plan called 'Eurocables concept' was hatched calling for extensive cooperation with several European cable producers. The aim was to establish Nokia Cables as a strong and equal competitor in the European cable markets through a 'controlled acquisition policy'. At the time the leading European cable makers included Alcatel of France, BICC of Britain and Pirelli of Italy. Each of them doubled its net sales between 1987 and 1989.

Following complicated evaluations and negotiations, Nokia acquired a majority stake in NKF, the Dutch cable manufacturer, in 1989 for about €100 million. This paved the way for a determined penetration of the liberalized cable markets in Europe. Nokia's expansion strategy would probably have been less ambitious without the comfortable cushion provided by the profitable trade with Moscow. The NKF acquisition committed Nokia to the cable industry for a few more years.

As Vuorilehto saw it, Cables continued to play an important role in Group strategy but in the early 1990s the former growth industry and cash cow began to cause problems, too. Several factors contributed. First, the European cable cartel was dismantled primarily at the demand of the competition authorities of the European Community (later EU). Second, the collapse of the Soviet Union in 1991 wiped out Nokia's important markets in the East. The third, and perhaps most important, change was the economic downturn, which compounded the problems of overcapacity and considerably weakened the company's profitability.

Nokia Cables had its own problems – its home market was suffering from a deep recession. Internally there were management and administrative problems at the recently acquired NKF. The merger of NKF into Nokia Cables was not completed as planned, and the two units continued to operate as separate companies. Nokia's corporate management disagreed on a cable strategy – Vuorilehto and Isokallio crossed swords at several Board meetings during the autumn of 1991 on whether Nokia should acquire PKI, the cable manufacturing operations of Philips. The chief executive had the last word and nothing came of it.

Facing the need to divest

● When he took over as chief executive of Nokia in spring 1992 Jorma Ollila still considered Cables as one of the company's core businesses. Two years later the strategy was reversed and he decided to divest the cable and cable machinery business altogether. This was one of the company's turning points.

Ollila presented his plan for focusing Nokia on the Telecommunications and Mobile Phones divisions, and divesting all other business areas, at a Board strategy meeting in Hong Kong in May 1994. This was the first time the management had seriously proposed its revolutionary plans to the Board. On the block were to be Cables, Cable Machinery, Tires, Industrial Electronics, Power and Consumer Electronics. The Board hesitated (see pages 148–150) but eventually the fire sale got under way. The bearer shares in Nokia-Maillefer cable machinery operations were sold to a group of investors in 1995. Likewise, Nokia Cables was sold to international investors in 1996. Prices received were low compared to investment made in the business areas, but nevertheless helped to cover losses at Consumer Electronics.

A simultaneous rapid rise in Nokia's overall profitability facilitated the divestitures and the bold shift of focus, and Nokia was able to set new and much more ambitious targets.

CHAPTER 8

Building on technology

Throughout its history, Nokia has placed great importance on technical excellence. The wood processing business, which gave birth to Nokia in the 1860s, was part of the revolution in pulp and paper production technology that brought the explosive growth in paper consumption and applications. Likewise, the rubber industry, one of the original core businesses of the group, was highly demanding in technical terms. Companies jealously protected technological innovations that helped to widen their portfolio of rubber products.

When three companies were merged to form Oy Nokia Ab in 1966, top management recognized the importance of continuing research and development in all business areas. In the 1970s R&D in electronics made the longest strides. Yet it can be said without exaggeration that real change in the historical context did not take place until June 1983. Up to that point, Nokia's chief executives had mainly been concerned with the availability and price of raw materials, such as copper and raw rubber, and particularly energy. Now the focus quickly shifted to research and development and upgrading of education both inside Nokia and generally in Finnish society. Knowhow was becoming Nokia's primary competitive edge.

Cheap energy was one of the main concerns of the Finnish executives. Björn Westerlund, Nokia's chief executive, had been the key player in the decision to build two private nuclear reactors in Finland in the 1970s. His successor, Kari Kairamo, was equally keen to ensure that cheap energy was available for Finnish industry, which in practice meant lobbying for a fifth reactor.

Led by Kairamo, the Energy Policy Committee of the Confederation of Finnish Industries published a paper on energy policy in June of 1983 which argued for more nuclear power capacity in Finland. It met with strong political opposition, particularly from the agrarian Center Party, one of the key parties in the coalition government, and the initiative was stalled. Further complications were created by international factors, such as the Chernobyl accident, which increased anti-nuclear sentiment at home and abroad. The debate continues into the 21st century and Finland still has no fifth nuclear reactor despite substantial imports of energy and prompting by the country's forest products industries.

It is interesting to note in the historical perspective that Kairamo seemed to lose interest in nuclear energy soon after 1983 although he remained active in industrial policy. He opposed the dominant position of the state-owned energy companies Neste Oy (oil) and Imatran Voima Oy (electricity), but that position was part of a wider campaign by private industrial companies opposed to the excessive role of state-owned companies in the Finnish economy.

RESEARCH AND DEVELOPMENT EXPENDITURE IN SOME OECD COUNTRIES 1985–1999

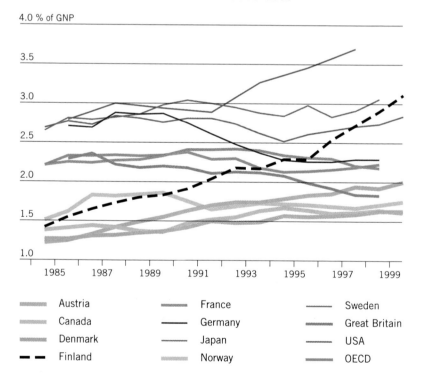

From energy to research

● The years 1982–1983 marked a turning point in Nokia's history as several developments touched both the company and Finland. Real interest rates, which had remained negative for years due to constant inflation, turned positive. This profoundly reshaped the economic landscape. Inflation no longer concealed debt or paid for investments. Companies faced new demands for profitability. Monetarist economic views and values were gradually hitting the shores in Finland, leading to the liberalization of financial markets and new opportunities in corporate finance. At Nokia, this development loosened the grip of the banks that were also its major shareholders.

Simultaneously, Europe began to wake up from its 'Eurosclerosis' as the integration of Western Europe gathered speed. At the same time a far-reaching transformation was under way at Nokia. Cheap energy as the focal point gave way to knowhow, and research and development became the nucleus of corporate development.

Research and development and technology matters quickly rose to the top of Kairamo's agenda. He also vigorously promoted education issues. In 1983 Nokia personnel in R&D totaled only 907, from a total workforce of 23,651. One impetus for raising this proportion was the high-tech policy discussions within the Paris-based Organization for Economic Cooperation and Development (OECD) as well as the industrial strategy symposiums of the Royal Swedish Academy of Engineering Sciences and the Royal Swedish Academy of War Sciences.

Nokia's research activity was headed by Viljo Hentinen, a PhD in telecommunications technology. He had extensive contacts in university research circles and of course at Nokia. In 1985 Hentinen prepared a memorandum, 'Technology Strategies', that divided Nokia's products into four categories:

- First-to-market
- Follow-the-leader
- Application engineering
- Me-too

Hentinen posited that Nokia had only three products that would fit the first category, and their share of the company's output was just 12 percent. Followers accounted for 46 percent of sales.

Change at Nokia came as part of the development that can be described as the birth of Technology Finland. As this chapter aims to explore the extent of public support for Nokia, it is necessary to shed some light on the government's activities in research and development.

Finland's public support of research and development has been routed through three channels. Unlike many other countries, Finland's expenditure in military R&D has been minuscule. Elsewhere, telecommunications and electronics companies have closely cooperated with the military, which has helped to generate substantial financing and orders for equipment.

Public R&D expenditure goes primarily to universities and the Technical Research Center of Finland. Funds have then been directed to special projects such as research connected to war reparations after World War II, and research on nuclear energy in the 1950s and 1960s. Public funds have also been channeled through the Ministry of Trade and Industry, which later established Tekes, the National Technology Agency, as a vehicle for public R&D investment.

According to Juhani Kuusi, the first director general of Tekes and later director of the Nokia Research Center, August 12, 1982 can be considered the birth of 'Technology Finland'. On that day the government made a far-reaching decision regarding the country's technology policy, among other things setting the target for Finland's R&D expenditure – public and private combined – at 2.2 percent of gross domestic product (GDP) by 1992 (it was 1.2 percent at the time). Besides establishing Tekes, the government decided to launch national technology programs and substantially increase international cooperation in technology issues.

In retrospect the progress has been impressive. By the end of the 1990s, R&D expenditure topped 3 percent of GDP, thanks largely to Nokia's role in the field.

Nokia's global success has sometimes been attributed to the support it has received from the Finnish government. This impression is false; Nokia has not grown with the help of public funds. Nokia's own research expenditure is substantially larger than the public support it has received. Compared with its competitors in Sweden, Germany and France, Nokia has received much less in government subsidies – direct or indirect. However, the effectiveness of public support has usually been high, since it has been targeted at risky key products and long-term research.

Nokia Research Center

● The roots of Nokia Research Center (NRC) reach back to 1979 when the company established an information technology unit aimed at developing new businesses in telecommunications and data processing. The unit was given five years to become commercially viable. Among products

Japanese Nokia researchers from left: Yoshiya Hirase, Dr. Takshi Iwamoto, Dr. Koichi Mori and Hiroshi Tobita at NERD (Nokia Exchange of Research and Development) in Helsinki in 2000.

it developed during the time was the electronic mail system NoteX. Overall, the unit was not a commercial success, and its position came under scrutiny. This led to the establishment, or re-establishment, of a common research and development unit in the Nokia Electronics division in 1986.

Here the unit's operating philosophy differed from that of many other electronics companies. IBM, for example, had established dedicated 'lab in the woods' research centers funded entirely by the central administration of the company.

NRC was quick to find its role in servicing business units and it grew at the brisk rate of 50 percent annually. It established extensive international links with projects such as the pan-European Eureka project and got seriously involved in the creation of international of standards. (Eureka is a joint public-private initiative established in 1985 involving the European Union and 31 other countries to fund market-driven research aimed at maintaining European competitiveness.)

Personnel at the NRC initially totaled only 50 but had increased to 200 by 1989. Nokia's financial position weakened considerably in 1989–1991 and corporate management decided to transfer the funding responsibility of NRC to the business units. This decision forced the research center to revise its strategy, and become more business-oriented. This took place earlier than at many other large international electronics companies, but it also led to shortsighted funding efforts.

The role of the NRC came under close scrutiny at a top management workshop in the spring of 1993. As Chief Executive Jorma Ollila saw it, the 1990s would be the decade of telecommunications, requiring the adaptation of new technologies. Nokia would increasingly have to rely on knowhow. Ollila believed that the creation of sufficient basic knowhow at Nokia would be a long-term effort and would require as much as a decade to accomplish, even though product cycles would only last about a year. Hence research would primarily have to be organized by independent business units, based on their R&D requirements and investment capabilities.

NRC was to become a knowledge center for the development of new technologies and R&D processes, and it would adapt the latest information from international markets for the use of Nokia's business units. Interestingly, an NRC Workshop memorandum stated as early as in 1993:

> Strategic alliances and partnerships will play a crucial role also in R&D projects, since they would provide information about basic technologies before they become public.

Numerous employees have volunteered to transfer from the research center to business units. About half of the transfers have taken place at the request of the individual or by appointment to positions in new projects. Others have resulted from structural changes such as the establishment of new business operations.

When Nokia's profitability got back on track in 1994, outlays for R&D increased substantially. In 2001 Nokia employed 18,600 people in research and development, about 35 percent of the workforce. It set up several research centers around the world during the 1990s, and by 2001 had 54 R&D centers in 14 countries.

Education and cooperation with universities

● Since 1987, Nokia has conducted limited academic education in technology, aimed at high degrees. Studies in these programs have turned technicians into engineers and engineers into post-graduate students, and some have gone on to doctorate level. Nokia's education programs in 1987–1993 included 260 people, who devoted an average of four working hours a week to their studies.

In advanced education, Nokia cooperated with the University of Oulu,

Tampere University of Technology and Helsinki University of Technology.

In the 1980s, Kairamo dedicated a great deal of time to international education issues and links between industry and universities. He was in charge of education issues at the European Round Table of Industrialists (ERT) and invited training directors of member companies to Finland for brainstorming sessions. The cost of these projects exceeded ERT's budget, and Nokia made up the difference. One result of this networking was *'Education for Life: a European Strategy'*, a white paper edited by Kairamo. It was published posthumously in book form in 1989 (Butterworth Heinemann, London).

Nokia has always opposed the idea of establishing a new private university for Finnish industry. Instead, as Nokia became more and more research-intensive, the company built closer ties with existing universities and research institutions. Its objective was to influence the orientation and level of research in those institutions. At the same time, the need for better-educated employees grew rapidly, and Nokia lobbied strongly for the further development of education systems, quality of examinations and emphasis on educational programs.

Throughout the 1990s Nokia managed to find most of its required

R&D Engineers Carl-Magnus Fager and Teppo Aapro doing thermal testing of components at the Nokia Research Center electronics laboratory in Helsinki.

Dr. Yrjö Neuvo, chief technical officer, Nokia Mobile Phones, and member of the Executive Board.

R&D personnel in Finland. This is one of the fundamental reasons for maintaining the head office in the country of its birth. In 2000, some 63 percent of Nokia's R&D personnel were based in Finland.

In public, Nokia executives have consistently stressed the importance of systematic education and the development of knowhow. Nokia has focussed particularly on the general understanding of mathematics and the sciences by supporting various campaigns and donating appropriate literature to all Finnish high schools.

By the late 1990s, cooperation with both local and foreign universities was proving to be a big help in Nokia's recruitment, research and development and the education of its employees. Another objective was to secure facilities for Nokia's own research and development in the long term. Most of this kind of cooperation with technical universities and faculties takes place in countries where Nokia has its more extensive operations.

Nokia's recruitment activities have included various events and visits to campuses. The introduction of student trainees proved to be one of the most successful recruitment activities in Finland. In the late 1990s some 1,000 students annually prepared their theses while working at Nokia, and after graduating most of them stayed on board.

Cooperation in research and development took different forms. Nokia commissioned research as plain subcontracting while also working with consortia involving several partners. International research projects have usually provided a framework for the larger research and development projects involving universities and other companies.

The foundation for the international expansion of Nokia's R&D activities was laid even before Finland joined the European Union, but its membership in 1995 enabled Nokia to engage actively in the EU's telecommunications and information technology R&D programs. Nokia has since led several key development programs in telecommunications. In addition Nokia's R&D experts frequently meet with professors and university researchers to gauge the future direction of research.

Gradually, Nokia's own education programs failed to satisfy the rapidly growing demand for an educated workforce. The needs grew as Nokia pulled itself out of its financial difficulties and focussed on telecommunications. As early as in 1995 Nokia estimated the need for new technically trained staff would reach 2,000–2,500 annually when total recruitment totaled 3,000 per annum. Hence Nokia would watch closely and aim to influence Finland's education policy, particularly the training for technical personnel.

The need for educated personnel continued to grow, and by the end of 1997 Nokia estimated that it would need some 6,500 highly educated experts during 1997–2000. At that time the total number of corresponding graduates from Finnish universities/polytechnics would be 9,550. In 1998 both the number of graduates and Nokia's recruitment needs totaled 2,000 people.

Nokia preferred to direct public education systems toward its objectives rather than develop its own competing education programs. In 1997 Nokia spent approximately FIM 550 million (€98 million) on internal training, and every employee spent on average 11 working days per year in further education.

Internal training often involved Nokia's own research community. For example, in autumn 2000 it organized a large internal symposium called Nokia Exchange of Research and Development, or NERD (pun intended). Over one thousand researchers and product developers from around the world gathered in Finland to listen to some 50 presentations and 40 demonstrations.

Meanwhile top management were trained in programs such as 'Landscape' and 'Panorama'. These focussed on themes like 'How to become the employer of choice in the US', 'Understanding the strategies of fast-growing high technology companies in the US', 'Distribution channel management' and 'Emerging opportunities in the US communications market'. Some 30 Nokia managers at a time took part in these sessions.

The most significant education venture in the late 1990s was the supplementary education program for information technology. The program was launched by the Ministry of Education in 1998 as a result of an analysis of future knowledge and education requirements as well as active lobbying by information technology companies. The objective was to substantially increase both the quality and quantity of education at universities and polytechnics in the fields of electrical and electronics technology, telecommunications and information technology.

The program called for the number of places at universities to be increased by 1,000 and in technical schools by 1,400 by the year 2000 at a cost of some FIM 3 billion (€505 million) in 1998–2006.

About 20 Finnish electrical and electronics industry companies took part in this 'joint venture' by upgrading laboratory equipment for technical universities and faculties through equipment and software donations worth a total of FIM 50 million (€8 million) in 1998–2006.

Nokia assumed a pivotal role in both the supplementary education of information technology and in equipment donation. The magnitude of the program compares with the size of an average Finnish university. Hence these ventures can justifiably be called 'the university of the 1990s' for Finnish information technology companies. The success of these programs partly explains why Nokia has remained in Finland, and why its core is still very much Finnish: constant renewal of knowledge is the primary resource of a rapidly developing technology company.

How research is linked to standardization

● Nokia's continuing investment in research and education naturally aims at supporting product development. Its second objective is closely linked with the development of international standards. A prime example is Nokia's key involvement in creating the standard for the third generation cellular phones.

One of Nokia's greatest breakthroughs in standardization took place in October 2000 at the 3GPP (the Third Generation Partnership Project) codec meeting in Osaka, Japan. (Digital signal processing in mobile phones is done in tandem with sophisticated compression techniques mediated by the codec (acronym for compressor/decompressor) unit of the phone.) The company's speech and voice laboratory at Tampere had worked for several years on the standardization of a broadband speech code for 3G and GSM systems.

Mobile phones currently use narrow bandwidth (300–3,400 Hz) for voice, which is transmitted over ordinary telephone networks. The next step will be the introduction of broadband speech (50–7,000 Hz), which improves the quality of speech to the level of television standard. The difference in voice quality is similar to a television news program in which an anchor person speaks in the studio and a reporter speaks on the telephone.

The committee responsible for standardization accepted Nokia's proposal for the new 3GPP and GSM codec standards and the decision at Osaka was unanimous. It was based on test results that Nokia won by the largest margin in the history of codec standardization. All in all there were 11 entries, of which 5 were chosen for closer scrutiny. The five included Nokia, Ericsson, Motorola, Texas Instruments and the FDNS consortium (including France Telecom, Deutsche Telekom, Nortel Networks and Siemens). The tests were expensive, demanding and extensive involving three continents and five languages. There was a total of 160 individual test cases. The table below indicates the number of failures for each applicant.

This was the first time an applicant passed all tests without failure. At the conclusion of the listening tests, Nokia's figure of merit was in a class of its own.

The achievement marks the culmination of Nokia's technology strategy. Nokia believed that following the choice at Osaka the 3G and GSM standards would remain fairly stable in the foreseeable future. This also marks the point at which 3G standardization would move from speech to multimedia. Nokia's next objective was to introduce the broadband standard as the standard for the Internet. Then there were a number of smaller codec standardization issues, and application of existing standards to practice.

Research plays a vital role in the choice of worldwide telecommunications standards and Nokia understood this at an early stage.

Osaka 3G voice codec tests in 2000

	% of failure	Figure of Merit
Nokia	–	60.4
TI	14.4	32.0
Motorola	14.4	19.6
Ericsson	20.0	19.0
FDNS	35.6	6.8

CHAPTER 9

GSM opens a window
to the future

The factors behind Nokia's success can be traced to the second half of the 1980s when digitalization emerged as the way forward in the electronics industry. Secondly, deregulation on the national level opened markets to competition, both domestic and foreign. Thirdly, international borders opened as the European Community evolved into the European Union and protectionist trade barriers were gradually removed.

Finally, the overheating of the western economies seemed to bring on a sense of invulnerability among successful managers and what some observers today call 'speed blindness'. The pressure to grow and expand internationally through acquisition was part of this trend.

Much of Nokia's global success stems from the fact that it has kept its roots firmly in Finland where deregulation began earlier and was implemented more consistently than elsewhere. This forced Nokia to adapt to the dynamism of open competition ahead of its competitors. Additionally, Finland is such a small marketplace that Finnish companies had to seek growth beyond their home borders.

Dismantling operator monopolies

● Finnish authorities began to dismantle operator monopolies by first deregulating telefax transmission. This led to open competition in data transmission in 1988. The first political debate to break the monopoly concerned the license application by Datatie Oy, which had built a nationwide infrastructure for private telephone companies in 1985. Soon an even fiercer battle over cellular phones ensued. After a fight over the mobile license for Radiolinja, the cellular phone operator established by

Mobira Talkman roadside ads in 1986. The analog NMT mobile phone system intro-duced in Scandinavia in the early 1980s was the decisive background for Nokia's rise in mobile phones and mobile networks. It was mainly used in cars.

private telephone companies, the government decided in principle to throw all telecommunications services to open competition.

From the equipment suppliers' perspective the entry of new operators opened a new chapter in telecommunications. Nokia saw the potential to grow quickly, and strengthened the position of cellular phones and tele-communications in 1986 by elevating their status to a 'major division'. In its first meeting, the internal Board of Nokia divided the Electronics divi-sion into three industrial divisions: Nokia Information Systems, led by

Kalle Isokallio; Nokia Mobile Phones, headed by Jorma Nieminen, and Nokia Telecommunications, led by Sakari Salminen.

This industrial structure had been in preparation for several years. Certain individual business operations were switched progressively from one group to another over the years. But the essential question was the development of innovation, not of organization. The change that largely determined the future of Nokia was the breakthrough of digital mobile communications.

Telecommunications and Mobile Phones, the two core businesses of Nokia's future, mainly relied on organic growth. Telecommunications did search for acquisition targets, and one candidate was studied very carefully,

GSM infrastructure customers 1989–2001

1989
- Radiolinja/Finland

1990
- Cellnet/UK
- Vodafone/UK

1991
- Orange/UK
- Sonofon/Denmark
- Hongkong Telecom Mobile Services
- Europolitan/Sweden

1992
- KPN Telecom / Holland
- Optus/Australia
- Vodafone / New Zealand
- Sonera/Finland

1993
- E-Plus/Germany
- Globe Telecom / Philippines
- Pannon/Hungary
- TAC/Thailand
- Cegetel/France

- Telia Mobile / Sweden
- TCI/Iran

1994
- Omnitel Pronto / Italy
- Telenor Mobil / Norway
- NetCom GSM a/s / Norway
- LMT/Latvia
- North-West GSM / Russia
- Beijing TA / China
- AIS/Thailand

1995
- Zhejiang PTA / China
- Shanghai Unicom / China
- Henan PTA / China
- Jiangxi PTA / China
- Modi Telstra Ltd / India
- Fujian PTA / China
- Sky Cell/India
- Time Wireless / Malaysia
- Radiolinja/Estonia
- Swiss PTT / Switzerland

- VoiceStream/USA
- PTT/Morocco

1996
- Mobile One / Singapore
- Hunan Unicom / China
- Yunnan PTA / China
- Belgacom/Belgium
- Aerial/USA
- EuroTel Praha / Czech republic
- Polkomtel S.A. / Poland
- Fascel Ltd / India
- Tata Communications / India
- BPL US West / India
- Telefónica Móviles / Spain
- Uzmacom/Uzbekistan
- New World PCS / HK
- Evergrowth Telecom / India
- Bouygues Telecom / France

but in the end Nokia failed to find companies that would clearly add value. Instead, Telecommunications grew consistently through strategic investments in operations, targeting the development of new products based on the latest technology as well as geographical market expansion. These investments amounted to 25 percent of net sales in network operations and 10 percent in the Mobile Phones division.

The Mobile Phones division saw more acquisitions. First Nokia and Salora joined forces in Mobira. This was followed by the acquisition of Technophone. But the division's growth was always more organic than acquisition-driven.

Internal knowhow accumulated, which in turn boosted competitiveness.

111 operators in 50 countries

1997
- Shanghai PTA / China
- Shanxi PTA / China
- Telia/Finland
- Wireless Alliance / USA
- Mobilix/Denmark
- Cosmote/Greece
- VIAG Interkom / Germany
- Telsim/Turkey
- Mobilkom/Austria
- ONE/Austria
- Telkomsel/Indonesia
- Digital Phone Company /Thailand
- Centertel/Poland

1998
- Omnitel/Lithuania
- NingXia PTA / China
- BEN / Holland
- diAx/Switzerland
- Mobile Telecommunications / Kuwait
- Iowa Wireless Services / USA
- Orange Communications / Switzerland

- Finnet-group/Finland
- Corporacion Digitel C.A. /Venezuela
- Smart/Philippines
- StarHub/Singapore
- Telecom Cellular / Malaysia
- SOL Communications / USA

1999
- KG Telecom / Taiwan
- China Unicom An Hui / China
- China Unicom Gan Su / China
- China Unicom / China
- Inner Mongolia
- Amena/Spain
- VimpelCom/Russia
- Primatel/Hungary
- Tele Danmark / Denmark
- LUXGSM/Luxemburg

2000
- Blu/Italy
- Elca/Venezuela

- Nuevatel/Bolivia
- Partner Comms. / Israel
- Viag/Liechtenstein
- 2G/Finland
- Hainan/China
- Max.mobil/Austria
- Eircell/Ireland
- Digiphone/Ireland
- Guilin/China
- Chonqqing Mobile
- AT&T/USA
- AMC/Albania

2001
- Heilongjiang Mobile / China
- Mobinil/Egypt
- TIM/Peru
- MegaFon/Russia
- Telemar/Brazil
- Liaoning Unicom/ China
- Saudi Telecom Co/ Saudi Arabia
- Yunnan Unicom/China
- Zheijang Unicom/ China
- Cingular/USA

This principle differed from some other industrial divisions where growth was mainly achieved through acquisition. The opening of the west European markets in 1988 gave a further boost to the growth of Telecommunications.

Nordic NMT

● The pan-Nordic NMT, the analog Nordic Mobile Telephone system that was introduced in 1981, in many respects laid the foundation for future development of the coming digitized mobile phone systems.

'The role of NMT in the Nokia success story is difficult to overestimate', says Lauri Melamies, who was director in charge of the development of Nokia's cellular networks. 'It was not only a question of how smart our choice of certain details in the standard was – they are always debatable – but also the economy of scale in the standard that was originally created to become international.'

The pan-Nordic NMT system became a standard, and it provided easy carry-over from one country to another through international roaming. Luckily, it also adopted the 'calling party pays' principle, which facilitated the spread of mobile phone numbers on business cards and the like. This differs from the United States where in some regions the receiver pays part of the cost of the call, making many mobile phone users reluctant to give out their phone numbers.

On the back of the successful NMT system, Nokia's Mobile Phones division grew rapidly. Nokia allocated all available programming resources to NMT exchange production when they had finished other projects. Demand for programmers far exceeded supply even then.

Following numerous internal discussions, Nokia decided to expand production to facilitate the first bid for an NMT exchange in 1984 followed by the first contract in 1986. This broke the virtual monopoly position of Ericsson as the supplier of NMT networks.

NMT rapidly spread to various parts of the world, including the Far East where Thailand became an important market for Nokia. With the help of NMT, Nokia for the first time reached market share in a segment that was (at least to some extent) global. A key element in the system was international mobility. This feature provided one of the key elements for the coming GSM system, the next generation mobile phone networks with a more complex architecture.

Former Finnish Prime Minister Harri Holkeri making the first GSM call on 1 July 1991 in Helsinki. His role in opening mobile phone competition in Finland was significant. Holkeri was president of the United Nations' General Assembly in 2000–2001.

The map of global mobile phone standards was very colorful in the early 1980s. The United States had a system called AMPS, while the British adopted TACS, derived from the American version. Meanwhile Germany, France, Italy and Japan had their own indigenous systems. NMT, AMPS and TACS were among the few systems that gained footholds outside of their original home base. Nokia manufactured handsets for most systems, but focused only on NMT in network equipment at the time since the required investment in several systems was considered too high.

Today those systems are commonly called first generation mobile phones. Technically they all used an analog signal although the network exchanges were already digital.

GSM takes off

In 1982, the European Conference of Postal and Telecommunications Administrations (CEPT) launched a program for the standardization of the second mobile phone generation. The working group was named 'Groupe Spécial Mobile' (GSM). It later lent this name for the mobile phone standard, although it was redefined as 'Global System for Mobile Communications'. The objective was to create a common bandwidth that would facilitate pan-European roaming, create mass markets that would result in cheaper calls, and, more generally, adopt the latest available technology.

In December 1986 the Commission of the European Community set July 1, 1991, as the target date for the inauguration of the new system. In February 1987 the working group chose the digital TDMA (time division multiple access) as its common system. It was relatively close to the proposal by Nokia and the Nordic countries.

One important milestone in the development of the GSM mobile phone systems took place in October 1987 when 13 European countries signed a Memorandum of Understanding that defined the essential standards and the timetable of GSM. This started the race for the development and introduction of the new system.

The phenomenal success of GSM was crucial to Nokia for two reasons. First it provided a large enough market to justify substantial R&D investment to create long product lines. From this perspective the choice of GSM was not a decisive factor; the same goals would have been achieved with any widely accepted standard. On the other hand, Nokia's familiarity with the GSM standard helped it in the battle for market share. It had actively taken part in the development of the technology of the GSM standard, and the transition from the NMT systems was relatively smooth in terms of user culture.

The development of a new standard for networks was much more complicated than the development of handsets. Hence it was vitally important for Nokia that the standard of network it focussed on would gain a leading position globally. Along with the success of NMT, Nokia had made plans to develop other systems for the first generation of mobile phones. But in the early spring of 1988 these plans were shelved and the top management of the Telecommunications division decided to concentrate on the GSM system.

Soon thereafter the goal was set out in an internal memorandum more precisely:

> On July 1, 1991 Europe's first GSM network, supplied by Nokia, will be inaugurated.

This was one of the most far-reaching decisions in the history of Nokia. Surprisingly, the target was achieved, probably because the operator Radiolinja, the joint venture of private telephone operators and a new player in the newly opened market, was eager to inaugurate the network on schedule.

Radiolinja thus had the distinction of opening Europe's first GSM network and the former monopoly state-owned Post and Telecommunications Administration was left behind. At the time it was content with the rapid growth of the NMT user base and network capacity, and had planned to move onto the GSM network only in the mid-1990s.

Like all equipment suppliers, Nokia was prepared to sell products to all operators and buyers, although competition between buyers did not make life easy. It had to balance the interests of competitive customers while also maintaining good business relations with everyone.

Because this was a new technology for a new market, GSM sales forecasts were rather erratic. Estimates in 1987 and 1988 put the figure of European GSM subscribers in 2000 at 10 million, seemingly on the high side. In fact, the figure that year was far higher. There were several tens of millions GSM subscribers outside of Europe. In other words in the early 1990s Nokia was in the throes of huge growth that somehow had to be managed. So there were lots of surprises, but overall Nokia's visions and strategies for the future were pretty much on the mark.

GSM became successful in Europe largely because all key players including governments (regulators), service providers (operators) and the industry (suppliers) were committed to it. The other reason was the choice of the digital standard. This enabled the development of services, encryption of voice and data, additional capacity, reduction of the size of base stations and lower prices.

Meanwhile, the development of handsets surprised nearly everyone. Their size and weight shrank, prices came down steadily and the number of subscribers grew faster than anyone could have anticipated. They became mass-market products with an increasing number of new features and services such as SMS, the text message service.

In the autumn of 1987 Nokia established Nokia Cellular Systems Oy for the manufacture and sale of telecommunications products and services. The company's Board consisted of Timo H.A. Koski, Sakari Salminen and Sari Baldauf, who also became president.

This was preceded by the Finnish government's decision to sell the

The target was to sell 400,000 of these Nokia 2100 series phones, but they sold 20 million. The series was introduced in 1994.

remainder of shares in Telenokia to Nokia, which helped to streamline the business operations. The roles and responsibilities were at last clarified, with the Mobile Phones division focusing on handsets and Telecommunications on infrastructure. A new and fast-growing business required a smoothly run organization to meet the considerable challenges ahead.

There were two reasons for establishing Nokia Cellular Systems. First, a new and fast-growing business required a separate, more efficient unit to meet the challenges. Second, the new structure enabled it to engage in strategic partnerships without affecting the ownership structure of the entire operation.

In October 1987, two of Nokia's top executives featured prominently in Geneva. Chairman and CEO Kari Kairamo gave the keynote address at Telecom 87, the international telecommunications conference and exhibition organized every four years by the International Telecommunications Union (ITU). The first Finn ever to represent the global telecommunications industry, Kairamo called for the liberalization and deregulation of telecommunications, emphasizing the importance of the GSM and ISDN.

Nokia, Alcatel, AEG consortium

● Also at Telecom 87, Nokia, Alcatel and AEG announced the establishment of a European mobile phone consortium. Nokia's director in charge of the negotiations was Sari Baldauf. As she recalls, the final handwritten agreement was signed in an Orient Express railway car hired by Alcatel. The press release estimated that 'the system will require several hundreds of exchanges and over 5,000 relay stations. Over 10 million subscribers are estimated to join the GSM network.'

Nokia was relatively small compared with the other two well-established electronics giants, but it was accepted as a partner due to the advanced technology of its Mobile Phones division. Alcatel was Europe's largest telecommunications group with 1986 sales of €16 billion and 150,000 employees in 110 countries. AEG was also a sizable firm, with sales of €6.7 billion, a workforce of 80,000 and activities in 111 countries. In comparison, Nokia's sales in 1987 amounted to €3.4 billion and it employed 29,000 people.

Nokia's primary objective in the consortium was access to European markets. Alcatel and AEG were more focussed on cooperation in technology. Nokia aimed to become more European and gain exposure and international credibility. The agreement certainly helped create both. The other positive aspect of the agreement was seen internally as internationalizing Nokia's personnel. Lauri Melamies, the director closely involved in the process, describes it:

> Being part of the Nokia success story has been a learning process for many men and women from the Finnish backwoods. GSM was one big school of internationalization. European airports were full of mainly young Nokia employees traveling to and from standardization meetings, the ECR consortium (the cooperation project with Alcatel in the early stages of GSM), or meetings with customers. These trips would teach you agendas, action points, contributions and other English terminology that would penetrate the Finnish language. White cotton tennis socks would gradually change at least to blue as the sartorial requirements of international meetings became more familiar. You would also learn to lobby effectively in the corridors of standardization meetings.
>
> Unnecessary inferiority complexes, sometimes appearing as arrogance, vanished when you learned that the guys on the other side of the table were just ordinary people, albeit pretty smart ones. This process has paved the way to the Nokia of today, a multicultural company with all memorandums written in English, a company where you would as easily hear Hindi as you would Hungarian.

However, the Nokia-Alcatel-AEG consortium did not work quite as well as planned. Practical research and development turned out to be particularly sticky. In this field Nokia felt that it didn't get much out of the cooperation. As a result Nokia drew the conclusion that R&D is better conducted primarily alone.

Since its inception, Nokia's mobile phone business had grown at a 30–50 percent rate annually. But still in 1988 it only accounted for some 5 percent of the Group's net sales. The fastest growing part of the business was still the handsets for the analog NMT networks. However, a major change was brewing under the surface. The whole operating environment was changing with the move to the digital pan-European GSM system. At the same time, the deregulation of network operators was spreading from country to country. This was the development that made Nokia's mobile phones a truly great business.

Nokia was regarded as the world leader in mobile phones in 1988 with a 13.8 percent market share followed by Motorola (13.4 percent), NEC (11.9 percent) and Panasonic (9.4 percent). Then Nokia lost its leading position to Motorola, which became the top supplier in the early 1990s. Although Nokia was No. 1 in the Scandinavian NMT networks, the markets were insufficient to generate competitive sales, particularly in the United States, which was beginning to see serious growth of cellular phones.

In the spring of 1989, Antti Lagerroos, member of the internal Board, was appointed president of the Mobile Phones division. The move was part of CEO Simo Vuorilehto's plan to assign the full-time board members operational responsibilities. Lagerroos embarked on an extensive cost reduction campaign. He removed non-performing assets, eased bottlenecks in research and development, renewed the organizational structure, changed people in key positions and clarified responsibilities. Mobile phone production capacity rose by nearly 100 percent in 1989, which was partly due to the introduction of two shifts.

The year 1989 was a difficult one. As the annual report puts it:

> The operative result was weaker than the year before, and operating profit was slightly negative. The group will now focus on the mobile phone business in which Nokia is one of the world's top three manufacturers.

The new mobile phone strategy was designed in the summer and autumn of 1989 by Antti Lagerroos, Kari-Pekka Wilska, Markku Alasaari, Kaj Lindén and Leenamaija Jarenko. The strategy was based on the assumption that mobile phone markets would grow at an average rate of 30–50 percent annually, and in the United States by as much as 100 percent annually.

The team made these pledges:

- 'We will focus on CMT (cellular mobile phone) knowhow and CMT business
- All non-core business operations are/will be sold (Airtime, Mobitex, Cordless, Cue) in order to focus scarce resources and management time more efficiently
- We will strengthen basic technical knowhow
- We will search for partners for cooperation
- Acquisition: Technophone?'

At the time when Nokia's problems in Consumer Electronics emerged, these other sectors provided brighter prospects. A memorandum on investment plans stated in December 1990:

> Digital systems will completely change the whole system side and will create new demand for systems and handsets... Sales of handsets may grow faster than we can anticipate.

In January 1990, the Supervisory Board approved the new strategy. Soon after, Vuorilehto prompted Lagerroos to leave Nokia. Lagerroos's departure was not related to the performance of Mobile Phones but rather to differences of opinion with Vuorilehto over corporate strategy on the internal Board. Lagerroos was replaced on March 1, 1990, by then-CFO Jorma Ollila.

Focus on the Nokia brand

● Throughout the 1990s, Nokia worked diligently to build its corporate image and that of the Nokia brand. The aim was to promote sales of products with a positive brand name, and promote investment in Nokia shares.

The Nokia brand has roots going back to the beginning of the 20th century. But in the 1980s Nokia manufactured television sets under seven brands and mobile phones under two brands. They all were national labels and none was Nokia. A concerted effort began to build a global Nokia brand. The brand was also connected to the reorganization of the distribution network.

Led by Jorma Ollila, the Mobile Phones division started to invest more heavily in the Nokia brand in 1991. Ollila asked Anssi Vanjoki to organize a 'brand afternoon'. Vanjoki had joined Nokia from 3M to prune the excessive international sales network and build a brand strategy. He took time to examine the success of such international brands as Nike, Daimler-Benz and Philip Morris.

Branding combines the name of a product with visual appearance to add value and give the product identity. Anssi Vanjoki defined branding in a memo as:

> An act of consistency and continuity along predetermined dimensions to achieve customer satisfaction.

When the product and the company share a name, the corporate image and ultimately the company's credibility are essential parts of the brand.

In October 1990 Vanjoki received an internal memo entitled 'Building of the Nokia CMT brand' which set an ambitious target: Nokia CMT will in two years have a better brand awareness and brand image than Motorola has in Europe and in Asia-Pacific. For a company slogan the memo proposed either 'Nokia – The Eurotechnology group' or 'The future is looking good'.

Vanjoki worked on the issue and finally came up with a slogan: 'High technology with human touch'. He may have borrowed it from Nokia Data, which had used the slogan 'High Tech with a human touch' in its international advertising in June 1991. Vanjoki presented his brand strategy in June 1991.

In advertising, he made clever use of the company's limited resources. One of his ideas was to place one-column advertisements in the grey pages of business papers where small-font market quotations were listed. They caught the reader's eye more effectively than Motorola's big ads lost in a sea of other colorful ads.

Brand dimensions

High technology
- Superior functionality
- Balanced for total concept
- Unique product features
- User friendliness
- Pride of possession
- Ease of use
- Non-pollution
- Faultless automation
- New to the world

Nordic
- Artistic design
- Modern and light styling
- Design for functionality – hand and face informality and flexibility – of company culture
- Conditions requiring quality
- Pioneer in cellular technology
- Green values emphasis

Individual
- Technical service requirements
- Selection and functionality of accessories
- Product upgrading possibility
- Ease of purchasing product
- Dealer profile and territory coverage
- Physical environment at point of sale

Freedom
- Basic offering of a cellular phone
- Contacts and product usage at all environments
- Charging, interfacing, security aspects of the product
- Customizing

Enduring quality
- Dependability
- Products built for long term
- Stated technical quality
- Reliable distribution solution
- First class manufacturing

Market segmentation

- **Cityman, latest technology**
- **Freedom, attract large number of potential customers**
- **Talkman, reserved for mobile terminals only**

In June 1992, Nokia's Executive Board committed itself to further investment in the brand. Later that year the company adopted a new English-language slogan, 'Connecting People' and it has proven durable. In German the same message was translated as 'Die gute Verbindung von Mensch zu Mensch'. There was no Finnish language version, and the German one was gradually phased out.

An internal memorandum in 1995 outlined far-reaching plans to 'improve Nokia brand recognition in the key export countries to pave the way for the success of improved export efforts'. At that point Nokia was a more familiar brand than Motorola only in Germany and Sweden. According to a US survey, the Motorola brand reached a score of

63 percent in the category 'total awareness, all adults' while Nokia trailed well behind with a score of 10 percent. By 2000 Nokia had become one of the world's most valuable brands, ranking fifth in some surveys. In terms of brand recognition Nokia dwarfs its closest competitors (see page 220).

Anssi Vanjoki's brand strategy (extracts), June 3, 1991:

> The brand is Nokia... Brand management is a necessity in the class of technological leadership and low-cost manufacturing for us. It is an element of survival and prosperity in our business.

Nokia's main goal in mobile phones was to penetrate the United States, potentially the world's largest cellular phone market at that time. Preparations included personal contact in March 1989 with the country's seven largest operators, GTE, PacTel, US West, McCaw Cellular, Southwestern Bell, Bell South and Nynex to get a first-hand feel for the US market and potential future customers.

An important acquisition helped Nokia in the effort. In March 1991 the Mobile Phones division acquired Technophone, the British mobile phone maker, a deal which had nearly been clinched a year earlier. Technophone had a firm foothold in the United States and it was competitive particularly in car phones. Technophone was in the right place at the right time, just as the market began to grow. The purchase price of Technophone was FIM 238 million (€46 million). In 1991 the company's net sales amounted to the equivalent of €58 million, and its personnel totaled 750. It had manufacturing plants in Camberley, England, and in Hong Kong.

Nokia sold mobile phones under various labels until 1995. Handsets sold to operators were labeled Nokia, but the Technophone brand was changed to Nokia only after the company made a decision to introduce the Nokia brand globally.

Penetration of the US markets required the removal of trade barriers. American competitors often used legalistic delays as well as the country's economic might and political lobbying to keep new entrants from the market.

As expected, when Nokia's market share reached 10 percent nationwide in the United States, Motorola sued Nokia in April 1988. The lawsuit was based on Section 337 of the US Commercial Code, which decrees that importation of a product that infringes on a US patent as deceptive competition. Hence it could be denied access to the market separately from a patent dispute. The matter would be dealt with at the US International Trade Commission (ITC) in Washington, where a demand banning imports would be filed. Following the procedure at the ITC a civil suit on patent infringement would be filed in Chicago, Motorola territory.

As Nokia saw it, Motorola aimed to stop its product development by tying it to a patent dispute. This conclusion is based on the fact that Motorola sued Nokia instead of the Japanese company that made the component in question. Antti Lagerroos, who dealt with the matter at Nokia, was familiar with the strategy as he had fought a similar battle in Germany. Working at Salora, Lagerroos had encountered German efforts to stop imports of Salora television sets.

At the preliminary hearing, a temporary import embargo was imposed that would have stopped Nokia imports. Following tough negotiations, Nokia and Motorola reached an out-of-court settlement under which Nokia paid some $20 million as compensation, in effect buying a truce for three years. During that time Nokia changed suppliers of the disputed component, and a cross-licensing agreement between Nokia and Motorola was signed in 1993. Nokia thereafter resolved to launch a large-scale effort to build up its own patent portfolio.

GSM network deliveries since 1989 to the rapidly growing markets were the engine for the development of the company's telecommunications business and the whole Nokia group during the first half of the 1990s. And yet more growth was to come.

CHAPTER 10

Ollila the man, his team and his strategy

Jorma Ollila became chief executive officer of the Nokia Group in January 1992 following his success at the Mobile Phones division that he had headed for about two years. Ollila's assignment at Mobile Phones, based away from corporate headquarters in the Finnish town of Salo, had started with a challenge. As he recalls those days:

> What I was told by my superiors was, 'Look, you've got six months to make a proposal on whether we sell it or what we do with this business'. After four months I said, 'No, we're not going to sell this one'.

As Ollila saw it, the main problems at Mobile Phones were low morale and a lack of integration with the Nokia organization. His solution was to set about generating enthusiasm and streamlining the organization. One of his objectives was to encourage the research and development operations to meet the challenges of the European GSM standard.

Ollila was de facto elected CEO at the beginning of December 1991, although the appointment would not take effect until mid-January 1992.

The position he assumed at the age of 41 was highly prestigious in Finland but the company itself was in disarray. He was obliged to dispose of traditional businesses and refocus efforts on telecommunications. Under his guidance Nokia not only recovered but went on to become the world's leading mobile phone maker and No. 2 supplier of mobile/cellular networks.

Ollila's leadership style is typified by two strengths: his ability to maintain a certain equilibrium around him, and his ability to articulate and simplify key objectives. His top management team remained unchanged throughout the 1990s, only rotating their positions.

His guiding management principle of equilibrium was critical as he gradually led the diversification of Nokia's shareholder base from predominantly Finnish institutions to a vast number of international investors. The explosive growth of the company also called for a balance between mass production efficiency and segmented marketing.

With his extensive international education, Ollila represents a new breed of business leader. He is at once intellectual and acutely aware of the psychology of the international capital markets.

Ollila seems to have been a model citizen from a young age. In his early years he was active in the Boy Scouts and belonged to his school's nature club. His father was a maintenance manager at a local cotton mill and both his mother and father graduated from high school but Jorma was to be the first family member to achieve a university degree. An avid pupil at school in Vaasa, on the west coast of Finland, he received a scholarship to study at a special international school, Atlantic College in Wales in the United Kingdom, at the age of 17. Pentti Kouri, who became an international investor, economics professor and a Board member of Nokia, studied at the college at the same time.

After his British experience, Ollila went on to plunge into the study of political science and economics. Some of his theses were nothing short of prophetic. His Master of Science thesis at the Helsinki University of Technology was entitled 'The Optimization of Economic Growth as a Control Theoretical Problem', while his Master of Political Science thesis at the University of Helsinki, awarded the highest marks of the faculty, was entitled 'Uncertainty in the Theory of International Economy'. In addition he earned a Master of Science degree from the London School of Economics.

Amid his studies, Ollila was actively involved in student politics, which provided valuable experience in his later career. This culminated in his election as chairman of the National Union of Finnish Students and as secretary of International Affairs of the Center Party. During his stint in mandatory military service, Ollila followed the path of his Nokia predecessor Kari Kairamo, as chairman of the Student Corps of the Reserve Officers' School.

Ollila began his professional career by returning to Britain where he joined Citibank in the City of London. To take advantage of the deregulation of the Finnish money markets, Citibank opened an office in Helsinki where Ollila was placed as part of the team. Working at the hub of the financial world during the era of global liberalization, Ollila absorbed valuable lessons in finance and global business operations.

In 1985 he moved over to Nokia to manage international operations. One of his first major projects was to expand Nokia's ownership base with a private placement with funds managed by George Soros, the

Ollila heading for his first press conference as CEO in February 1992. Times were critical which can been seen from the faces. Following Ollila, Group Controller Hannu Bergholm, Vice President of Communications Matti Saarinen and Senior Vice President, Finance, Olli-Pekka Kallasvuo (Lehtikuva/Pentti Koskinen).

Hungarian-born investor based in the United States. In 1986 Ollila became Nokia Group's vice president, finance. In that capacity he was a key player as Nokia expanded rapidly through its big acquisitions at the end of the 1980s.

In early January 1992, a week before he was appointed, Ollila presented ideas for Nokia's future development to Board members Casimir Ehrnrooth and Yrjö Niskanen, who had been instrumental in his appointment. This memorandum can be regarded as the basis for Nokia's strategy in the 1990s:

Development model for the Group
- The group will be developed on the basis of the current structure so that we will tie up no more capital in operations until the group's profitability stabilizes on an acceptable level;
- For our shareholders, we will aim to secure cash flow that actively follows positive development of profitability;

- The group's core businesses will have substantial investment needs in the next few years. This, together with the comment above, will in practice require clearer decisions on prioritization of allocations than before;
- Withdrawal from certain business areas totally or through joint ventures;
- Possible stock market listing of certain business operations in the mid-term;
- Continuous structural cost savings, particularly in businesses where this can be achieved without jeopardizing operational development.

Development model by business area

Consumer electronics. The possibility of withdrawal from the business will be re-examined immediately as the first priority. If withdrawal proves unviable we will look for a solution based on cooperation, which is commercially sensible also in the short term and which enables withdrawal in the next few years.

The current situation at Consumer Electronics requires large non-recurring write-offs at the corporate level.

Cables and Machinery. The strategic position requires us to continue substantial investments in the group's main business area, the cable business, and at the same time examine possibilities for releasing capital from the division's other business operations.

Telecommunications. This is a core business area, particularly as regards the mobile phone networks. It seems probable that securing the group's development and growth would require engagement possibly in even large-scale cooperation arrangements. Considering the large investment in development and the growing risks, we may have to consider disposing of the business unless its profitability reaches an acceptable level in the required timeframe.

Mobile phones. This is also a core business area, and there is no reason we should consider giving it up. The objective is to at least retain the current global position.

Basic industry. This is not a core business area. Decisions concerning it should be taken pragmatically. Divestiture of the tire manufacturing operations should be examined without delay.

Since Ollila became chief executive, one of his closest colleagues has been CFO Olli-Pekka Kallasvuo. In the spring of 1992 Ollila and Kallasvuo recognized that shareholders were unhappy with the company, so they decided to start building a base for significant improvement in stock performance as the first priority of the corporation.

To attract the interest of US institutional investors, Ollila had to tell a good story, and the old one, 'We are a Finnish conglomerate with some tech stuff', would not cut it. Within a few months his team had devised an even more stripped-down strategy: 'Focus, global, telecom-oriented, value added'.

Ollila's leadership style was value-driven from the beginning. In the 1992 annual report he said:

The Nokia way of operating is based on a flat, decentralized organization, with emphasis on efficient teamwork and entrepreneurial spirit. Flexibility, being able to innovate, react speedily and make fast and effective decisions are the central features of Nokia's way of operating ... continuous learning, improving skills and quality, ambitious goals and respect for the individual.

The strategy was based on a vision of development in the 1990s. As early as 1993, at an internal seminar discussing the future of the Nokia Research Center, Ollila said he believed that Nokia's business, manufacturing and research and development would all become global. New active players, such as the computer industry and consumers would emerge in the field of telecommunications. And most importantly, new technologies and product concepts would sprout at an increasing pace.

Loss-making 1991 – share price falls

● In January 1992 Jorma Ollila took the helm of a leaking ship. Nokia's top management tried to be realistic about the problems it faced and in retrospect it appears they were on the right track – they just were not moving fast enough. The problems at Consumer Electronics, Nokia's largest business unit, were worse than expected. Nokia had failed to turn it to profit or dress it up for a quick sale.

In his last management group meeting as chief executive at the beginning of January, Simo Vuorilehto had grim news. Sales in 1991 had declined all around except at Mobile Phones. Sales at Consumer Electronics were down by 18 percent, while sales at Telecommunications had sunk by 28 percent. Sales to Russia were FIM 1 billion (€190 million) lower than the previous year, while cable and machinery declined by 13 percent and basic industries by 17 percent. In addition the divestiture of Nokia Data removed annual sales of FIM 5 billion (€970 million) and the establishment of joint venture for Chemicals of FIM 600 million (€116 million) from the group's total net sales.

At Nokia's Annual General Meeting a few months later, Vuorilehto told shareholders that comparable group net sales had declined by 16 percent from the previous year. Consumer Electronics, he acknowledged, was 'deep in red ink', while other business operations reached a 'positive return on equity'. On a more positive note Vuorilehto said the company's liquid assets had increased to FIM 3.7 billion (€716 million) from FIM 3.2 billion a year earlier. Debt to equity ratio had gone down to 51 percent from 67 percent a year earlier.

Thus Jorma Ollila's tenure began dramatically. The morning after the appointment, Nokia's share price fell by 10 percent, recovered in the afternoon, but closed with a 4 percent decline for the day. The *Wall Street Journal* account was headlined, 'Nokia Appoints Jorma Ollila to Top Post; Unexpected Reshuffle Sends Stocks Falling'. Yet, stock market analysts seemed to prefer Ollila over Kalle Isokallio, the previous president.

'With Mr. Ollila it will be more back to nuts and bolts – rather than grand plans of expansion, which Nokia can't afford any longer anyway,' said Dennis Exton, an analyst at Merrill Lynch in London. Ollila himself quickly acknowledged the back-to-basics principle. He stressed the importance of doing small things right, to allow little streams to grow into a major river of profits.

Healing the inflamed situation at the top was an urgent priority for the new management. Reshuffle of the Board helped accomplish this. Under the terms of the agreement made a year earlier, Casimir Ehrnrooth, chairman of Kymmene, was elected chairman while Yrjö Niskanen, CEO of Pohjola, became deputy chairman. The two had executed the top management change according to plans outlined by Ahti Hirvonen, CEO of Union Bank of Finland (UBF), Nokia's largest owner. New members of the Board included Pirkko Alitalo, senior vice president of Pohjola, and Björn Wahlroos, senior vice president of UBF.

Nokia at the start of Jorma Ollila's tenure as CEO

Nokia's net sales and operating profit January–May 1992, FIM million

Business divisions	Actual	Variance with budget	Variance with previous year
Net sales			
Consumer electronics	2,000	-186	-464
Mobile phones	1,131	29	-25
Telecommunications	790	-26	82
Cables and machinery	1,678	25	-220
Basic industries	494	-31	-170
Other	59	-22	13
Nokia Group	**6,077**	**-219**	**-560**
Operating profit			
Consumer electronics	-303	-93	-242
Mobile phones	142	71	57
Telecommunications	1	73	20
Cables and machinery	-24	-18	-40
Basic industries	72	9	-14
Others	-88	-5	0
Nokia Group	**-200**	**38**	**-219**

Departing Board members included Mika Tiivola, former CEO of UBF and Jaakko Lassila, former CEO of Kansallis-Osake-Pankki (KOP) who had been fierce rivals on the Finnish banking scene. Instead the top positions on the Board were shared between Ehrnrooth and Niskanen. They were no longer direct representatives of the commercial banks, which made a break with past practice and created a major opening for Nokia's corporate governance. Ehrnrooth's explicit aim was a 'shared chairmanship' with Niskanen so that 'we would not pull the strings in different directions'. He also wanted to eliminate the friction between the Board and management by discussing with the CEO in the executive committee as often as possible and always with all three key men present. Together with Ollila they made up the new executive committee of the Board of Directors.

Casimir Ehrnrooth recalls: 'With the disturbing factors eliminated on the Board and top management levels, morale improved surprisingly quickly and we started doing the right things.' While the Board felt it was less and less necessary to get involved in operational management, the number of preparatory committee meetings also declined rapidly. Ollila felt the need to share management of Nokia with the Board only until he considered that the management's competence was established and trusted.

By the spring of 1992, some large international electronics groups speculated that Nokia was a target for acquisition. In mid-June, Ollila was visited by the deputy chief executive of Siemens, who asked for Nokia's response to an earlier proposal to acquire Nokia's Telecommunications division. Ollila declined the offer. Nokia's top management was aware that at least three investment banks were peddling ideas about Nokia as a potential acquisition. The situation was so critical that Ollila decided not to mention the Siemens case to the Board – out of fear that they just might be prepared to consider a sale.

Nokia's results in January–April 1992 were the weakest in the company's history: a loss of FIM 178 million (€34 million), compared with a profit of FIM 119 million (€23 million) in the previous year. The new chief executive had the unenviable duty of announcing the figures in June. Release of the news was timed for late afternoon on the day before Midsummer Eve, one of Finland's biggest festivals. Understandably most journalists had already started festivities, and coverage of Nokia's news the next day was modest. But after the midsummer weekend the subject surfaced again with bigger and more negative headlines. Now in addition to profitability problems, Nokia's new management faced a serious credibility gap.

Ollila wrote his strategy in the spring of 1992 and presented it to the Board on June 17, the same day it approved the interim report. The starting point was far from easy. The poor performance of Consumer Electronics stood out starkly, and both sales and profits were considerably lower than forecast. The business group had made a loss of FIM 300 million (€57 million) in five months. This boat was leaking badly.

Now Ollila presented a revised the budget for that year. He lowered the operating profit estimate for the whole year by as much FIM 267 million (€51 million). But the actual figure turned out to be FIM 500 million (€95 million) lower than the new forecast. The new budget was prepared by Hannu Bergholm, the former group controller who had recently been appointed head of the Consumer Electronics division. He emphasized that 'uncertainty in the markets does carry a considerable risk element', but in overall terms the budget can still be considered overly optimistic.

The revised budget had estimated the Nokia Group's profit to reach FIM 378 million (€72 million). The actual figure was FIM 288 million (€55 million). In the overall context the difference was rather small. This was due to positive surprises in other business sectors. Mobile Phones made a profit of FIM 437 million (€83 million), which was FIM 141 million (€27 million) higher than the budgeted figures. Telecommunications, which only broke even the year before due to the collapse of sales to Russia, reached a profit of FIM 427 million (€81 million).

Ollila puts his team together

● Throughout his tenure at Nokia's helm, Ollila has stuck with his original team of Olli-Pekka Kallasvuo, Matti Alahuhta, Pekka Ala-Pietilä and Sari Baldauf, all still young, but seasoned veterans at Nokia who had suffered and survived the storms of the 1980s.

However, the establishment of the top management was preceded by some significant personnel moves. Noels, who had headed Consumer Electronics since summer 1988, was relieved of his duties at the beginning of February 1992 and was replaced by Hannu Bergholm, Nokia group controller. Prior to joining Nokia in 1987 Bergholm was controller at Kone, the Finnish elevator manufacturer, for 13 years.

Noels' strategy had never won unanimous approval of the top management. Antti Lagerroos, member of the internal Board, was never a fan, nor did Noels get support from Kalle Isokallio, president of Nokia. Only Chief Executive Simo Vuorilehto wanted to give Noels his support but in practice he personally meddled in formulating the strategy at Consumer Electronics.

The Nokia Executive Board in 1999. Sitting from left: Matti Alahuhta, Sari Baldauf, Jorma Ollila, Pekka Ala-Pietilä, standing from left: Olli-Pekka Kallasvuo, Veli Sundbäck, Yrjö Neuvo, Anssi Vanjoki, Mikko Heikkonen.

Noels' grand scheme was aimed at gaining synergies by merging the Mobile Phones division into Consumer Electronics. As his successor, Bergholm faced a tough challenge. One example of the great difficulties was that even Bergholm, with a number-cruncher's background, was too optimistic in his forecasts.

Pekka Ala-Pietilä, MSc (Economics), head of product marketing at the Mobile Phones division, was the next key appointee to the group's top management. He became president of Mobile Phones on March 1, 1992. Ala-Pietilä had joined Nokia Data in 1984 and moved on to Mobile Phones in 1988. His duties had included development of product marketing and corporate planning.

Three months later, Tapio Hintikka, MSc (Engineering), was appointed head of the Cables and Machinery division in August 1992, replacing Seppo Ahonen, a favorite of Vuorilehto. Hintikka had started at Nokia in August 1990 as head of Basic Industries. Prior to that he had worked for Rauma-Repola, the Finnish engineering group, as development director and head of an industrial group.

In November 1992, Dr. Matti Alahuhta was appointed head of Telecommunications. At the beginning of 1993, moving up from the No. 2 position. Dr. Yrjö Neuvo, research professor at the Academy of Finland, was appointed Senior Vice President, Technology, of Nokia Group. A year later Neuvo became head of research and development of the Mobile Phones division. Sari Baldauf, head of Cellular Networks, was appointed member of the Executive Board in January 1994.

Balanced leadership, Ollila's ideal

● In management studies, there is often a gap between what leaders claim to do and what they actually do, or what takes place in an organization. In this book we have focussed on the latter. Nevertheless it is interesting to look at some of the general ideas that prevailed within Nokia's top management in this period.

Ollila emphasizes balance and equilibrium in his management style, taking an equally keen approach to numbers-based management, and focuses on productivity indicators, as well as the inspiration and motivation of individuals. He has surrounded himself with a well-schooled lot. Three top Nokia executives have prepared their doctoral dissertations while working at the company. In Kairamo's time, Timo H.A. Koski, just before his death, completed his dissertation on *Ownership Strategy and Competitive Advantage* (1988). Matti Alahuhta studied challenges for small and medium-sized companies in his dissertation *Global Growth Strategies for High-Technology Challengers* (1990). Mikko Kosonen, corporate planner who had held various positions at the group, earned his doctorate with his dissertation *The Internationalization of Industrial Systems Suppliers* (1991).

Nokia values

- Customer satisfaction
- Respect for the individual
- Achievement
- Continuous learning

Ala-Pietilä, who headed the Mobile Phones division until 1998 and was appointed deputy to the CEO, then president of the Nokia Group a year later, has published articles in publications of the Helsinki School of Economics. His theme in the *The Systems Group* publications dealt with supply chain management under the fast growth of the Mobile Phones division. In 1990, he wrote: 'The speed of product development is the key in the manufacture and sales of mobile phones. It has to meet the markets' constant demand for new products.'

In 1993 the company implemented *The Nokia Way – The Common Core of the Nokia Management and Leadership Approach,* which has been continuously updated. Its contents were introduced as an extensive planning process throughout the organization. In 1994 the chosen theme was Excellence in Performance and the objectives were Customer Satisfaction, Operative Efficiency and People Involvement. Ollila's management style led to the introduction of a systematic, sustained and broad-based program.

'This is the biggest thing ever'

● Nokia Group's operational results finally took a positive turn in the summer of 1992. The main engine was Telecommunications, which grew by 73 percent on an annual basis. The most notable performer within Telecommunications was Nokia Cellular Systems. Sales of mobile phones increased at a rate of 45 percent per annum. At the same time the expansion of the GSM mobile phone standard was beginning to have an impact on Nokia.

Nokia's cumulative results for the first eight months of 1992 were at breakeven, compared with the heavy losses during the first tertial of the year. The turnaround was unveiled at a company seminar in October and media coverage was positive.

From 1990 to 1993 the finance department was primarily concerned with Nokia's credibility, as this was a company in financial crisis. Nokia had built its financing on bonds in the optimistic 1980s. Now the international banks were not committed to the company while domestic banks – fighting for survival in their own banking crisis – lacked the capability and probably also the will to help Nokia. Hence Nokia depended entirely on its own cash flow, and when this slowed, the company faced problems. As CFO Olli-Pekka Kallasvuo recalls, one bank after another told Nokia that credit taps would be turned off.

The spring of 1993 was a turning point. Presenting its annual result for 1992, Nokia for the first time released specific figures for business areas.

The reason for this move was to highlight the difference in performance between divisions. While Consumer Electronics had made a horrific loss of FIM 783 million (€149 million), Nokia was able to focus financiers' and investors' interest on the operating profit of FIM 437 million (€83 million) in Mobile Phones and the profit of FIM 427 million (€81 million) in Telecommunications.

In April 1993 Kallasvuo met with Laurence I. Solomon, a California-based fund manager, who had looked at the figures and exclaimed: 'This is the biggest thing ever.' Since then, Solomon attended every Nokia presentation in Europe, and even proposed to subscribe one entire Nokia share issue for the funds under his management. Nokia politely declined, but Solomon kept buying Nokia shares on the open market for two years and made a substantial profit on his investment as Nokia shares underwent a phenomenal rise.

Currency rates also helped in Nokia's recovery. The external value of the Finnmark fluctuated wildly in 1992–1994. The value of the Finnmark sank by as much as 50–60 percent against leading currencies. This naturally boosted Nokia's export income and consequently profitability. The flip side of the issue was the subsequent strengthening of the Finnmark, which at the end of 1994 had reduced Nokia's operating result by FIM 400 million (€73 million).

A day in Hong Kong in May 1994

● Exceptionally, Nokia's Board meeting on May 12, 1994, was held in Hong Kong. Participants remember the meeting particularly for one overhead slide. It proposed for the first time a detailed schedule for the divestiture of other business areas, and a new and exclusive focus on telecommunications and mobile phones.

Present were Chairman of the Board Casimir Ehrnrooth (chairman of Kymmene Oy) and Deputy Chairman Yrjö Niskanen (CEO of Pohjola Group) as well as Board members Pirkko Alitalo (senior vice president of Pohjola), Edward Andersson (professor at the University of Helsinki), Ahti Hirvonen (chairman of the Board of Unitas Oy), Jouko K. Leskinen (CEO of Sampo Group), and Vesa Vainio (CEO of Unitas Oy). Representatives of Nokia included Chief Executive Ollila, CFO Olli-Pekka Kallasvuo, Telecommunications President Matti Alahuhta, Mobile Phones President Pekka Ala-Pietilä and Harry Collin, secretary of the Board.

The slide presented by Jorma Ollila was part of the proposed strategy of the Nokia Group over the coming ten years.

Divestiture of other business operations will be considered:

Cables	94–95	Industrial electronics	94–96
Cable machinery	94–96	Power	95–97
Tires	94–95	Consumer electronics	96–97

Nokia's Board members were cautious about the grand plan. This was hardly surprising, considering the experience of recent years: the massive losses of Consumer Electronics, a business that had been acquired with such fanfare; the deep recession in Finland, and the difficulties in international markets.

Ollila was not springing the plan without preparation. He had shared his vision privately six months earlier with the chairman and vice-chairman of the Board. They regarded the idea of Nokia becoming the global champion in mobile phones so new and bold that they asked the consultants McKinsey & Co for an independent assessment.

McKinsey went along with Ollila's vision but when the plan was presented to the Board, caution still reigned. The Board asked for a more detailed version for the next June meeting. As insurance, it also asked for an alternative plan in case the cash flow and growth in the Mobile Phones division were not as good as expected.

The minutes of the Board meeting reveal this attitude of caution:

> Following a discussion the Board decided that the chief executive will prepare a more detailed summary of the group strategy for the June meeting; that an alternative strategic plan will be prepared taking into account the possibility that growth and cash flow figures turn out to be considerably lower than now forecast, and the eventuality that competitors offer considerably attractive financing plans to customers; that once a year the Board will get a special report on actual development and that the Board will not make a decision on the divestiture proposal made by the chief executive.

The profit figures presented at the Hong Kong meeting provided reason for optimism. The result for the first four months of 1994 was FIM 406 million (€74 million) higher than the budgeted figure, and FIM 457 million (€84 million) higher than in the same period a year earlier. The forecast for the full year was FIM 941 million (€173 million) higher than the previous year.

Nokia had clearly reached a turning point. It had restored profitability and was able to set more ambitious targets than in the preceding years. Ollila had good reason to be confident.

CHAPTER 11

The rise of Nokia

The information technology era has been described as the third industrial revolution – the impact of computers and telecommunications as the leading global industries from the 1980s onward. In each of the industrial revolutions, new technologies emerged, leading to the rapid introduction of innovative products manufactured by new industrial giants that were nimble enough to grasp the opportunity.

Nokia is just such a company, a major industrial firm that is focussed on making and selling products for telecommunications. Demand for Nokia products grew to worldwide proportions, which made it a truly global giant enterprise.

Nokia is treated in this study as a traditional industrial company. It always was and still is such a company, in the sense that it manufactures tangible products – mobile phones and telecommunications systems such as exchanges, base stations and transmission equipment. The increasing sophistication of software helped develop new properties for this equipment, and R&D played a key role in the process.

And yet the reasons behind Nokia's rise must be examined through the logic of the manufacturing industry, rather than via some abstract theory or a mystical secret of success. Nokia as a mobile phone maker simply got it right, making good products at the right price for a receptive market. Although Consumer Electronics was Nokia's largest division, the fastest growth since 1992 has been generated in networks and mobile phones. Year after year the share of mobile phones in group sales, and especially in operating profit, increased (see Appendix).

The other half of Nokia at this time consisted of such traditional business operations as cables and machinery, tires, and power. The company also produced steady profits but they were modest compared with the explosive growth of the telecommunications businesses. As discussed in previous chapters, Nokia's biggest problem in the first half of the 1990s was the Consumer Electronics division and its money-losing television set business. These massive difficulties were however offset by the triumph of Telecommunications.

In the mid-1990s even Mobile Phones encountered problems that could be called growing pains, and simultaneously the Basic Industries division was affected by the global economic downturn. As a result, Nokia's profitability stagnated, and even had a downturn in 1996. Nevertheless, the company kept producing a respectable profit, so these problems cannot be compared with the losses of the Consumer Electronics division a few years earlier.

Toward the end of the 1990s the growth of global telecommunications turned into rapidly growing sales and profits for Nokia. This has been particularly evident in the Mobile Phones division since 1997.

New operators as new customers

● It is easier to prune a tree than grow a new one but slimming down cannot alone explain the coming Nokia success. Divestitures only helped Nokia cut losses and allow for the allocation of capital to the remaining areas.

One common feature behind the success of the two core divisions is that both went through their own serious crises. They managed to pull out of their respective difficulties and developed production and operational processes to a new level of efficiency, paving the way for future success. Telecommunications crashed in 1991 when the Soviet Union, the biggest market area, collapsed. The group was therefore forced to restructure its operations completely in 1991 and just managed to stay alive.

Reorganization considerably improved the group's operating efficiency and it managed to gain new market share elsewhere and improve profitability in the following years.

Problems at Mobile Phones started in the mid-1990s as the so-called logistics crisis. This forced the company to improve the ways and means of production, which formed the basis for the strong and profitable growth in the latter half of the decade.

The growth of the Telecommunications division is equally instructive. The infrastructure industry develops, manufactures and sells equipment, systems and services for networks. The main customers are telecom operators, that offer services to corporates and private consumers. A second customer base consists of the users of professional mobile radio networks, such as rescue and law enforcement authorities or utilities.

In March 1991, just as the collapse of the Soviet Union started to deprive Nokia's Telecommunications division of its market, the division was in the middle of creating a new strategy for the future. The biggest hopes were placed on deregulation, the opening of competition in Western markets. Ambitious growth targets looked over the horizon to 1999. A strategy memorandum of the group concluded: 'Thanks to changes in the structure of our customer base we have a 10-year window of opportunity to become a leading supplier to new operators by year 2000.'

In April 1992 the Telecommunications division estimated that in the following 10 years new telecom operators would become its most important customers. After that, the consolidation would leave the markets with only a few strong operators.

In the business environment, three important changes were taking place, making the newly established independent telephone operators a highly important target group for Nokia. First, the collapse of the old markets and the recession in the Nordic countries. Second, the rapid growth of the mobile phone business and third, the increase in global competition. These developments led the Telecommunications division to search for more efficient operating models – from technology to production. As early as in 1991 the group managed to cut fixed costs by 20 percent without reducing the level of service.

In practice, the opening of competition meant granting operating licenses to new operators. Typically, the new operators focussed on the services that provided the best yield. The operators had no historical or political ties with equipment suppliers. The competitive edge came from price and flexibility plus the speed and quality of the services they provided. They wanted to invest in comprehensive system packages, preferably financed by equipment suppliers. Operators also expected active service and training on concepts and functions from suppliers. And finally, the operators needed guidance in understanding the new features of new systems and where the services were heading.

Nokia's Telecommunications division saw this opportunity to work with new operators as its most important strategic challenge.

New operators aimed to build networks as fast as possible. A prime example in Finland was Radiolinja, which challenged the state-owned Tele in mobile phone networks. The requirement for speedy installation of turnkey systems was necessary to enable the massive investments to generate cash flow as soon as possible. New operators were faster and more flexible than the old ones in searching for solutions and services that produced quick profits.

Another feature of the telecom business was the deep division between the fixed line and wireless networks. It was evident in growth figures. Fixed lines were a mature business with large volumes but slow growth. In mobile phone networks, the growth was phenomenal compared with fixed lines and so was the profit.

In the spring of 1992, the Telecommunications division prepared a new strategy listing a number of strengths on which to build the future. It was well positioned in the field of new European telecom operators, it had developed a number of new innovative system solutions, it had a broad variety of wireless product and system solutions, and it had achieved a high degree of efficiency in research and development as well as in other operations.

The strategy started with careful management of the 'home base'. This meant close customer relations at all stages and at all levels of the project. The first such project was the mobile phone network commissioned by Radiolinja in 1989. Its competitor Tele also bought a sizable number of exchanges from Nokia as did the Swedish Telia (formerly Televerket), both of which had traditionally placed their orders with Ericsson.

The second step was to acquire a strong position in the Asia-Pacific region and in Europe. The main markets in Europe included Britain, Germany, France and later Italy. These were followed by the United States, Latin America and Japan.

The Telecommunications division was quick to realize that when it expanded from a European to a global company Nokia would be transformed from a challenger to a leading supplier. In the 1990s the Telecommunications group had prepared a global strategy that also set objectives by countries. The strategy was largely based on innovative new products and system solutions.

As part of its continuous development, Telecommunications focussed as early as 1993 on the question of compatibility between second-generation GSM and third-generation UMTS standards, which only became a major issue at the end of the 1990s. The issue was how to expand the GSM-based telecommunications systems flexibly toward the UMTS requirements. Nokia was also present early in the development of common system platforms and solutions.

Mikko Kosonen has studied sales growth at Telecommunications, where he was planning director before being appointed as vice president, development of Nokia. He listed the reasons for the growth as follows:

- Rapid deregulation, i.e. opening competition in telecom networks
- Escalation of GSM standard
- Nokia's early start
- Product leadership
- Customer orientation

Development phases at the group can be listed as:
- Early enthusiasm (1993–1994)
- Focussing on growth (1993–1995)
- Systematic development (1996–).

The first years in the Telecommunications division were difficult. Results in 1991 were catastrophic due to the collapse of trade with the Soviet Union, but as we have established, the group managed to make a profit by shifting attention to markets in western Europe. In 1992 the group's profitability well exceeded the budgeted figures.

In Germany, Telecommunications managed to gain a firm foothold in 1993 when it won a contract to supply the first stage of the country's third digital network. This FIM 700 million (€130 million) deal was a 'highly significant' spearhead in a new market area, as Jorma Ollila reported to Nokia's Board. Success in Germany was psychologically important for Nokia because at the same time Consumer Electronics was suffering badly in that country.

The year 1993 marks a major chapter in the history of GSM. Nokia initiated a project called GSM+, or GSM 2.5, which aimed to refine the GSM standard – a sort of midway point between the second and third generations. A key element of the process was lobbying for a new standard in various international regulatory bodies.

Compared with the old standard, the new GSM+ offered substantial additional features such as voice code and data transfer in GSM systems. Internally it helped Nokia to integrate the Research Center, the Mobile Phones division and Telecommunications to jointly research and standardize the GSM systems.

Nokia realized that standardization work would turn into a competitive edge. One notable area of development involved digital signal processing (DSP), which included development of voice codecs.

Finland – the pioneer in mobile phones

● When did Nokia evolve from a Finnish company into an international one? The summer of 1994 is as good an answer as any. That was the point at which the Board of Directors switched the language of its minutes from Finnish to English. As a decision it was small, but its symbolism was great. At the same time the use of English was encouraged all over the company wherever natural and possible. But the most significant move was becoming the first Finnish company to be listed on the New York Stock Exchange. Related to the listing, Nokia raised FIM 2.5 billion (€460 million) in an international share issue, two-thirds of which was sold to US-based investors.

Nokia's relationship with Finland is multifaceted – and more so than one might guess from the ownership structure or the choice of corporate language. Many reasons have been advanced for keeping the management base in Finland despite the fact that most shareholders reside outside the country, and sentimentality is not one of them. In previous chapters we have discussed the availability of a qualified workforce, the primary resource, in Finland. Corporate tax in Finland was favorable for Nokia and that was underpinned by the weak Finnmark. Thirdly, Finland's domestic market was also spearheading developments in telecommunications.

Of course the cellular phone as an international product is nothing new to Nokia. Nokia has been one of the leading global mobile phone manufacturers since the 1970s. In the early years markets were very small, although growth was rapid. The industry was originally hobbled by a multitude of standards and systems but Nokia manufactured handsets for all the most important analog and digital cellular systems.

The history of mobile phones is usually portrayed as the evolution of handset models, while in telecommunications the headlines are made of major deals between operators and suppliers and the development of new standards. However, a closer look at the business logic in handsets reveals an equally important relationship between operators and equipment manufacturers. As Finland has been the world leader in mobile phone penetration, it is worth examining how this interplay actually worked.

From about 1981 to the end of the decade, the mobile phone was an expensive piece of equipment mounted in cars. The high cost made it a small market. Equipment manufacturers sold the product directly to consumers; operators played no role in the process. Mobile phone calls generated limited cash flow for operators. Nokia's greatest breakthrough at

CELLULAR PENETRATION 1991–2001

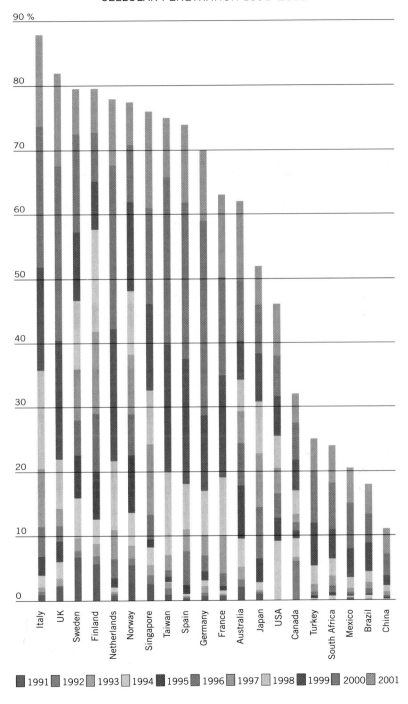

90 %

80

70

60

50

40

30

20

10

0

Italy · UK · Sweden · Finland · Netherlands · Norway · Singapore · Taiwan · Spain · Germany · France · Australia · Japan · USA · Canada · Turkey · South Africa · Mexico · Brazil · China

■ 1991 ■ 1992 ■ 1993 □ 1994 ■ 1995 ■ 1996 ■ 1997 □ 1998 ■ 1999 ■ 2000 □ 2001

this stage came when Britain opened its markets to competition. This provided a useful lesson for Nokia on how to operate in large markets. Britain has about 12 times the population of Finland. It also provided experience of how costly such a market entry can be.

At the next stage, the mobile phone was liberated from the car. The concept of the portable phone was born and the user base expanded considerably. Distribution channels became crucial and operators began to see opportunities in combining the sale of equipment and services. In several countries operators bought handsets in large volumes and sold them together with subscriptions. To avoid dependence on big operators, Nokia used its own advertising to influence consumers, which in turn created pressure on operators to offer Nokia handsets. One big breakthrough at this stage was in Italy where Nokia sold Cityman 100 handsets to the TACS network operated by SIP, now renamed as Telecom Italia.

The third stage started in 1994 with the runaway success of the digital mobile phone. It swept the world during the second half of the 1990s, elevating Nokia to the ranks of global industrial giants. An important early deal was the purchase of 20,000 digital handsets by Mannesmann. This deal became a key reference for Nokia as digital technology commenced its march to ultimate triumph.

Finland provided Nokia with an important pioneer market. At the beginning, mobile phone operations were a state privilege. The monopoly was held by the Post and Telegraph Administration, which later changed its name to Tele, Telecom Finland and finally Sonera, as it is called today. In 1971 it opened the first open mobile phone network called ARP. At its peak the network had 35,000 users. The pan-Nordic NMT network, a joint venture between Nordic telecom administrations, was introduced in 1981. By the mid-1990s it had attracted 440,000 subscribers. Tele was an important client for Nokia's NMT network solutions, helping it also to promote NMT handset sales. By contrast, GSM had a subscriber base in Finland exceeding 3 million in 1999.

In 1988 Finland's privately owned regional telephone companies established Radiolinja. This created an awkward situation for Nokia as its good client Tele strongly opposed granting a mobile phone network license to the newcomer. Radiolinja bought a digital GSM network system from Nokia in 1989, before it had actually been licensed to operate. Radiolinja subsequently received its license and opened the world's first GSM network in the summer of 1991, creating fierce competition between Tele and Radiolinja. Under the influence of heavy marketing and product

The Nokia 5110 was one of the best-selling handsets ever.

development, Finland quickly achieved the world's highest penetration of mobile phones.

Soon after, GSM networks were spreading all over the world. Yet GSM handsets were slower to enter the markets. The real breakthrough in GSM handset sales took place only in 1994–1995 when handsets became a mass-market product.

Mobile phones hit the mass markets

● In the early 1990s Nokia Mobile Phones had to face up to two major problems. First, the US giant Motorola occupied the dominant position in the mobile phone industry. It was the benchmark, the main competitor and model that Nokia bumped into everywhere. Second, Nokia was essentially a one-product company with only a few successful handset models. This made the company vulnerable, as became evident when it had to recall chargers made by the Norwegian Mascot Electronics for the top-selling Nokia 2110.

But Nokia was eager to spread its wings, to penetrate the United States, Motorola's home market. In 1984 it established TMC in Korea, the company that manufactured analog AMPS phones to be sold through the Radio Shack retail chain in the United States. By 1992 a total of 824,000 handsets had been sold under the Tandy label and another 885,000 under the Nokia label.

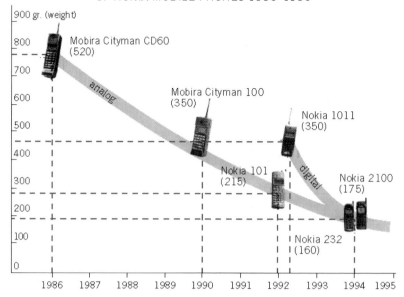

DEVELOPMENT OF SIZE AND WEIGHT
OF NOKIA MOBILE PHONES 1986–1995

900 gr. (weight)

800 — Mobira Cityman CD60 (520)

700

600 — analog — Mobira Cityman 100 (350)

500 — Nokia 1011 (350)

400

300 — Nokia 101 (215) — digital — Nokia 2100 (175)

200

100 — Nokia 232 (160)

0

1986 1987 1988 1989 1990 1991 1992 1993 1994 1995

The development of weight of Nokia handsets. The size in cubic centimeters is shown in brackets. Source: Mikko Koivusalo, Kipinästä tuli syttyi.

In January 1992 Nokia launched the model 101 in the United States and it became a breakthrough product. The marketing message was lower cost, better design and ease of use. Important steps in the US penetration included the acquisition of Tandy's share in the jointly owned manufacturing operations in 1994 and a major order from AT&T in 1995. Since then, AT&T has been among Nokia's biggest customers.

Cooperation with Tandy began in 1984 when the two established Tandy Mobira Corporation (TMC) in Korea followed by the establishment of the Tandy Nokia Corporation (TNC) joint venture in Fort Worth, Texas, in 1992. Both were owned 50–50, and they managed to meet the objectives of both partners surprisingly well. When Tandy redirected its strategy away from manufacturing and toward distribution, it was prepared to sell its stake in both ventures. This was compatible with Nokia's strategy in the United States and it bought the remaining half of the business from Tandy in 1994.

We have seen that in the early years the mobile phone business was developed in professional mobile radio networks operated by various authorities and utilities, and the original market was very much tied in with the automobile.

The more transportable and less expensive handsets entered the market only at the end of 1992. This gave birth to mass markets, and the nature of mobile phone sales transformed quickly from professional electronics to consumer goods catering to individual needs. The decisive advance took place in 1994–1995 when Nokia's handset sales doubled annually for two years in row.

From business tool to designer item

● A sea change took place when mobile phones became truly pocket-size. The role of design was suddenly determinant in a model's success. Earlier, design had been governed by ways of fitting the phone comfortably inside the car. Now the phone was an independent item to be displayed – a reflection of the user's personality. Handsets were progressively miniaturized, and now could fit in a pocket or a handbag. Nokia stressed the importance of industrial design from the beginning. As handsets became consumer goods, users began to ask for special features and functions.

It was a turning point, recalls Frank Nuovo, Nokia's chief designer and vice president. Since the late 1980s, Nokia had worked with Designworks USA/BMW Inc. for development of its look and feel.

Nuovo's career covers a wide range of products – furniture, consumer electronics, medical instruments, car interiors, air control equipment and instrument panels for power stations and computers. As Nuovo sees it, the car industry is 60 percent design and 40 percent industrial production. Every year new models are largely sold on the basis of attractive design.

Nuovo's design process values the visual element as well as functional simplicity and overall harmony. He comes from Monterey, California, an area known for harmonious beauty created by cypress groves, the ocean shoreline and steep cliffs running down to the water. He has an office and studio at home for maintaining his 'outsider's view' in the creation and development of form. This has become the essential thrust of his work at Nokia.

Nuovo worked initially on a consultancy basis but was hired in 1995. That year Nokia established the Nokia Design Center in Los Angeles. Assisted by Andy Wong, Nuovo designed the model 101. He has played a leading role in the design of the models 232, 2110, 2120, 1610, 8110, 3110 and 6110, among others.

The designers evaluating the Nokia 3210 Xpress-on covers at Nokia Design Center in Los Angeles. From left: Senior Graphic Designer Marni Mcloughlin, Chief Designer Frank Nuovo, Senior Industrial Designer Matthew Sinclair, Corporate American Design Chief Alastair Curtis and Senior Designer Gerardo Herrera.

In the 1990s Nokia hired several young designers from art schools in order to keep in touch with trends. The Nokia Design Center cherishes teamwork as the most effective way to produce results.

As cool design gave another impetus to this booming industry, operators competed with each other to add new services enabled by the GSM technology. Airtime prices plunged and consequently calls lasted longer. This created a virtuous circle – as the cost of calls fell, handset sales rose.

A professional tool thus became a mass-market product comparable to the wristwatch, even a fashion statement. This change was fastest in Finland but the same development soon took place across the world.

CHAPTER 12

The making of the 'Nokia millionaire'

The critical factors for Nokia's predecessor companies were global raw material prices. The Cable Works watched the copper prices closely and adjusted inventories accordingly. The Rubber Works depended on the price and availability of rubber, while Nokia Oy, the forestry products company, was concerned about timber prices and the cost of energy.

As its electronics business expanded to the level of the group's traditional basic industry companies in the 1980s, Nokia faced a new challenge among its critical factors: knowhow. Research and a qualified workforce became primary issues, and Nokia began influencing Finnish public education and research policy.

The basic challenges of industrial production were still the unchanged, however: production efficiency, sales and logistics were still the key issues. The problems in television sets were linked to productivity and to pricing in the fiercely competitive markets. In the mid-1990s Nokia confronted a similar problem in the rapidly growing Mobile Phones division. Cutting through this knot led to a new kind of thinking in the organization of the production chain. This is one of the reasons Nokia has been clearly more successful in the late 1990s than its competitors.

When one problem is solved, another often emerges. But in examining Nokia's difficulties in the 1990s the scale of the difficulties makes the difference. At the beginning of the decade Nokia struggled with enormous losses in television set production, and the entire corporation suffered financial problems. The crisis in the mid-1990s was about sales and profit figures coming in below budget although the company as a whole continued to make a strong profit. At the end of the decade, Nokia encountered market speculation typical of growth companies – highly volatile, with the share price alternately climbing and nosediving.

Growth created a cash-flow problem

● The rapid expansion of the Mobile Phones division was one of Nokia's key issues in the mid-1990s. In order to find the reasons for the group's problems we must look at how the character of the company changed in 1994 and how its budget forecasting, prompted by strong growth, became overly ambitious. When the growth rate failed to reach budgeted figures, problems emerged in production and logistics. This was the starting point for changes and improvements that finally led Nokia mobile phones to world leadership at the end of the decade.

By 1994, Nokia's outlook had become clearly positive. Profitability of the Telecommunications and Mobile Phones divisions was developing well. The group was on target for the refocusing of growth businesses and divestiture of non-core activities. The new situation gave the management leeway in developing its plans for the future.

Nokia's character changed as its traditional businesses were divested and the emphasis was placed on telecommunications. The listing on the New York Stock Exchange and the related share issue in 1994 was a turning point. It is no exaggeration to say that Nokia became a large start-up company able to finance operations with cash flow instead of borrowed funds. As CFO Olli-Pekka Kallasvuo recalls, investors were at last more interested in Nokia's growth prospects and its ability to manage growth than in the company's break-up value.

Financial management proved to be a great challenge. 'Although our profitability will be as good as planned, Nokia Group's cash flow will not be positive in 1994', Kallasvuo told the Board in a report in April of that year.

He continued:

> The primary reason for this is the very fast growth at NTC (Telecommunications) and NMP (Mobile Phones). In cash flow terms, this reveals an increasing need for operating capital and investment requirements. Furthermore, the reorganization measures decided for Consumer Electronics will have a FIM 550 million (€100 million) negative impact on cash flow, almost all of it for 1994. All in all, cash flow for 1994 (excluding possible acquisitions and divestitures) will be negative FIM 1.6 billion (€290 million). The situation will improve in 1995 but cash flow will still be negative.

To ease the shortfall, the Board authorized management to prepare a directed share issue in connection with the stock market listing in the United States. In the summer of 1994, Nokia raised a total of FIM 2,490.3 million (€457 million) through a share issue and the launch of American Depository Shares (ADS) at the New York Stock Exchange.

How to become a 'euromillionaire'

● As Nokia's valuation became less based on substantive value, the market's attention turned to management credibility and its preparedness to meet the challenges of growth. New incentives were then offered to Nokia executives in the form of stock options as part of their compensation package. In April of 1994, Nokia's Annual General Meeting decided to target a bond with warrants to 46 people in top management. Subscription for a warrant that would entitle the holder to subscribe 1,000 Nokia preferential shares for FIM 374 was priced at FIM 1,000 and it was exercisable between December 1, 1998, and January 31, 2000. The warrants that were offered varied from FIM 2,000 to FIM 12,000 depending on the person's position in the company.

The most popular Nokia mobile phones 1992–2000

	Network standard	model	units sold
1992	AMPS Mobile		395 000
	AMPS 101		190 000
	AMPS Kite		154 000
1993	AMPS Mobile		361 000
	AMPS 101		297 000
	AMPS 121		215 000
1994	AMPS		830 000
	DCT/GSM	2110	618 000
	AMPS	101	475 000
1995	AMPS EASY CALL		2,018 000
	DCT/GSM	2110	1,112 000
	DCT/GSM	2110	767 000
1996	GSM900	2110	2,387 000
	GSM900	1610	2,231 000
	AMPS	232	1,422 000
1997	GSM900	1610	3,346 000
	TDMA800	2160	2,691 000
	AMPS	636	2,634 000
1998	GSM900	5110	8,421 000
	GSM900	6110	5,161 000
	GSM900	3110/3810	4,566 000
1999	GSM900	5110	18,904 000
	GSM900/1800	3210	9,278 000
	TDMA	5120	7,934 000
2000	GSM900/1800	3210	31,825 000
	GSM900	5110	17,237 000
	TDMA	5210	12,261 000

Nokia's share splits

effective	split	nominal value before (€)	nominal value after (€)
31.12.1986	5:1	16.82	3.36
24.4.1995	4:1	3.36	0.84
16.4.1998	2:1	0.84	0.42
12.4.1999	2:1	0.42	0.24
10.4.2000	4:1	0.24	0.06

In other words, one FIM 1,000 warrant would entitle the holder to sub-scribe Nokia shares for a total of FIM 374,000. At the time of the decision Nokia's share price was €1.2 (taking the splits into account), but defying all expectations the price had climbed to €13.0 by the end of 1998 – when the subscription period had started. This first stock option plan proved very favorable for the top management and elevated Nokia's management com-pensation to a new level. The term 'Nokia millionaire' was born.

The stock option plans were further expanded so that numerous No-kia employees have benefited from the positive share price development. At the same time, a bonus plan was introduced to all personnel. A bonus of up to 5 percent of annual salary would be paid to all staff when a set target profit figure was exceeded.

In addition to managers and employees, the third and the largest group that got rich with Nokia's success was, naturally, the shareholders. In the 1994 share issue the price for a preferential share was set at FIM 432. At the end of 2000 the price was 42-fold, in other words FIM 18,075. Those who had purchased Nokia shares in 1990–1992 when the company per-formed very poorly profited far more.

One concrete example describes the price development. Had a person bought one Nokia share on July 30, 1991 at €10.59, the total number of shares in May 2001, after all the splits, would have been 64. On that day one Nokia share was worth €34.18, giving compound profit of 20,545 per-cent, and an annual yield of 71.87 percent. Had a person reinvested all the dividends back in Nokia shares the profit over the period would have been 23,370 percent resulting in an annual yield of 74.14 percent. To put it sim-ply, the investment would have grown 233 times over. Such an investor would have become a 'euromillionaire' on an initial stake of €4, 278.

Ownership moves abroad

● A majority of Nokia's share ownership shifted abroad during the 1990s. Finnish banks, insurance companies and other institutions gave way to mostly US-based investors. Nokia's management executed the change from a predominantly Finnish company to a typical US group through a few well-planned moves. The reasons behind the moves included long-term internal pressures as well as more topical reasons.

Finnish commercial banks had traditionally held industrial companies in their grip through lending and share ownership. This often caused friction between management and the banks. Nokia's situation was more complicated than usual as it had not one but two rival banks as its biggest shareholders. Nokia's management wanted to have more elbowroom, while the banks wanted to maintain the status quo. For instance, Union Bank of Finland (UBF), one of the two main banks, took a dim view of Kari Kairamo when, as chairman of the Confederation of Finnish Industries, he supported the proposed law that would lower the banks' maximum ownership in companies from 20 percent to 10 percent. When the law came into effect the banks were quick to place part of their holdings in proxy companies.

The unstable ownership situation in the early 1990s became evident to Nokia's management when the banks, UBF and KOP, first ended up in conflict, coming to a resolution only when KOP sold its stake in Nokia.

NOKIA'S STOCK PRICE 1991–2001

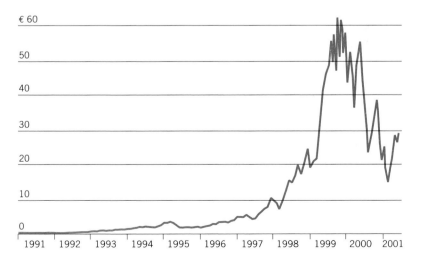

Nokia's largest international shareholders August 31, 1997

		million shares
1.	Fidelity Management & Research Co.	8.7
2.	Alliance Capital Management	8.6
3.	Capital Group	8.0
4.	Templeton International	6.4
5.	Jennison Associates Capital Corp.	4.9
6.	RCM Capital Management	3.2
7.	NordBanken Asset Management	3.1
8.	AIM Capital Management	3.0
9.	Morgan Grenfell Asset Management	3.0
10.	American Century Companies	3.0

Furthermore, UBF had also contemplated selling its stake in Nokia in 1991. The situation stabilized briefly in 1992 when UBF and a group of related companies supported by the insurance group Pohjola wound up in a dominant position as Nokia's owners.

At the beginning of 1993, the Finnish government removed restrictions concerning foreign ownership of companies. This opened the way for international investors, a crucial factor contributing to Nokia's future growth. At the same time, unrestricted foreign ownership brought along the threat of a hostile foreign takeover. Nokia therefore began a concerted effort to create an ownership policy that would be effective in thwarting unwanted suitors. As Nokia's management was aware, international institutions had already amassed sizable blocks of Nokia shares.

The third reason for the change in ownership policy was the decision in 1992 to start raising money on the international capital markets. The growth of Telecommunications and Mobile Phones reinforced management's belief that Nokia would pull through the difficulties, and that its further development would require substantial new capital. At the same time it decided to maintain the two-tier share structure, which would help keep decision-making, management and research and development in Finnish hands. Ultimately this would serve as a defense against hostile takeovers.

As Nokia grew and its biggest domestic shareholders suffered from a recession in the early 1990s, there was no way to retain Finnish dominance in Nokia's ownership indefinitely. In any case, Nokia's management was also working to widen the ownership base.

The Annual General Meeting in the spring of 1993 decided to add a redemption clause in the company statutes. If a new buyer/group acquired

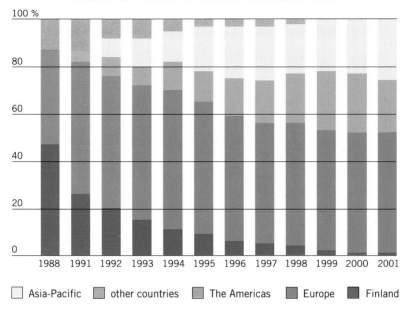

NOKIA'S NET SALES BY MARKET AREA 1991–2001

100 %
80
60
40
20
0

1988 1991 1992 1993 1994 1995 1996 1997 1998 1999 2000 2001

☐ Asia-Pacific ▨ other countries ▨ The Americas ▨ Europe ▮ Finland

Sales in Finland dropped below 10 percent of the total in 1995. Europe has consistently accounted for roughly half of the sales. The figure for Finland in 1988 includes other Nordic countries.

33.3 percent or over 50 percent (two separate triggers) of either shares or votes it would be obliged to make a bid for the remaining shares. The redemption price would be based on previous trading or the prevailing share price, whichever was higher. The same AGM decided to abolish the restrictions on foreign ownership, which the new law had already made obsolete.

Finland as home base

● Nokia raised a total of FIM 3.5 billion (€642 million) in 1993 and 1994 through share issues targeted at international capital markets. The issues raised awareness of Nokia internationally, particularly in the United States helped by the listing on the New York Stock Exchange.

By the end of 1997 foreign ownership in Nokia had already risen to over 70 percent of shares, but reached only 16 percent of the vote-rich

K-shares. The biggest Finnish sellers included the banks. The Union Bank of Finland, which was traditionally the dominant owner of Nokia, had held 12.1 percent of the shares and 16.3 percent of votes in 1988. By 1997 the holding of the bank, which had changed its name to Merita, had dropped to below one percent. Likewise a number of Finnish industrial and insurance companies reduced their holdings.

The Finnish government had become a shareholder of Nokia in 1987 when it received shares as payment for its stake in Telenokia. The government's holdings actually date back to 1981 when Nokia bought a majority of the state-owned Televa and the government became a minority shareholder in Telenokia. In 1992 the state's holding, 2.3 percent of Nokia, was transferred to the Finnish National Fund for Research and Development (SITRA), which gradually reduced its holdings throughout the 1990s. The Government Guarantee Fund received some 4.1 percent of Nokia shares when the ownership of Skopbank was restructured in 1993. These shares were sold in the next few of years.

In the United States, investors had begun to take an increasingly active part in annual general meetings but this trend did not reach Nokia. As Nokia saw it, the reasons were probably the mandatory share registration and other obligations in the book-entry system. An American shareholder willing to participate in Nokia's AGM would first have to convert his tradable American Depository Shares into ordinary shares, and after that register the shares in the company share register well before the AGM.

Participation of shareholders in General Meetings and shares present of all potential votes and shares 1988–1997

General Meeting	K-shares %	A-shares %	% of votes	% of shares
1988 (extrao.)	58.4	21.4	56.6	46.0
1988	57.0	29.0	55.6	47.7
1989	59.7	17.7	57.6	45.2
1990	57.4	26.7	55.9	46.8
1991	64.2	28.3	62.4	51.8
1992	49.9	14.6	48.1	37.7
1993	49.6	16.4	48.0	38.1
1993 (extrao.)	41.6	7.6	39.9	29.8
1994	38.4	5.9	36.2	25.3
1995	41.9	2.4	37.5	20.0
1996	41.4	1.5	35.4	15.9
1997	41.8	1.3	34.5	14.0

GEOGRAPHIC SPREAD OF NOKIA SHARES

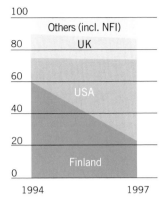

100
Others (incl. NFI)
80 UK
60
USA
40
20
Finland
0
1994   1997

NET SALES BY MARKET AREA 2001 (2000) %

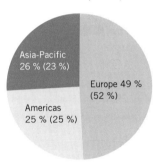

Asia-Pacific
26 % (23 %)

Europe 49 %
(52 %)

Americas
25 % (25 %)

VOLUMES OF NOKIA SHARES TRADED IN 2001 %

Stockholm
17 %

New York
31 %

Helsinki 52 %

Frankfurt 0 %   Paris 0 %

From 1994 Finnish ownership had shrunk by 20 percent but in voting power the decline was only 8 points. By early 1997 domestic investors still controlled some 60 percent of the votes in Nokia, so at that time Nokia was still firmly under Finnish control.

The question of domicile prompted long and earnest discussions at Nokia. Should Nokia remain in Finland for the long haul, or move its base abroad? In the autumn of 1996 Nokia made the strategic decision: to keep its head office in Finland, and move to 'Nokia House' at Keilalahti, a seaside location in the city of Espoo a few kilometres west of Helsinki.

Nokia informed Finland's president and a few key ministers of the decision, expressing the hope that Nokia would not be 'punished' for the decision with heavy taxation. A few months later Ericsson of Sweden threatened to move out of its home country – a notable difference in chosen lobbying methods. In the end, Ericsson also stayed put.

CHAPTER 13

Growth challenges lead
to efficiency gains

Corrective measures taken by the new management bore more fruit than expected in 1994. A combination of pruning and nurturing resulted in what became known as the year of the 'Nokia miracle'. And it was an interesting time, particularly because in the following year things started to go awry, leading to massive reorganization.

By the end of 1994 angst gave way to optimism in the top management. In March, Jorma Ollila reported to the Board:

> The Consumer Electronics division reports positive development in the home electronics unit. The flow of new orders at Telecommunications remains strong. Mobile Phones received a substantial order from Philips. Another highly significant order is expected to be received from AT&T. Order books at the Cables division have improved considerably from last year, and are higher than budgeted.

The long-term strategy that was presented at the Board's strategy seminar in Hong Kong in May 1994 by the top management, including Jorma Ollila, Matti Alahuhta, Pekka Ala-Pietilä and Olli-Pekka Kallasvuo, focussed on the strong growth prospects.

The leading theme, approved by the Board in June, was:

> Utilization of the growth potential at telecommunications by investing heavily in the development of telecommunications and mobile phones mainly through organic growth ... At the same time we aim to utilize the knowhow accumulated in consumer electronics when markets for multimedia products open after 1995 ... The growth strategy also means the divestiture of non-core businesses in 1994–1996.

As for income, Ollila calculated that by 2001 Nokia could reach an operating profit of FIM 5 billion (€920 million) on sales of FIM 65 billion (€11.9 billion). In retrospect the predictions, particularly on the development of profitability, turned out to be rather cautious. Actual operating profit in 2000 was €5.8 billion and sales totalled €30.4 billion.

In May 1994, the management estimated the value of Nokia's business operations at FIM 35 billion (€6.2 billion) of which Mobile Phones would account for FIM 15 billion and Telecommunications FIM 12 billion. Thus these two businesses accounted for 80 percent of Nokia's value in 1994.

During the first half of 1994 Telecommunications had exceeded the budgeted profits by FIM 105 million, Mobile Phones by FIM 68 million and the whole Group by FIM 162 million. Yet, the biggest news in the interim report was the FIM 700 million improvement of profitability at consumer electronics.

A few months later, Ollila defined his management philosophy:

> The management has become more convinced that it is inappropriate to devote the company's financial and intellectual resources to the development of all current businesses.

This thinking became reality when Nokia had to make a decision on the sell-off of tires and Nokia Power. The same thinking – focussing management energy and knowhow on core businesses – has been one of the cornerstones of management at Nokia during Ollila's tenure.

Good managers learn from their mistakes and problems, and the men running Nokia were fortunate to have this attitude when difficulties at Mobile Phones suddenly arose in 1995. Solving those problems in fact gave birth to new practices that catapulted Nokia to undisputed market leadership by the end of the decade.

The explosive growth at Mobile Phones had led to problems that required new ways of controlling the equation of growth and profitability.

The 'Nokia miracle' had already infused group management with a sense of optimism. The battle for survival had evolved into a major triumph. Externally, self-confidence showed as the company listed on the New York Stock Exchange. Internally it showed by setting even more ambitious targets and budgets for 1995.

Growth rate of Nokia's operating profit 1992–2001

Year	%	Year	%	Year	%
1992	385	1996	-15	2000	48
1993	509	1997	98	2001	-42
1994	146	1998	75		
1995	39	1999	57		

In December 1994, estimated Mobile Phones growth for the following year would reach as high as 85 percent. As Ollila told the Board:

> The sales budget for NMP (the Mobile Phones division) is aggressive and highly target-oriented. It is based on winning market share in a situation where we estimate our competitors to be production and partly distribution handicapped due to fast growth. Our estimated global market share in 1995 is 25 percent (in 1994 it was 21 percent).

Accelerating Mobile Phones sales required investment in production capacity. To meet this demand, in the spring of 1995 the Mobile Phones division decided to expand the Bochum plant in Germany. Why Bochum? Because Bochum was in good condition and Nokia did not want to increase the number of its plants. Production units in Asia had problems with logistics and trade barriers. The investment in Germany totaled FIM 387 million (€70 million). CFO Kallasvuo rolled out the numbers for the Board:

> The planned production capacity of NMP in Europe (Salo 8 million units annually and Bochum 4 million units) falls short of the budgeted sales (14 million units) in 1996. The required capacity for 1997 is estimated to reach 20 million units.

The steady increase in the number of subscribers and the expansion of networks demanded investment in new production capacity. At the end of March 1995 Nokia received its biggest order so far. E-Plus, the German mobile phone operator, increased investment in the GSM network, by placing an order worth FIM 2.5 billion (€450 million) with Nokia. The Nokia share price rose rapidly during the first half of 1995, giving the company an aura of unqualified success.

For 1994, the Mobile Phones division had budgeted for sales of 4.3 million handsets, while sales of 5.5 million units were achieved. The following year, 12.1 million units were estimated but the forecasters had overshot the mark – actual sales reached 'only' 10.5 million.

Stages of development in the mobile phone industry

- Initially, home market operations
- Slow international expansion by exports
- Manufacturing abroad
- Research and development abroad
- Management of explosive growth

Two profit warnings 1995–1996

● Then in the spring of 1995 the real difficulties with profitability at Mobile Phones began, and they worsened toward the end of the year. By February 1996 the Board declared it was facing a significant problem.

The situation was not helped by the fact that Consumer Electronics, which had briefly surfaced from the doldrums, returned to a deep loss. To solve that problem the company resorted to further reorganization, re-grouping Consumer Electronics (NCE), Industrial Electronics (INEL) and the Cable Industry (NCI) together as Nokia General Communications Products. The new group was headed by Tapio Hintikka. Meanwhile, no organizational or personnel changes were made at Mobile Phones, where the problems were attacked by other means.

The strains at Mobile Phones became evident when the division's performance fell short of budget. Sales for the first five months of the year were FIM 395 million (€72 million) and profit FIM 119 million (€29 million) below the budgeted figures. The corresponding figures at Telecommunications were FIM 109 million (€20 million) and FIM 134 million (€24 million) above budget.

CEO Ollila told the Board, 'We have nevertheless managed to increase market share'. He also said, 'The component problem has been solved and consequently production volume can now be increased to meet demand.'

The low Mobile Phones figure was the topic of the day at the Board's strategy meeting in Camberley in the United Kingdom in September 1995. By now it was clear that the ambitious budget was far from reality, even though annual sales growth in absolute terms was still quite impressive. Sales during the first eight months were FIM 3.5 billion (€640 million) higher than in the same period the year before. The problem was that the figure fell FIM 2.7 billion (€490 million) short of the budget causing considerable internal difficulties. Likewise, operating profit for this period was FIM 402 million (€73 million) higher than the year before, but FIM 267 million (€149 million) below budget.

Luckily for the company as a whole, the situation at Telecommunications was the reverse. Telecommunications' operating profit exceeded its ambitious budget by FIM 624 million (€113 million), even though sales remained unchanged. As other business units also exceeded their budgeted figures, Nokia's corporate operating profit at the end of August was FIM 570 million (€104 million) ahead of budget.

But problems persisted and the management was aware of them. In

October 1995, Ollila summarized the situation at Mobile Phones:

- Sales target for 1995 had led to high costs
- Logistics problems
- Component problems: radio interference, battery, charger
- Quality problems
- Growth of organization

Figures for January–November revealed that operating profit at the Mobile Phones division was FIM 550 million (€100 million) below budget. Yet, the group's profit was an impressive FIM 1,829 million (€332 million), an increase of FIM 51 million (€9 million) from the previous year. The loss of FIM 264 million at Consumer Electronics for the first 11 months was FIM 338 (€48 million) below budget and FIM 264 million (€61 million) lower than a year earlier. The figures were presented to the Board on December 14, 1995.

Ollila told the Board:

> In order to reverse the situation we will eliminate the technical and organizational problems by consolidating procedures and the organization even at the cost of losing market share if necessary.

The next day Nokia issued the Board-approved profit warning:

> Strong revenue growth continued throughout the autumn period in all of Nokia's main businesses with Nokia continuing to gain global market share in its main product categories. However, operating profits (profits before tax) for the third tertial are expected to be lower than in the same period last year.
>
> At Nokia Telecommunications, sales, profitability and order book have developed well and according to plan.
>
> Despite improvement in Nokia's US mobile phone business, growth and profitability in Nokia Mobile Phones have developed somewhat below plan.
>
> European color-TV markets in the final months of 1995 have continued to deteriorate. As a result, Nokia Consumer Electronics, a division of Nokia General Communications Products, will not achieve its set goals, and will incur a significant loss for the division for the whole of 1995. Steps are now being taken to rectify the situation.
>
> In 1996, Nokia is well placed to further improve its market position in growing and developing telecommunications markets.

In January 1996 Ollila told the Board that most of the shortfall in profitability was due to internal factors:

> First, the budget was aggressive since we expected that markets (would) continue to grow as during the previous year. Second the problems in the component, logistics and quality factors had adversely affected profitability.
>
> All in all, the proportion of fixed costs was excessive and we failed to adapt their proportion to the rapidly declining profitability. On the positive side, investment requirements in 1996 will be modest as the current capacity allows a

substantial increase in production. Of the external factors affecting profitability, the chief executive would like to point to the standstill of the US markets in summer. We have several measures going on to correct the situation, including strict restrictions in recruitment, cost cutting in marketing, more selective, market-oriented focussing of research and development, and changing the structure of the guidance system in order to underline profitability over market shares.

Problems existed also in financial management. Nokia's auditors later analyzed the situation in autumn 1995 as follows:

Net working capital of Nokia Mobile Phones increased substantially in autumn 1995 and measures were initiated to correct the situation. However, the group's information systems and the profit forecasts made on the basis of those systems failed to identify quickly enough the effects of the measures and other problems on the reportable profit figures. So the substantial decrease in profitability became evident only in reports given after year-end.

Deviation from forecasts – a crisis analysis

● Ala-Pietilä, head of the Mobile Phones division, analyzed the situation for Nokia's Board at the end of February 1996:

Although the Mobile Phones division remained very profitable in 1995 and managed to increase profit over the previous year, the massive shortfall from the budgeted targets constituted a major crisis in itself. The reasons behind this help us understand the key element in mobile phone business: adapting production to unpredictable and rapidly changing demand.

NOKIA SHARE PRICE SEPTEMBER 1, 1995 – MARCH 29, 1996

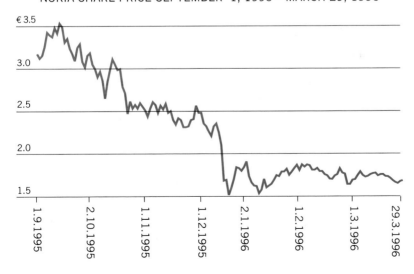

In Ala-Pietilä's analysis, the crisis stemmed largely from the constant growth of demand for mobile phones that kept exceeding forecasts, and the wide variations between various forecasts. Nokia had underestimated market growth more than once. Forecasts for mobile phone sales in 1995 varied between 45 and 60 million units.

Geographical differences did not help in the forecasting effort. American sales developed markedly slower than anticipated, Europe was rather on the mark while the Asian market grew much faster than forecast. Although Nokia doubled its mobile phone sales from 5.5 million to 10.5 million units, it was still 1.6 million units behind budget.

The mistakes, calculated Ala-Pietilä, cost Nokia FIM 500 million (€91 million) in Europe, FIM 330 million (€60 million) in Asia and FIM 100 million (€18 million) in America totaling FIM 930 million (€169 million). Nevertheless Mobile Phones made a profit of FIM 1,754 million (€319 million) in 1995. In addition, Ala-Pietilä reminded the Board that price erosion, a typical feature in the business, was about 20 percent both in 1994 and 1995.

What conclusions did Ala-Pietilä draw? In addition to the short-term measures, in the longer run management of growth was seen to require reorganization, increasing resources in logistics, lower recruitment and investments, and sharpening the focus on profitability.

In conclusion, Ala-Pietilä said that 'profitable operations mean focussing on profitable segments', and 'conservative volume growth estimates form the basis for planning profitable operations'.

The overhead slide presented by Pekka Ala-Pietilä, president of Nokia Mobile Phones, to the Board of Nokia on February 28, 1996

Short term corrective measures

1. Estimation of market growth	→	From growth-oriented to profitability-oriented goal setting
2. Product mix (USA)	→	Narrowed product mix and new business focus
3. RFI	→	Supply quality – with special resources and according to special programs
4. Product quality	→	Under special observation • programs for reduction of unit costs • quality of components • mechanics

Mobile phone markets and Nokia's sales 1994–1995

millions of units

	estimated world sales for 1995	actual world sales 1995	Nokia's budgeted sales for 1995	Nokia's actual sales in 1995	difference	Nokia sales in 1994
Americas	23	18	6	4.6	-1.4	2.7
Europe	12	11	4.0	3.7	-0.3	2.1
Asia	10	13.4	2.1	2.2	+0.1	0.7
Combined	**45**	**43.1**	**12.1**	**10.5**	**-1.6**	**5.5**

At the end of February 1996, Nokia had to issue a second profit warning. CEO Ollila said:

> We estimate the profit for the first two quarters of this year to remain well below corresponding figures in 1995.

The *Financial Times* of London regarded this warning as 'substantial'. The Nokia share price had now dropped to half the value of the previous September.

New logistics and new goals
– a turn for the better in 1996

● The budgeting failures in 1995 obviously had an impact on planning for the following year. Based on past experience and the situation at the end of 1995, the outline for the budget was cautious. CFO Kallasvuo explained the background for budgeting:

> The growth rate is estimated to decelerate substantially in all the group's main business areas. At the same time, price competition will increase in all markets… Profitability will remain at a good level but it will clearly decline at somewhat faster rate than forecast … The budget can be called cautious rather than aggressive. The conservative basic nature of the budget is justified as a guiding principle for keeping costs in check in an environment of fast growth.

But despite the caution, the year began with grim news. In January-February 1996 the Mobile Phones division made a loss of FIM 260 million (€47 million), a negative difference of FIM 439 million (€79 million) with the budget and FIM 625 million (€112 million) below the figures a year earlier. Telecommunications made a profit of FIM 36 million (€6 million), but that was FIM 188 million (€34 million) behind the budget, and FIM 269 million (€48 million) below the corresponding figures in 1995. Nokia

Group made a loss of FIM 269 million (€48 million) in the first two months, instead of the budgeted profit of FIM 350 million (€63 million). The difference with the previous year was FIM 955 million (€172 million).

Understandably, the interim report released in May 1996 explained the problem in delicate terms:

> The decrease in Nokia's operating profit was mainly attributable to Nokia Mobile Phones, which recorded a slight operating loss attributable to slower sales growth, price declines and logistical issues.

However, it was not simply a question of logistics, but of a deep and serious crisis that swept through the Mobile Phones division.

Ollila now listed a number of reasons for the problems. They included overly ambitious forecasting and the related cost increases, particularly in recruitment, attitude problems, and serious quality problems internally as well as in the supply chain. He paid close attention to management information and reporting systems, and the ability of middle management to bring about corrective measures. Ollila also mentioned price problems and delays in new product launches.

Production and logistics were fundamentally refocussed in 1996. The program dealt with all parts of the production chain. Key people involved in the process were Pekka Ala-Pietilä, president of Nokia Mobile Phones; Frank McGovern, head of operations, and Pertti Korhonen, head of logistics. The measures proved successful. As a result, profitability of Mobile Phones turned the corner, and the steep rise has continued ever since.

What was actually behind the improved profitability? The Board received the following explanation:

Ten largest customers of Nokia mobile phones in 1996

	million FIM		volume, units
Telecom Italia Mobile spa	774		454,000
NTT DoCoMo	729		411,000
France Telecom	518		361,000
RadioShack	470		603,000
Orange	398		337,000
AWS	393		337,000
Fleggaard Indkøb A/S	329		178,000
R.F. Telecommunication, S-Africa	323		184,000
Telecom, Germany	309		169,000
Eurocom, Israel	306		211,000
Combined	**4,551**	(€819 million)	**3,145, 260**

Ten largest customers accounted for 21 percent of the sales and volumes of Mobile Phones division.

From right: Pertti Korhonen, senior vice president, who is in charge of Mobile Software Unit with Pekka Koponen, responsible for strategy, and Niklas Savander. Korhonen is known as The Man Who Saved Nokia *in the transformation of supply chain management in the mid-1990s.*

> As a result of the measures, production time per unit has declined markedly. In addition we have achieved substantial growth in production volumes with less production workforce. Essential parts of the process include smaller inventories in materials, components and finished products. As for finished products we have managed to halve their inventory costs. The role of subcontracting is growing and we have increased cooperation with our suppliers.

The changes were achieved through more efficient inventory control, and replacement of the centralized system with a new Regional Demand/Supply Process. Orders were precision-targeted by better management of materials in order to reduce required inventories. Contacts with suppliers and cooperation between plants was increased. The worldwide logistics system was named the Integrated Supply Chain.

As an illustration of the depth of the changes and success of the measures taken, internal measurements showed that production efficiency improved by 40 percent in the third quarter of 1996 compared to the same quarter in 1995.

Throughout this turmoil, Nokia mobile phones sold well. In the middle of its problems the Mobile Phones division signed a major deal with AT&T Wireless Services Inc. (AWS) for its network, which was operating both analog and digital services at two different frequencies.

The crisis had a significant impact on values and attitudes both at management and shop floor levels. It is safe to say that the entire Mobile Phone unit went through a renewal process as a result of which a considerably more efficient production and sales machinery emerged. The renewed Mobile Phones division was also considerably more efficient than its competitors, which became evident in faster growth of sales and profitability in the months and years ahead.

Throughout the 1990s, the organization of mobile phones has relied on strong process management. The chart below explains the main features of development.

Several special features separate Mobile Phones from other business operations. It is a global business with vast variations between markets. Demand and sales have grown fast. A number of different standards dot the markets, and new ones are on the drawing board. Intensity of research and development is high. And last but not least, brand, distribution channels and new customer segments play a vital role.

Production efficiency in Nokia Mobile Phones

Changes achieved in 1996
- Smaller inventories released FIM 2.5 billion (€450 million)
- Inventory cycle reduced from 154 days to 68 days
- Raw material cycle reduced from 86 days to 26 days
- Cash flow FIM 4.6 billion (€830 million) positive in 1996 (FIM–3.2bn in 1995)
- Inventory costs down from FIM 200/handset to FIM 100/handset.

New production goals
- The number of parts down from 900 to 400 (DCT3) and below 200 (DCT4)
- Production time from 40 minutes to 4 minutes
- Production start-up time and efficiency (at the beginning of the 1990s six months, now one month)
- Improvement of production yield from 30 percent in the early 1990s to 90 percent with the latest products
- Improvement of line efficiency from 35 percent to 92 percent
- The hourly performance of SMD pick-and-place machine from 15,000 to 40,000
- Line capacity from 35,000 units in 1992 to 110,000 units (DCT3) in 1997
- New production test equipment, reducing testing time by 30–50 percent
- The number of mechanical parts reduced by 20–30 percent.

The key metric: increase in productivity

● Nokia's financial control systems have focussed on various aspects of the business over the years. In the 1990s the accounting systems remained largely unchanged. Processes have become faster and more efficient but annual profit and loss accounts have in practice been comparable. Nokia has employed the International Accounting System (IAS), and also presented results according to the Finnish Accounting Standards (FAS).

But CEO Ollila has added one measurement, Added Value/Total Wages and Salaries to his bag of tools. And that is the ratio he has followed keenly. The formula goes as follows: first, all external purchases (components, goods and services) are subtracted from total sales. This figure is divided by salaries and wages including pension and social security contributions. If the result is 1, personnel has managed to add value equaling only their salaries and wages. If it is 1.5, more value has been added. In other words, the higher the figure, the more efficient production. In addition to productivity of labor, Nokia's financial management keeps a sharp eye on return on capital employed.

As Ollila sees it, his ratio is a better instrument for measuring productivity than the popular sales/employee or similar formulas, many of which can be manipulated by outsourcing production.

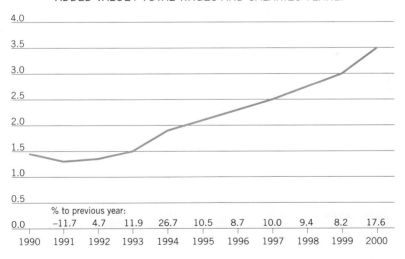

ADDED VALUE / TOTAL WAGES AND SALARIES YEARLY

	1990	1991	1992	1993	1994	1995	1996	1997	1998	1999	2000
% to previous year:		−11.7	4.7	11.9	26.7	10.5	8.7	10.0	9.4	8.2	17.6

One of Jorma Ollila's most important management tools is the ratio that measures change of productivity.

CHAPTER 14

Modus operandi changes
as personnel expands

The Nokia personnel count expanded rapidly in the 1996–1999 period, as both Telecommunications and Mobile Phones doubled in size. Recruitment of this highly educated workforce gathered pace toward the end of the decade, with many of the new recruits joining research and development. The effect of investment in R&D on overall profitability is an interesting area but is difficult to prove with numbers. Instead we will look at the increases in R&D personnel and how that began to transform the very nature of Nokia.

At the end of 2000, Nokia employed some 58,700 people including 27,400 in Mobile Phones, 23,500 in Networks, 2,200 in the Nokia Ventures Organization and 5,600 in other operations. Almost 20,000, or 32 percent of the workforce, were in research and development – a large proportion for any company in this sector. Nokia's R&D expenditure amounted to €2,584 million, about 8.5 percent of turnover.

Focus of R&D

● What was the focus of Nokia's R&D investment? Some outsiders have calculated that Nokia spent more on research and development than all of Finland's universities and other institutions of higher education put together. This comparison is misleading, however, because Nokia focuses its R&D on product development while universities and other institutions undertake basic research. Only a fraction of Nokia's R&D expenditure is allocated to basic research.

In the second half of the 1990s, Nokia understandably channeled more of its R&D into the basic development of mobile phones and mobile data communications than before, and it paid off. One way to analyze the success of this strategy is to look at the number of patents Nokia has received. Since the patent dispute with Motorola, all of Nokia's business units have consistently built up their patent portfolios. (See chart below)

In 1999 Nokia's R&D was organized on two levels. The company had its Nokia Research Center (NRC) and at the same time business units operated 44 additional research centers in 12 countries around the world. NRC 'sold' some 70 percent of its services to business units. Medium-term research connected with the development of product generations took about half of the NRC's research activities paid for by business units. As Juhani Kuusi, head of NRC, put it, about one-quarter of the work consisted of 'fire brigade jobs', solving urgent problems in the business units. The remaining quarter was devoted to long-term research preparing for the future and was financed at the corporate level.

As the corporate focus changed in the 1990s, so did personnel policy. In the past Nokia had old, established businesses with clearly defined jobs and professions, and personnel was traditionally organized in the appropriate

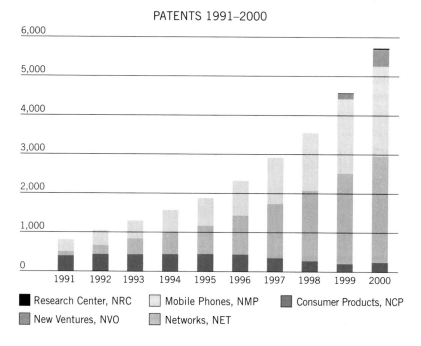

PATENTS 1991–2000

Legend:
- Research Center, NRC
- New Ventures, NVO
- Mobile Phones, NMP
- Networks, NET
- Consumer Products, NCP

The activity of Nokia's research and development was evident in the constantly increasing number of patents. This was significant not only for protecting its innovations but also in talks with other companies. A sizable patent portfolio was a useful bargaining chip in negotiations for cross-licensing.

unions. The situation changed considerably in the 1990s when personnel grew rapidly, the average level of education rose, job descriptions became more flexible, career moves came more quickly, the average age of employees dropped and the compensation policy became more versatile.

Labor relations – strikes and avoiding them – have featured prominently in the earlier history of Nokia. Detailed analysis of labor union activity is not possible in this book; suffice it to say that certain principles have remained unchanged throughout the years. The most important feature is the continuous dialog between management and labor organizations.

One of the most significant changes in the 1990s has been the growing number of non-Finnish employees on the Nokia payroll. Although the Executive Board is still Finnish and retains an essential homogeneity, management and employees reflect a truly global perspective.

Since the mid-1990s, Nokia has held an annual Nokia Euroforum, a two-day event for the exchange of information between management and employees. The events are based on a directive of the European Union that obliges larger companies to organize an annual briefing with 30 employee representatives. Participants are chosen by country quotas based on the extent of Nokia's international operations in the European Union. The event includes a management briefing on topical issues and the company's economic outlook.

Cooperation also extends to compensation. In parallel with the management stock option plan, Nokia introduced an employee bonus plan linked to earnings per share (EPS). Several larger high technology companies have similar plans. Nokia adopted a two-tier scheme. Employees ranked in lower job grades are included in the global bonus plan, under which they would receive an annual bonus based on an increase in EPS. Employees ranked in higher job grades are included in the stock option plans.

A new modus operandi

● Decentralization and centralization often come and go in cycles in the management of a large, diversified company. At times management prefers to clamp down on business units for the unification of the group's practices and operating procedures. In other circumstances, fast decision-making requires delegation to lower levels. Nokia has tried both. There is no single model that has spanned corporate history. A global company also faces the constant challenge of how to mix a function-based organization and a region-based hierarchy. Grouping by business operations underlines the

Product range

DCT 0	DCT 1	DCT 2	DCT 3
2 products	1 Product/ standard	1–3 Products/ standard	2–3 Products/ standard
GSM	GSM	GSM	GSM
	DCS 1800	DCS 1800	DCS 1800
	DAMPS	DAMPS	DAMPS (800+1900)
	PDC (800+1500)	PDC (800+1500)	PDC (800+1500)
		CDMA	CDMA (800+1900)
		DCS 1900	DCS 1900
		(EFR)	GSM/DCS 1800
		(HR)	GSM/DECT
			(AMPS MOD)

Nokia has consistently aimed to simplify mobile phone production platforms. The emphasis is on the development of platforms, that will enable as cost effective production as possible. This table was presented by Pekka Ala-Pietilä and was included in the minutes of the Board meeting on March 24, 1998.

specific branch of expertise while a regional and customer-oriented organization focuses on overall responsibility and customer service.

Perhaps change itself has been more important than the actual form of the renewed organization. A carefully planned and well-timed switch from one model to another can shake up the organization, preventing the spread of complacency and rigid bureaucracy.

Nokia was highly decentralized at the beginning of the 1990s. The same applied to the ownership base when the management aimed to attract new international investors to finance the company's growth. On the other hand the abolition of the restrictions on foreign ownership brought another threat, that of a hostile takeover.

The pendulum swung the other way in the mid-1990s. As of the beginning of 1997 Nokia strengthened top management control of operations in Asia Pacific and in the Americas. In practice, CFO Kallasvuo became responsible for operations in the Americas and Sari Baldauf, a member of the Executive Board, assumed responsibility for Asia Pacific, which initially included Japan, Korea, China, Hong Kong, Taiwan and India. Both Kallasvuo and Baldauf reported to CEO Ollila.

Ollila described the new structure to the Board as a 'market-oriented approach'. He added that the change 'will improve the utilization of the group's knowhow in telecommunications, streamline the decision-making process, and improve the ability to take regional characteristics into account'.

In connection with the regional arrangements, Nokia also redefined its core businesses. The focus would be on network infrastructure, terminals and integrated solutions. The last term was more abstract and difficult to define. On the one hand it involved preparation for technological changes – discontinuities or disruptive change, as they have been called. On the other hand it included the belief, which originated in the 1980s, that as a result of digitalization various kinds of communications equipment will converge and integrate.

Ollila also aimed to clarify Nokia's management culture. As he told the Board in November 1998, the cornerstones of Nokia's management were:

- Openness
- Collegial operation of the Executive Board
- Business-oriented management
- Speed, proactive approach
- Head office made up of support functions, active recycling of positions, no predetermined career ladder

In 1998 the organization was again rotated. Pekka Ala-Pietilä, who had led the Mobile Phones division, was appointed deputy to the chief executive and head of new product areas. He was replaced at Mobile Phones by Matti Alahuhta, head of Telecommunications. To complete the reshuffle, Sari Baldauf became head of Telecommunications. Meanwhile Kallasvuo returned from the United States to the position of CFO.

Communications shifts to market analysts

● Nokia has been listed on the Helsinki Stock Exchange since 1915. For decades the company's external communications effort was primarily targeted at the media. It was not until the 1990s that the focus shifted to investors and equity analysts. The change was largely prompted by the growth of foreign ownership, particularly in the United States, which was enabled by the abolition of foreign ownership restrictions in 1993 and Nokia's share issue in 1994.

Nokia says it has aimed to be as honest and transparent as possible in communicating its results and future outlook. It sought to provide equal information to the capital markets and the media. Yet Nokia's credibility among the media suffered a major blow in December 1995 when the company issued a profit warning. An internal memorandum at Nokia quoted a London-based analyst as saying: 'Nokia made a catastrophic communications mistake in connection with the profit warning.'

Nokia came to the conclusion that it had to pay more attention to investor and media relations. The company also wanted to improve communications to customers and to its own personnel. Later Nokia also acknowledged that it had not been sufficiently aware of its investors' decision-making processes – based not only on facts and figures but also on rumors and market gossip.

Investor relations is more codified and developed in the United States, and Nokia was keen to learn more about it. It was particulary important to understand how equity analysts operate. Sell-side analysts working for investment banks specialize in business sectors following from 10 to as many as 80 companies in the same field. In 1997 some 50 analysts followed Nokia. Analysts collect information through various sources including discussions with companies, their suppliers and distributors.

Institutional investors have become a more fragmented and diverse target group for companies. They build their portfolios on narrow criteria such as stock price movements, dividend or the combined yield. This makes dialog with the target groups more difficult. In addition, investors include active players who buy and sell their stakes several times a day, and turn their portfolio over 10–15 times a year. These fast movers increase share price volatility on the market.

Nokia's conclusion from the events in 1997 was that 'the company image is more and more personified by the top management, which underlines the importance of a more consistent message and style of communication'. Hence responsibility for public statements was primarily placed with CEO Ollila and CFO Kallasvuo.

Investor relations has expanded the field of corporate communications. It included delivering material, phone and video conferences, electronic communications on the Internet and by e-mail, regular meetings and conferences, corporate advertising, providing service to investors, and dealing with Nokia's suppliers and other stakeholders.

Growth of brand awareness 1994–1996

In brackets the brand awareness in absolute figures at the end of 1996 as percentages of population investigated.

Nokia	74 (65)	Ericsson	132 (41)
Motorola	80 (55)	Sony	25 (25)

As Finland became a member of the European Union the focus of lobbying shifted from Finland to the EU. Veli Sundbäck, undersecretary at the Ministry of Foreign Affairs and the key civil servant in Finland's entry negotiations, became Nokia's 'foreign minister'. He replaced Paavo Rantanen, another previously high-ranking appointment from the Ministry of Foreign Affairs who had briefly also been Finland's foreign minister. One of Sundbäck's first tasks was to increase Nokia's influence in the European Union.

He felt that Europe had lost too many industrial battles in global competition. This sorry track record includes the textile and clothing industries, the steel industry, consumer electronics, shipbuilding, and the car industry. Sundbäck formulated Nokia's message in spring 1996 as follows:

> Europe cannot afford to lose its strong position in the global competition in the fields of telecommunications and information technology. Maintaining the position requires measures from both the industry and the European Union.

Investor relations became more systematic and measures bore fruit. In spring 1999 *Investor Relations* magazine awarded Nokia the prize for best investor relations by a European company listed in the United States, an award it continued to win for the next few years.

Long term brand development

● Nokia learned that investors don't necessarily read a message the way it is written. Martin Sandelin, head of Nokia's investor relations based in Irving, Texas, in the 1990s, recalls a few examples. When Nokia said it will 'invest in the future', investors interpreted the message as higher costs and lower profits. 'The future is uncertain' is a message that starts a stampede out of the stock. Words such as 'good', 'sound' and 'stable' are seen as a signal for profits exceeding expectations.

As Nokia's Mobile Phones division became a world leader, the role of the brand grew correspondingly, and in doing so accounted for an increasing proportion of the company's total value. Anssi Vanjoki, head of brand development, focussed Nokia's branding on 'individualism, desire for the new, human scale technology, high quality, and the ability to be mobile with the product'.

Brand awareness was increasingly surveyed on a global basis among various consumer groups. Nokia understood that building a brand name

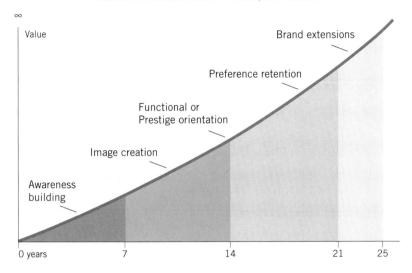

BRAND DEVELOPMENT CYCLE, 25 YEARS

Value

∞

Brand extensions

Preference retention

Functional or
Prestige orientation

Image creation

Awareness
building

0 years   7   14   21   25

requires consistent work and that global awareness cannot be established in a few years. The timescale can extend up to 25 years for a worldwide name.

From the brand development perspective, two technical innovations, e-mail and the Internet, have helped tremendously in communications. Much of the emphasis has shifted from the traditional print and electronic media to the new media. At Nokia the Internet has revolutionized advertising, recruitment and general communications. Internet-based communication now supplements traditional channels in internal and external publications.

CHAPTER 15

How the Internet changed the operational environment

'The current technological development is no longer just a rising tide, it is a storm of tidal waves. Likewise, the real emergence of the Internet will form the basis for a new technological order.' This is how Juhani Kuusi, head of the Nokia Research Center, describes the Internet revolution, which has led companies to rethink their ways of operating. Internet tools now dictate much of internal and external communications and contact with business partners and customers.

Technological development and the relevant standards form the basis for the design and manufacture of telecommunications networks and mobile phones. The Internet, which connects computers creating a global network, became the platform for worldwide telecommunications revolution in the second half of the 1990s. It evolved at astounding speed from an e-mail network between a few scientists and computer specialists to a global communications network linking offices and homes alike.

Short Messaging Service (SMS), the fastest growing service in mobile communication, was just an appetizer for things to come. It was estimated that some 250 billion messages were sent worldwide in 2001 from GSM networks alone.

The Internet has had a profound impact on Nokia. As an example Nokia introduced the new WAP (Wireless Application Protocol) mobile phone in Cannes to only 3,000 visitors, and some half a million members of the public logged on to the Nokia website to see the new product.

The new era at Nokia began in 1997 when the Internet was sweeping the world. The Nokia of old was gradually being swept aside by the 'new' Nokia.

The Communicator was the Nokia product that first bridged data transmission with voice. Launched in 1996, the Communicator included an Internet search engine, telefax, e-mail service, calendar and, of course, a regular mobile phone. It entered the market years before the network operators were providing all the functions it could perform. Nokia's corporate image has been built on avant-garde products such as the Mikro Mikko computer and the Communicator, although profits and volumes have come from elsewhere.

New strategy: 'Leading position in the most attractive fields of global telecommunications'

● Recovery from growing pains put the Mobile Phones division back on track for global leadership. At the same time Nokia became one of the world's most valuable companies by market capitalization. Yet the growing pains also proved that the company is vulnerable: it can be hit suddenly by enormous problems. The difficulties of the Mobile Phones division pointed up the dangers of being overly dependent on one business. Nokia's recovery was helped by its telecommunications networks, which performed exceptionally well and helped the recovery.

Nokia became a world-class corporation, and began to be compared with other leading high-tech companies such as Microsoft, Intel and Sony. In 1996 Nokia ranked 19th on the list of the most valued companies in Europe compiled by Price Waterhouse and the *Financial Times*. In electronics, Nokia trailed only Siemens and Electrolux. Jermyn P. Brooks, director for Europe at Price Waterhouse, said: 'Nokia is a company that has managed to combine technology and reliability. You cannot be at the technological peak unless you are able to provide after-sales service and security.'

The ranking was based on three main criteria. First, the company must have a clear vision and the ability to achieve it in practice. Second, its management must be flexible, adopting different management methods as required. Third, the company must have the skills to manage investor relations.

In the second half of the 1990s Nokia achieved a position in Finland similar to that of Volvo in Sweden at the beginning of the 1980s. 'In those days no company was more attractive in Sweden than Volvo', recalls Pehr Gyllenhammar, group chief executive of Volvo during the 'golden decade'. At a time when automobiles were the world's leading industry Gyllenhammar was the leading Nordic industrialist, and he also wielded influence on the European continent. Yet Volvo never gained a position in the car markets equal to that of Nokia in mobile phones and telecommunication networks in the 1990s.

In 1997 Nokia adjusted its strategic goals to become the global leader in the most attractive areas of telecommunications. This was to be achieved by anticipating and rapidly fulfilling evolving customer needs, quality in products and processes and solutions, and openness with people and new ideas.

Nokia's profitability rocketed in 1997. Operating profit in January–August 1997 exceeded the budget by as much as FIM 1,781 million (€318 million) while net sales topped the budget by a mere FIM 6 million (€1 million). As Jorma Ollila explained it, the result was largely due to 'several software deliveries at high margins' at Telecommunications while Mobile Phones had the benefit of a 'more optimal product mix and higher prices than forecast'.

Ollila told the Board that Nokia's challenges in 1997–1999 were to maximize shareholder value, and to maintain a strong financial position and a balanced expansion on a global basis. Ollila also stressed the stabilization of profit development at the Mobile Phones division. This was to be achieved through the development of operating processes and strengthening Nokia's position as a pioneer in high value-added mobile phones.

Among telecommunications operators, Nokia aimed to strengthen its position through a partnership strategy. Finally, it was also important to succeed in the choice of standard as the standardization of cellular phones proceeded via UMTS development. Finally, it was also crucial for Nokia to reduce its reliance on Mobile Phones by strengthening the fixed-line network business.

Acquisition of Internet technology

● Major acquisitions were conspicuously absent from Nokia's strategy in the 1990s. At the beginning of the decade the company simply could not afford them. The balance sheet was weak and Nokia aimed to get rid of the loss-making consumer electronics business. Gradually Nokia's financial position improved and the management turned from the remaining small divestitures to possible acquisitions. One milestone in this process was Ollila's report to the Board in September 1997, perhaps echoing Nokia's experience of the 1980s:

> Acquisitions remain one way to develop corporate structure but they are not the top priority.

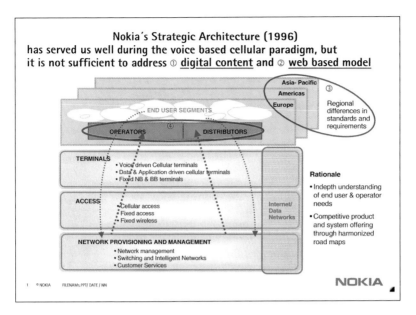

In 1996 Nokia based its strategic thinking on the challenge of digital technology and the Internet. A slide by Pekka Ala-Pietilä.

Nokia began acquiring companies that could be considered vanguards in Internet technology. This concept assumed that the future of telecommunications would increasingly be based on Internet solutions. At this point Nokia's business operations seemed to divide into two separate areas. On the one hand there were the highly profitable and fast-growing mobile phone and network operations. On the other, Nokia searched for new footholds in the latest technology. However, the two areas were in different leagues. In the year 2000, the new ventures accounted for only 3 percent of the group's total sales.

One era in Nokia's history came to an end in autumn 1997. Automotive Electronics, which was started with high hopes in cooperation with Volvo, was sold to Autoliv of Sweden, and audio electronics was acquired by Harman International of the United States. Nokia received FIM 300 million (€53 million) (book value FIM about 150 million) for the loudspeaker business, and FIM 55 million (book value FIM 37 million) for Automotive Electronics.

The division had manufactured and sold speakers and sound systems as well as Automotive Electronics to the European car industry. It employed some 1,400 people in Germany, Sweden and Hungary. Autoliv already

Tatyana Freitas at the Nokia Mobile Phones factory in Manaus, on the Amazon River, Brazil.

owned 50 percent of the unit, which manufactured electronics for air bags.

The division's total net sales amounted to FIM 770 million (€137 million) and operating profit to FIM 41 million. Hannu Suominen, head of the division, explained the reasons for the divestiture:

> Profitability is coming down largely due to the strong price squeeze from the car industry. As the car industry moves toward system deliveries, the position of component suppliers becomes more difficult. The division needs a dedicated partner or owner who can offer the clients total audio systems, not only loudspeakers.

In September 1997 a strategic outline set the goal of strengthening the 'product and knowhow base in the packet-switching networks of telecommunications'. One step along that path was the acquisition of the Silicon Valley-based Ipsilon Network Inc., for $120 million.

Mikko Kosonen, vice president for corporate development and a key person in the negotiations, explained the reasoning behind the move:

> Data transfer within the corporate sector and the manufacture of appropriate equipment is the fastest-growing segment in telecommunications. The engines of growth are digitalization and several other new applications based on packet-switching technologies, as well as services such as the Internet.

This segment is important to Nokia not only for its high growth potential but also for the fact that the traditional circuit-switching telecommunications technology will gradually be phased out by the so-called packet-switching technology ... They are also important for wireless telecommunications ... Up until now Nokia has not been active in the development of intranet solutions for companies. The main players in the market were companies supplying circuit-switching exchange networks (such as Ericsson), and the mostly North American suppliers of packet-switching data networks (including Cisco).

Ipsilon was heavily involved in Internet technology as well as in the application of ATM technology for increasing the performance of the Internet. The company employed some 120 people but had not yet attained a significant position in any customer or market segment.

In an internal memorandum, the importance of Internet technology was likened to GSM technology:

Hundreds of Nokia employees have been involved in the development of the GSM standardization. All the connected telecommunications protocols are considered to be strategic knowhow, which must stay in our control. The situation with the Internet is very much the same. If Nokia wants to be involved in the telecommunications business it must have expertise in all relevant parts of the Internet technology. One cannot outsource this technology.

Matra Communications, the joint venture of Northern Telecom and Lagardère, wanted to sell its GSM terminal business operations to Nokia. In June 1998 Nokia acquired only its research and development center, a 250-employee unit based in Ulm, Germany, for $24 million. Originally a unit within AEG Mobile Communications, the center had over 10 years' experience in the development of GSM technologies.

The pursuit of global leadership

● Tapio Hintikka, the member of the Executive Board who finalized the restructuring and divestiture of Consumer Electronics, moved on to the chief executive position at Hackman, a Finnish household goods manufacturer, in 1997. He described his former employer in an interview in *Nokia People* magazine in February 2000 as follows: 'The atmosphere was excellent, totally different from the past. It was something I had never seen in my life and I have seen a number of companies.'

The crisis in the mid-1990s had strengthened Jorma Ollila's role as the company's chief executive. Ollila can be described as a player-coach. He does not stand still and shout orders from the sidelines. Neither

The Sydney Olympics was the first truly wireless Olympics. The Telstra system handled some 125,000 mobile phone calls within Stadium Australia where 110,000 spectators saw the opening ceremony. The system was based on the MetroHopper base station supplied by Nokia.

does he take a seat up in the lecterns and criticize the coach. Ollila plays on the field. Although he has a strong team around him, he directs the game by setting objectives and placing the players in appropriate positions.

The key players have clearly defined roles. CFO Olli-Pekka Kallasvuo seems to be Ollila's closest confidant, an 'administration director' without direct business line management responsibility. However, he has a pivotal role in investor relations and monitoring profitability.

Matti Alahuhta is assigned to run Mobile Phones, the largest business division. His predecessor Pekka Ala-Pietilä became president in 1999 and remained a kind of development director as he had been in the second half of the 1990s, leading the search for new business areas and the preparation for the changes in the technological environment.

The career of Sari Baldauf is closely linked to Nokia's breakthrough in the expansion of the GSM networks, which was facilitated by the new standards. At the end of the 1990s, when the world was heading toward the third generation mobile phone standard, she was appointed head of Network division.

Ollila has described the watershed in the mid-1990s as a balance between value-based leadership and fact-based management. As he puts it, in 1992–1996 Nokia was in an 'entrepreneurial growth period', which called for value-based management. 'One had to tolerate an element of chaos, too,' he recalls. Yet toward the end of the decade it gave way to a more fact-based management, and in the closing years of the 1990s Nokia strengthened the role of common corporate functions such as information management, business control and human resources.

In the autumn of 1998, Nokia produced a comprehensive Internet strategy. According to this document, Nokia's aim was to become a significant player in the Internet within three to five years. Network security became a key element in the strategy.

Internet technologies have a way of changing telecommunications markets and the companies involved. At the highest level are carriers and the Internet service providers. The former offer transfer capacity while the latter buy the capacity in bulk as cheaply as possible and refine it to sell on packets of it at a higher price to the consumer.

Service providers build their networks by using routers, and they buy the connection between the routers from operators. The connecting parts can be copper cables, optical fibre, SDH (Synchronized Digital Hierarchy) connections, frame relay connections or ATM (Asynchronous Transfer Mode) connections. The last three are becoming increasingly popular as they enable the operator to sell capacity of one connection flexibly and simultaneously to several users.

Routers sold to service providers and ATM switches sold to operators represent different technologies that help achieve different things.

Even in the middle of the Internet revolution, Nokia maintained its focus and marched on to become the world leader in its primary business area, mobile phones.

CHAPTER 16

Nokia takes the leadership in mobile phones

C EO Jorma Ollila first announced it in the October report of 1998, and the news was powerful indeed:

> Market information for the first nine months of this year provides us with the basis to assert that we have significantly increased our global market share in mobile phones and become the world's biggest manufacturer of mobile phones.

Ollila's bland language, typical of his management style, meant that Nokia achieved one of the most coveted goals in business: world leadership in a major industry. This was perhaps the most significant milestone in the company's long history, and since then Nokia has moved to consolidate and strengthen its position.

Nokia was the strongest player in the negotiations over digital GSM 900/1800 standards, and those systems grew at the fastest rate in the mobile phone business. Nokia's strong leadership at the end of the 1990s was based on healthy, profitable growth. Ollila had succeeded in gaining market share without sacrificing profitability.

Forecasting growth is one of the biggest challenges in the mobile phone business. In the early days market growth was usually underestimated. As the stock markets overheated, the growth of mobile phone markets became a popular object of speculation.

Motorola of the United States and Ericsson of Sweden were Nokia's fiercest rivals in mobile phones. In network equipment the closest rival was Ericsson. In the second half of the 1990s mobile phone markets were often volatile, and consequently competitive positions have varied throughout the years. Nokia's position weakened in the mid-1990s when it failed to forecast market growth accurately but the loss of ground was reconquered within one year. Meanwhile Motorola has continued to lose market share, and in 1998 it relinquished global market leadership to Nokia for the first time.

Development of Nokia's mobile phones

Mobira Talkman   Mobira Cityman   101

Classic

2110   8110   6110   6210   6310   6510

Basic   **Expression**

2010   1610   3110   5110   3210   3330   3510

Tough   **Active**   **Imaging**   **Fashion**

6250   5210   7650   8210   8310   7210

Premium   **Communicator**

8810   8850   8910   9000   9110   9210

Mobile phones have developed in three different ways: they have become smaller, they have been segmented according to different user groups, and their features have increased. One key to Nokia's success is the ability to develop a multitude of models without losing the benefits of mass production.

Ambitious goals

● Nokia has been determined to grow and has set itself quite ambitious goals in mobile phones. The first target was global market leadership, and the next target was to become one-and-a-half times bigger than the next rival. This milestone was passed in 2000, and was followed by yet another target – to increase sales to twice that of the nearest competitor.

How did Nokia manage to gain market share and simultaneously reach higher profitability than its main competitors in a business that is highly volatile and vulnerable to abrupt changes? Matti Alahuhta, head of Nokia Mobile Phones, explains that Nokia appreciated the importance of gaining a continuous, competitive edge simultaneously in three fields: products, branding and logistics. The Mobile Phones division relies on these three parameters for measuring and developing its position.

Motorola was weakening as Nokia edged ahead. As Nokia sees it, Motorola lost its position because its mobile phones were not as competitive, its distribution did not function properly and it had focussed on analog technology for too long. Motorola also lost its position in infrastructure because it lacked exchanges and it had technical problems with digitalization and software.

Nokia also took a close look at the second wave of mobile phone sales – how soon consumers might swap their handsets for a newer model. Nokia estimated that the life cycle of a mobile phone would be 25–30 months and getting shorter. In 2001, Nokia estimated that 45 percent of mobile phone customers were not first-time buyers.

'We wanted to create a phone that would communicate style and enduring quality ... a beautiful object that you desire', said Frank Nuovo, Nokia's Chief Designer, in Newsweek *in December 1998, commenting on the award-winning Nokia 8810 model.*

Digital mobile phone markets exploded globally in 1996–97, based on the GSM 900/1800 standard that allowed the triumph of Finnish mobile phones. The penetration quickly spread to Europe, as is evident in the table below.

The critical year in Nokia's breakthrough was 1998. As its competitors stumbled, Nokia stayed focussed and managed to increase both market share and profitability. Competitors' problems were not solely attributable to the mobile phone industry. Other problems in their businesses impaired their ability to invest in the mobile phone operations.

In the summer of 1998 Nokia's biggest competitor Motorola issued a profit warning and said it would cut 15,000 jobs. In early autumn, Alcatel also announced that its profitability would decline. As a result its share price dropped by 30 percent. In October, Philips canceled the mobile phone cooperation agreement with Lucent of the United States. In November, Siemens announced a reduction in its workforce. And in December Ericsson, one of Nokia's main rivals, also issued a sudden profit warning and decided to reduce its workforce by 10,000.

Reasons for the companies' problems varied. In the case of Ericsson one reason may have been its failure to adapt to the change from

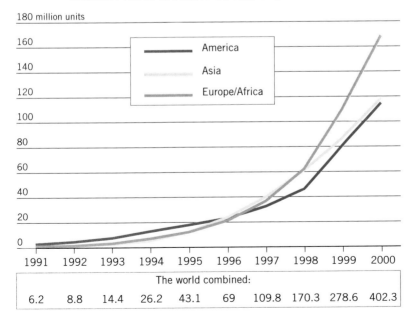

MOBILE PHONE MARKETS BY REGION, 1991–2000

180 million units

Legend:
— America
— Asia
— Europe/Africa

	1991	1992	1993	1994	1995	1996	1997	1998	1999	2000
The world combined:	6.2	8.8	14.4	26.2	43.1	69	109.8	170.3	278.6	402.3

Mobile phone markets by standard, 1991–2000

millions of units

	all	analog combined	digital combined	CDMA	GSM900/1800	GSM1900/TDMA	PDC	US dig ESM
1991	**6.2**	6.2	0.0	–	–	–	–	–
1992	**8.8**	8.6	0.2	–	0.2	–	–	–
1993	**14.2**	13.0	1.3	–	1.2	0.1	–	–
1994	**26.3**	21.5	4.8	–	3.8	0.4	0.5	–
1995	**43.1**	29.8	13.3	–	9.1	1.1	2.9	0.1
1996	**69.0**	31.1	37.9	1.0	23.0	2.1	11.7	0.2
1997	**109.8**	29.9	79.9	6.5	45.5	6.6	20.3	1.0
1998	**170.3**	27.1	143.1	18.1	80.0	15.6	27.7	
1999	**278.6**	24.7	253.8	41.2	145.8	35.1	29.2	
2000	**402.3**	11.5	390.8	62.4	226.2	62.5	35.4	

technology-driven mobile phone markets to the lifestyle- and market-driven business that it had become.

Meanwhile, Nokia's superior performance was due to several factors. In a newspaper interview, Ollila explained the excellent 1999 results:

> If one can manage growth of this magnitude, and the organization operates sharply, that alone facilitates the increase in the margins. It appears that we have succeeded in our operating philosophy in volume production and in organizing logistics. This paves the way for improved productivity. In addition, when things go smoothly employees are happier in their jobs. All that shows in the operating profit. And when you add successful marketing and strong products, that's it.

The qualitative factors behind Nokia's rise are much more difficult to assess than those that can be measured in numbers – production efficiency, market share or profitability. Nokia's pioneering position in mobile phone design, materials, colors and user-friendliness and constant renewal, are at least as important as production efficiency. As mobile phones have turned into fashion statements Nokia's trend-setting position has become more important.

Nokia in Europe, Asia and the Americas

● Now established as a global company, Nokia aimed at developing its three main market areas – Europe, Asia Pacific and the Americas – in a balanced way. Sales in Europe amounted to roughly half the total while Asia and the United States accounted for about one-quarter each.

Having joined the European Union (EU) in 1995, Finland set its next target as joining the European Monetary Union (EMU), the precursor of the European single currency, as of the beginning of 1999. This was desirable from Nokia's perspective as it would reduce currency risks and cash management costs. At the time Finland made the formal decision, some 60 percent of Nokia's net sales were in Europe. Nokia had about 60 legal entities in Europe including about 40 based in countries likely to join the EMU.

The eurozone developed pretty much as expected, and Nokia was among the first companies to adopt the common currency in its accounting. One unexpected development was that Sweden – and Ericsson – remained outside the euro, having decided, as did Britain and Denmark, to wait and see before abandoning their national currencies.

At least in the initial stages, the euro served as another catalyst to Nokia's growth. The weakness of the euro against the dollar increased export income of companies based in the eurozone.

In the United States, Nokia became a household brand by 1999. According to a survey made by Strategy Analytics, the US-based research company, 43 percent of mobile phone users were familiar with Nokia and 14 percent considered the product as good. Recognition of Motorola

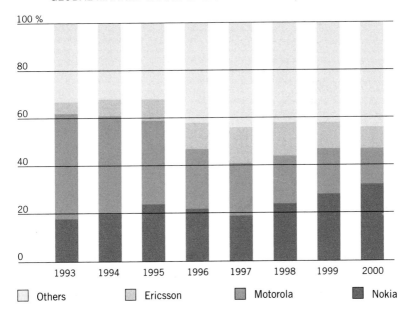

GLOBAL MARKET SHARE OF MOBILE PHONES, 1993–2000

From left: Research Engineers Li Chun An, Huang Hui, Shi Yi and Wang Hao in the Internet technology laboratory of the Nokia Research Center in Beijing in 2000.

reached 58 percent among those surveyed. The Nokia brand gradually strengthened in all areas while the attractiveness of Motorola, the biggest rival, declined. The Ericsson brand developed slowly and unevenly in various geographical areas.

Managing logistics

● One mobile phone includes 300–400 components depending on the model. Kari-Pekka Wilska, president of Nokia Americas, says the mobile phone business amounts to a large-scale logistical exercise. He announced in May 2000: 'We must have 100 million components in the right place at the right time. And now we have.'

Nokia's customers in the United States include large operators such as Sprint, Southwestern Bell and AT&T. For example Southwestern Bell has a huge logistics center near Nokia's plant in Dallas, guaranteeing quick marketplace feedback. Says Wilska: 'It is very important to be included in operators' campaigns. Otherwise it is very difficult to sell in price-driven markets.'

Mobile phone markets in the United States differed from those in Europe. The most notable example is digitalization, which progressed more slowly than in Europe. Nokia Mobile Phones division had a 21–22 percent share of the analog AMPS markets. In the digital markets the company's market share rose quickly to over 40 percent. The real breakthrough took place in 1998 when Nokia's overall market share in the United States increased by 15 percentage points, from 21 percent to 36 percent. Meanwhile Motorola's market share declined in the same period from 37 percent to 26 percent.

The challenges and successes of the Mobile Phones division are dependent on the ability to take advantage of changes in the marketplace. By the end of the 1990s a new era had emerged – integration of multimedia communications technology and wireless communications, and Nokia was prepared to make the investments for this promising new market.

Brand awareness 1999

	The World	Europe	Asia-Pacific	The Americas
Nokia	62	67	72	46
Motorola	72	60	83	74
Ericsson	60	59	75	55

CHAPTER 17

In search of new technologies and markets

N okia managed to ride the crest of the GSM wave and become the world leader in mobile phones as the world went crazy for mobility in personal communications. At the same time Nokia emerged as one of the two leading network suppliers in the world.

In this period of rapid growth, Nokia's top management put the emphasis on speed and agility. Business units were given new autonomy in their day-to-day decision-making. As Nokia became a large group even by international criteria, it also began to search for economies of scale internally. A parallel development was helpful: the proliferation of the Internet, e-mail and e-commerce that enabled and sometimes forced companies to unify their information management and corporate culture.

Nokia and many other companies were heading into uncharted waters in the late 1990s. New technologies, particularly those connected with the Internet, would change the operating environment in ways that required prompt response. Nokia concluded that its customer base, and consequently the markets and competitors, would be more difficult to identify, opening an era of less predictability. Nokia's top management regarded the change to be as important as digitalization and GSM were 10 years earlier.

Nokia's responses to this challenge were threefold: to acquire companies involved in the new technologies, establish joint ventures with other companies and set up its own New Venture Fund. These measures were part of Nokia's strategic outlines aiming to gauge future business opportunities. Pekka Ala-Pietilä, who had led the Mobile Phone division since 1992, was appointed head of these new operations. At the same time Ala-Pietilä became executive vice president and deputy to the CEO. Internally, he has also been nicknamed 'growth matrix director'.

Nokia management was well aware that the world of high technology favors companies that recognize windows of opportunity and know how to seize them. The history of technology companies indicates that leading firms have developed and adopted technologies that were often risky, complex and expensive. This helps explain how the largest companies with the deepest pockets managed to maintain their positions. One book that was particularly dog-eared at Nokia was *The Innovator's Dilemma: When New Technologies Cause Great Firms to Fail* by Clayton M. Christensen (published by Harvard Business School Press).

Nokia took these ideas on board in its analysis of the future and a 1997 memo by Mikko Kosonen, vice president for corporate development, defined the dilemma:

> Leading companies have focussed too deeply and for too long on being best in their chosen business area without focussing sufficient attention or funds on new growth areas or possible new technologies that may render existing technologies obsolete.

Nokia had correctly observed that the telecommunications giants had considered GSM as a marginal phenomenon until it was too late. This was not going to happen to the Finns. In April 1998, Nokia established the New Venture Fund with a capital of $100 million. Its mission was to 'search for new business operations, new technologies and long-term growth potential in new business areas'.

At the time Nokia was convinced that information technology, data communications and telecommunications would integrate.

In order to secure their future, such giants of technology as Microsoft and Intel had acquired minority stakes in companies outside their core businesses in order to hook them in the Windows operating system. Nokia's strategy, says Kosonen, was to 'complement its own product and business development by investing early in new and attractive technologies and businesses'.

The New Venture Fund was complemented in December 2000 by the establishment of another $500 million development fund. Unlike the original fund totally controlled by Nokia, this one also included Gold-

---

Objectives of Nokia Ventures Organization in 2000

- Foster Nokia's growth opportunities beyond the natural scope of existing businesses.
- Strategic IP oriented products and solutions for Enterprises and Managed Service Providers.
- Facilitates internal and external venturing.
- Piloting new applications and solutions.

Credibility of management is crucial for growing technology companies in search of additional capital. The other important factor is growth of operating profit. Nokia has built its corporate image around Jorma Ollila. This has been supplemented with public appearances by Pekka Ala-Pietilä, Matti Alahuhta, Olli-Pekka Kallasvuo and Sari Baldauf. Ollila became the first Finn to be featured on the cover of Business Week *on August 10, 1998. The improvement of Nokia's profitability in the early years of Ollila's tenure helped Nokia to raise new capital. By the end of the 1990s Nokia had become strong enough to manage its investments without external financing.*

man Sachs, BMC Software and CDB Web Tech.

Unlike the Funds, Nokia established a third 'division', a development group called Nokia Ventures Organization (NVO). This 'greenhouse' provided Nokia's management with a tool for exploring the future. Pekka Ala-Pietilä, head of both the Fund and NVO, explains that the Fund invests in businesses not directly connected with Nokia's existing operations. With the help of these investments, Nokia aimed to learn about the latest developments sooner than its competitors. As the market for Nokia's existing businesses became increasingly volatile, the establishment of these activities took on greater importance.

Ala-Pietilä explained the change from the past:

> Some five to ten years ago, you would set your vision and strategy and then start following it. That does not work anymore. Now you have to be alert every day, week and month to review your strategy on the basis of your vision, and changes in the markets.

Initially Nokia invested about one-tenth of one percent of net sales in the NVO. It was a kind of debating forum, an intellectual, technological and economics exercise aimed more at information-gathering than expanding business areas. When Ala-Pietilä was appointed president of Nokia Group, the matter received additional weight but it was too early to say whether the development funds and the development group would become Nokia's third leg. Or whether they have even been meant to become that.

Nokia and Microsoft
– the choice of operating systems

● As the properties of mobile phones developed, their operating systems became increasingly sophisticated. The Communicator and smart phones required different features in the operating system than the traditional mobile phones which used the more rudimentary Nokia Operating System (NOS). New demands from the marketplace included compatibility with computers, connection to the Internet, and compatibility with the most commonly used solutions.

The structure of the computer business, largely divided into equipment and software suppliers, means that when software companies were doing well, equipment manufacturers were stuck with more modest growth figures. Nokia saw the threat that Microsoft, the giant in computer operating systems, would pose if it established its Windows CE as the proprietary operating system in mobile phones. Along this road, software and component suppliers would achieve a dominant position.

Nokia aimed to develop a common platform for the Communicator and smart phones together with the leading companies in the business. However, Nokia and other manufacturers did not want to start an all-out war with Microsoft, and continued to use Microsoft products in areas where they were the best choice.

Nokia's attitude can be compared with the company's decision in the 1970s to begin to manufacture telephone exchanges although Siemens and Ericsson dominated the business. The difference here is that Nokia Mobile Phones already led the US market. It had a 30 percent share of the analog mobile phone market and almost 40 percent of the digital market. Nokia's overall market share in the United States was 34 percent, exceeding that of Motorola, the traditional number one on its home turf.

Timing of the initiative was interesting. The move was made in June 1998, just as US federal authorities were taking a close look at Microsoft, accusing it of abusing its dominant position in computer software. Public opinion largely echoed the sentiment. Microsoft was the world's leading company in its business by a wide margin, and opposing it would be a significant move. Yet Nokia thought that to compete with Microsoft it had to remain independent in the development of mobile phone properties. Nokia invested $47 million, which bought it a 30 percent share in the new software joint venture Symbian. The other partners were Psion PLC (40 percent) and Ericsson (30 percent). Motorola joined the new venture immediately after, and Matsushita in 1999.

The Nokia 9210 Communicator had a host of properties, which brought the handset closer to computers. Hence its operating system became increasingly important.

'Nokia on a collision course with Microsoft and Sony', read a headline in *Digitoday.fi*, an Internet newsletter, in January 2001. The newsletter referred to an article in *Business Week* headlined 'Is Nokia's Star Dimming?'

Business Week wrote about the development of the mobile phone as a radio-based product moving closer to the enchanted world of computers and consumer gadgets – from digital cameras to micro-sized videos – where all products fluently communicate with each other. The magazine concluded that in this world Nokia, which knew the old world so well, would compete head-to-head with the established giants such as Microsoft and Sony.

The acquisition of Vienna Systems Ltd. of Canada in December 1998 exemplified Nokia's new thinking. Nokia aimed to put more emphasis on the Internet Protocol (IP) telephone operations. The change from speech-driven development to data- and IP-driven development can be compared with the jump from analog to digital mobile phone standards, which had enabled Nokia to gain a major market share in voice transmission.

Because of its strategic importance, Nokia paid a relatively high US$90 million for the company. Established in 1996, Vienna Systems employed 189 people and its sales in 1998 totaled C$20 million. Its market share was 12 percent and cumulative losses amounted to C$15 million.

Strategy at crossroads in Beijing: wireless or the Internet?

● China had been important to Nokia for many years, but in the 1990s its importance steadily increased. Nokia had established the first links with China in the 1950s in cable exports. This was followed by telecommunications networks and cable machinery in the 1980s and mobile phone networks in the 1990s. In 1997 Nokia established a regional organization that made China one of the company's most important markets. Nokia underlined cooperation with local authorities and localized as much of its operation as possible.

Nokia's top management recognized China's importance by organizing a Board strategy seminar in Beijing in September 1998. The Board of Directors and members of the top management also met with high-ranking Chinese officials. As background for the strategy, Nokia was doing well at the time. Profits at both the Telecommunications and Mobile Phones divisions exceeded budgeted figures. In a sense, the situation was comparable to that in the 1980s when the main business was cables, which

NOKIA IN CHINA

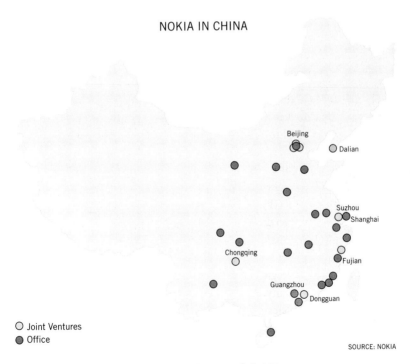

By the end of 2001, Nokia employees in China exceeded 5000.

NOKIA'S NEW BUSINESS DEVELOPMENT

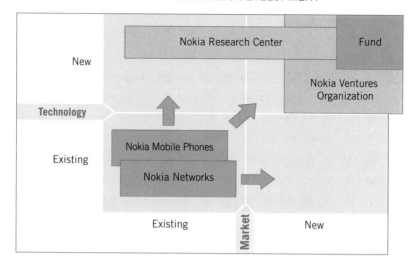

was successful due to its profitable trade with the Soviet Union. But, now as then, Nokia had to prepare alternatives.

The relatively small new venture funds and new business organizations amounted to a mere warm-up for what was to be a grand strategic choice. The question was: how long could Nokia bet its future on the profitability of network and mobile phone products? The key challenges were e-commerce, the development and future sales of mobile phones in a ten-year perspective, the impact of the Internet phone calls on the wireless world and the future structures of the consolidating telecom/datacom industry.

At the strategy seminar in Beijing, Ollila declared that Nokia was at a strategic crossroads. To him, it was a simple matter of choice: Nokia could remain predominantly a wireless player, or it could expand into the new markets opened by the IP technology.

The first choice was not without its attractions. A company focussing on wireless solutions and third generation technologies could achieve substantial growth and profitability in the mid-term. But slower growth later on could jeopardize profitability and render Nokia a takeover candidate.

Ollila said another alternative would be to exploit the paradigm shift as traditional telecom and IP-networking converge. This strategy would entail penetration of the IP area through acquisitions and a strong presence in the United States. It was obvious that this strategy would carry greater risks, in part because of the required acquisitions, but if successful, it could establish Nokia in a long-term sustainable growth position.

Global social responsibility

In the spring of 1998 Nokia publicly defined its corporate citizenship in these terms:

> Nokia, on behalf of itself, its affiliated organizations, its directors, officers, managers, and employees, is committed to being a good citizen, an ethically sound business, and to being a strong supporter of the rule of law wherever it does business. Code of conduct: Ethics and Law, Conflicts of Interest, Gifts and Bribes, Human Rights, Workplace Practices, Implementation.

On the basis of these Nokia published a booklet *The Nokia Way*.

In addition to business strategies, Nokia undertook the mapping of its corporate future environment from other perspectives. Ollila takes (seriously) his role as manager of Nokia's reputation and corporate responsibility on a global scale. The company's corporate culture, ethics and social responsibility are based on four basic values that were adopted at the beginning of the 1990s and have been hammered home on a daily basis. These values aimed to guide employees' actions in their relationship with

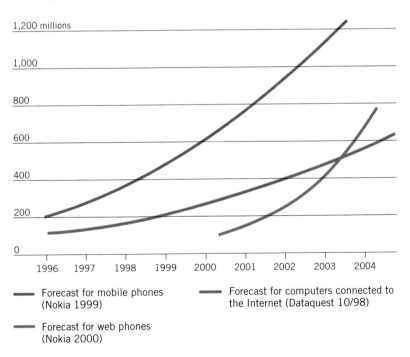

DEVELOPMENT OF INTERNET CONNECTIVITY 1996–2004

customers, colleagues, top management and society. In April of 1999, Nokia's Executive Board approved the company's 'Fundamental Principles and Code of Conduct'.

At the end of the 1990s Nokia produced its first comprehensive environmental report. In cooperation with the International Youth Foundation, Nokia began the 'Make a Connection' program. The first phase of the program was implemented in China, South Africa, Germany, England, Brazil, Mexico and Poland.

In August 2000, the Executive Board approved a refined approach as its guide to corporate social responsibility. It included economic, environmental and social aspects of work life. Nokia has received recognition for its social responsibility and ethical behavior. In June 2000 Nokia joined the World Business Council on Sustainable Development. The same year Nokia was included in the Dow Jones Sustainability Index, and in July 2001 the FTSE4Good index ranked Nokia as one of Europe's 10 leading companies in social responsibility. In 2001 Nokia became the first Finnish company to adopt the Global Compact declaration initiated by the Secretary General of the United Nations.

CHAPTER 18

Living with global share price fluctuations

The stock market is another environment where Nokia felt the impact of the forces of great change. In the late 1990s, share prices of technology companies in the United States rose rapidly, generally much faster than traditional industrial shares. The prices were no longer directly linked to the companies' underlying performance.

The Nokia share price began to climb in the autumn of 1998 as a result of growth prospects of the telecommunications and high technology businesses and Nokia's credibility in managing its growth. When growth expectations rose, the share price rocketed; a more modest growth outlook then caused the share price to plunge.

Share price volatility has constantly increased. For example, in 2000 Nokia shares reached a high of €64.88 and dropped to a low of €39.50. To even out these movements, Nokia took some measures in line with the market rules and regulations. For example, it brought forward the release date for its interim results (for the third quarter in 2000) and announced annual phone sales volumes prior to the release of annual results (in January 2001).

Diversification of the ownership base has increased the influence of independent market analysts. The equity analysts tell investors and the general public their views on which shares are on the rise and which are on the decline, and why. Since individual retail investors do not take a management role in the company and seldom participate in annual general meetings, the analysts, whose comments often move markets, acquire a stronger voice. Indeed, analysts' opinions have become an important counterweight and a controlling force on management.

In the late 1990s Nokia remained domiciled in Finland but its ownership was predominantly American. The Board of Directors was also structured to reflect the wider ownership base, with four nationalities

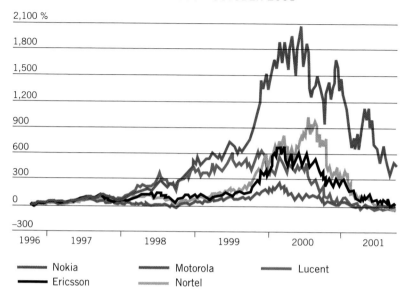

NOKIA AND ITS PEER GROUP SHARE PRICES,
OCTOBER 1996 – OCTOBER 2001

——— Nokia   ——— Motorola   ——— Lucent
——— Ericsson   ——— Nortel

represented among its members. This made it more international than many of the US multinationals.

During the 1990s, Nokia became one of the world's most valuable companies by market capitalization (share price multiplied by the number of shares). In addition to a company's profitability, market capitalization is to a large extent based on the value of its brand. The Nokia brand rose to the top global ranks during the decade, and the real breakthrough took place in 1999–2000.

Members of Nokia Board of Directors 2002

- Jorma Ollila, 51, chairman since 1999, member since 1995
- Paul J. Collins, 65, vice chairman since 2000, member since 1998
- Georg Ehrnrooth, 61, member since 2000
- Bengt Holmström, 52, member since 1999
- Per Karlsson, 47, member since 2002
- Robert F.W. van Oordt, 65, member since 1998
- Marjorie Scardino, 54, member since 2001
- Vesa Vainio, 59, member since 1993
- Arne Wessberg, 58, member since 2001

From large Finnish institutional owners to American retail investors

● Nokia's ownership base has changed profoundly since 1992. The first phase was the reduction in the Finnish institutional ownership and corresponding increase in the holdings of American institutional investors. Nevertheless, Finnish institutions continued to control the high-voting shares despite the constant stream of shares abroad.

The rapid rise in Nokia's share price elevated it to a class of its own in the Finnish economy. The local press welcomed the 1997 results, which had almost doubled from the previous year. *Ilta-Sanomat*, Finland's second biggest newspaper, calculated at the time that Nokia's market value was equal to the combined value of Finland's forest and metal and engineering companies as well as the banks and insurance companies.

Finland's traditionally important forest industry has played a major role, directly and indirectly, as owner of Nokia. UPM-Kymmene, one of Finland's largest – and now one of the world's largest – forest products group, had traditionally held a sizable stake in Nokia. In the spring of 1996 the membership of the Board started to change. Yrjö Niskanen, a former chief executive of the insurance group Pohjola, was not re-elected to Nokia's Board of Directors. His seat was taken by Iiro Viinanen, his successor at Pohjola. However, at Nokia's following annual general meeting in 1997 Niskanen was again elected, this time as representative of UPM-Kymmene.

The reason for the choice dates back to the early 1990s when Niskanen played a key role in the stabilization of Nokia's ownership base and top management base. Meanwhile, Casimir Ehrnrooth, the retired former chief executive and chairman of Kymmene, and a highly influential power broker in Finnish industry, continued as chairman of the Board at Nokia. When the executive committee of the UPM-Kymmene's Board was dismantled, Ehrnrooth moved his office from UPM-Kymmene to Nokia House in Espoo.

Meanwhile, Jorma Ollila was elected member of UPM-Kymmene's Board of Directors in spring 1997. As of summer 1997, UPM-Kymmene began to sell parts of its stake in Nokia, which loosened the historical connection between the two companies.

Nokia's ownership base changed substantially at the end of the 1990s. The number of individual US retail shareholders rose from 30,000 to

130,000 in the 12 months preceding the Annual General Meeting of 1999. In the second half of 2001 the number had jumped to 1.5 million.

Another traditional Nokia shareholder, the Pohjola group, sold some 14 million Nokia shares in February–March 2000 for a price of FIM 17 billion (€2.9 billion). Pohjola had been a key player in the ownership arrangement in 1991 when it distanced itself from the KOP camp and remained a shareholder in Nokia. This helped stabilize Nokia's ownership base. Pohjola's chief executive Yrjö Niskanen and his successor Iiro Viinanen served as vice chairmen of Nokia's Board. The price Pohjola got for its stake was about 400 times higher than it would have got back in 1991 when KOP sold its holding. Niskanen's decision to hold onto the shares was probably the best business decision in the history of Pohjola.

As Nokia's ownership base changed so did its corporate governance model. In the first phase, two large Finnish commercial banks had a direct hold on Nokia. They owned major stakes in the company and their respective chief executives were members of the Board and the Board's executive committee. In the second phase, much of Nokia's shares were bought by US pension funds that had no interest in nominating candidates for the Board. The funds confined themselves to stating their investment policy to the management. If they are not happy with the company, they sell their stakes.

In the third phase, Nokia attracted a huge number of individual retail shareholders. This group lacked a concerted view over management of the company yet they can sometimes act collectively by following the share price development, dividend payout and by following analysts' recommendations.

The world's most valuable brands, 1999–2001
(values expressed in billions of dollars)

			1999	2000	2001
1.	Coca-Cola	USA	83.8	72.5	68.9
2.	Microsoft	USA	56.7	79.2	65.9
3.	IBM	USA	43.8	53.2	52.8
4.	General Electric	USA	33.5	38.1	42.4
5.	Nokia	Finland	20.7	38.5	35.0
6.	Intel	USA	30.0	39.0	34.7
7.	Disney	USA	32.8	33.6	32.6
8.	Ford	USA	33.2	36.4	30.1
9.	McDonald's	USA	26.2	27.9	25.3
10.	AT&T	USA	24.9	25.5	22.8

The value of the brand has been ranked by Interbrand and it is based on the market value, results and other performance indicators.

Nokia used its own shares as payment when it acquired Finlux, the television set manufacturer, in 1992, and since then has paid for all acquisitions with its own shares.

In April 1981 Nokia introduced a dual share structure. This was seen as a move by the banks to consolidate their control at a time when the company needed capital. It included the ordinary K-shares with ten votes each, and the preferential A-shares, each of which had one vote. In 1994 it became possible to exchange K-shares for A-shares. Until then, Finnish shareholders controlled 64 percent of votes in Nokia even though only 33 percent of the shares remained in Finland.

Large Finnish institutions such as Merita bank (the amalgamation of the early chief rivals Union Bank of Finland and Kansallis-Osake-Pankki, later renamed Nordea) and UPM-Kymmene sold large blocks of Nokia K-shares in a period of just a few years. This led to a situation in which a blocking minority of one-third of the votes could have been purchased just by acquiring half of the K-shares, that is for one-tenth of the company's market value. The required investment was so small in global terms that it posed a serious threat of a hostile takeover.

In March 1999 the K-share was abolished through consolidation of the two share classes. At the same time another technical but symbolic measure was taken: the Nokia share became denominated in euros, then at the nominal value of 24 euro cents.

Among the world's 100 largest public companies, Nokia's domestic ownership proportion is the smallest, and Ollila has expressed concern over the Finnish institutions' desire to sell Nokia shares. This deprives the company of a 'safe haven', a shelter against storms in the equity markets. Ollila believes this has put enormous pressure on Nokia. By comparison, about half of Ericsson's shareholders are still Swedish.

On the other hand the ownership structure has made Nokia a pioneer in one sense: it has consistently built its operations according to market expectations. This is also evident in the restructuring of Nokia's corporate governance.

Board of Directors and corporate governance

● Corporate governance creates a framework and guidelines for the Board and top management. Under the rules of procedure confirmed in spring 1997, the Board of Directors would confirm the strategic guidelines, approve annual budgets and action plans as well as investments or

Nokia Board of Directors and Executive Board in front of the Palace on Water in Warsaw, Poland, in 1999. From left: Olli-Pekka Kallasvuo, Yrjö Neuvo, Vesa Vainio, Paul J. Collins, Sari Baldauf, Robert F.W. van Oordt, Iiro Viinanen, Anssi Vanjoki, Jorma Ollila, Veli Sundbäck, Pekka Ala-Pietilä, Matti Alahuhta, Pirkko Ali-talo, Mikko Heikkonen, Edward Andersson, Bengt Holmström, Jouko K. Leskinen and Ursula Ranin.

divestitures exceeding FIM 100 million (€17.8 million) or that were not included in the overall investment frame approved by the Board.

Previously, Nokia had changed its corporate governance structure in 1986 by creating a Supervisory Board and an internal Board of Directors. The roles of chief executive and president were divided between two executives. This model survived until 1990 when the Supervisory Board was replaced by a non-executive Board of Directors. In 1992 the two-pronged top management was dismantled when Jorma Ollila succeeded Kalle Isokallio as president and Simo Vuorilehto as CEO. At the same time a personnel committee was established within the Board of Directors. The Board's audit committee was established in 1996.

The Board was supported by three committees. The traditional executive committee was composed of the Board's chairman, vice chairman and Nokia CEO. The personnel committee was responsible for monitoring the company's personnel policy and making proposals for compensation packages for the CEO and members of the Group Executive Board. The audit committee met with the company's auditors and monitored internal control and supervising systems. The Board normally met eight times a year and a strategy discussion was held at the September meeting.

In December 1997 Casimir Ehrnrooth, chairman of the Board of Directors, made a proposal for Nokia's new corporate governance model. Preparations for the proposal had taken more than a year, and the document included an extensive memorandum, prepared by Ursula Ranin, secretary of the Board and vice president and general counsel, on corporate governance models and discussions on the subject in other countries. Ehrnrooth's proposal aimed to pave the way for the appointment of Nokia's No. 2 executive, and to discuss principles and procedures for considering new Board members.

The new model was influenced by the general principles prevailing in the United States, where more and more of Nokia's ownership was shifting. The most influential document at the preparation stage was probably the recommendations issued in 1997 by the Business Roundtable (BRT) in the US.

Ranin's background memorandum included views and experiences of merging the functions of chairman and CEO. On the positive side the model personified the highest decision-making power and representation. It also provided a good opportunity to carry out the company's vision and focus strongly on the chosen areas.

On the negative side, the model was criticized in cases where the company's poor performance might be attributed to the chief executive, and the Board would be too slow or weak to make the necessary changes. The risk was particularly great in companies where the Board was not independent enough. For instance, it could be composed of people dependent on the top management or who had other strong links with the company. Likewise, the supervisory role of the Board could be compromised, as its chairman is actively involved in running the company. Critics were concerned that excessive concentration of power in one person would weaken the Board in its primary tasks.

Ehrnrooth's model included limitation of Board members' tenure to one year. This was aimed at increasing shareholder influence and providing an opportunity to judge the model's practicality. In addition the

Casimir Ehrnrooth was instrumental in stabilizing the corporate governance of Nokia. He was a member of the Board in 1990–1999 and chairman of the Board from 1992–1999.

Board's executive committee was considered unnecessary and it was discontinued.

Finland's Companies Act requires that the roles of chairman of the Board and president be separated in a publicly quoted company. Following the proposal to appoint Jorma Ollila as chairman and CEO, Nokia needed a new president.

The March 1998 Annual General Meeting approved the proposal for a new corporate governance model. Pekka Ala-Pietilä was appointed executive vice president and deputy to the chief executive officer. Two non-Finnish members, Paul J. Collins and Robert F.W. van Oordt, were elected to the Board, and the official language of Board meetings was changed to English.

Casimir Ehrnrooth's tenure as chairman of the Board came to an end at the 1999 AGM. He had chaired the company since spring 1992, and had been instrumental in the ownership and top management arrangements a year earlier. The Board became more cohesive and effective during Ehrnrooth's watch. The relationship between the Board and top management was smooth and free of conflict. Nokia's ownership also changed during his tenure from Finnish to totally international, corresponding with Nokia's growth to a giant global corporation. All the major governance changes were carried out in a controlled manner, and at the company's own initiative.

Ollila becomes chairman and CEO

● Jorma Ollila's role as the undisputed No. 1 at Nokia was strengthened in March 1999 when he was appointed chairman of the Board of Directors. He continued as chairman of the Executive Board and chief executive officer. At the same time Pekka Ala-Pietilä became president.

This removed the Board's role as traditional counterweight to the operational management. Since the only body remaining above the CEO was the Annual General Meeting of shareholders, the Board's internal control and supervisory functions were strengthened. Iiro Viinanen, deputy chairman of the Board, chaired the Board's personnel committee. Edward Andersson continued as chairman of the Audit Committee, and Iiro Viinanen headed the new Nomination Committee. Compensation for the Board members was also changed; part of their fee would now be paid in Nokia shares.

As Jorma Ollila told a press conference following the decisions concerning a new governance model, the development of the new model began in summer 1997 when Casimir Ehrnrooth expressed his wish to step down. The first move was to abolish the Board's executive committee. The president became chairman and CEO. 'In the end', he said, 'we have ended up with the American chairman-CEO model.'

Ollila stressed that he would retain a firm grip on operational matters. In addition to day-to-day management, Ala-Pietilä was responsible for Nokia's ability to adapt to future changes. Casimir Ehrnrooth called the move a new way of also giving Ollila more recognition and reward for a brilliant job.

Nokia's competitive position

Mobile phones
　　Nokia strong leader,
　　Motorola attempts a comeback, danger from Japan
Wireless infra
　　Nokia strong No. 2 in GSM,
　　competing against Ericsson, Lucent and Nortel
IP networking
　　Nokia focussed player,
　　business dominated by Cisco, Lucent and Nortel
IT-software
　　Nokia in partnerships,
　　business controlled by Microsoft, IBM and Oracle

The headquarters of Nokia Americas in Irving, Dallas.

'Only the titles changed,' headlined *Talouselämä*, the Finnish business magazine, and to some extent this was true. The same people continued to report to Ollila. In addition to Ala-Pietilä they included heads of the largest business units and key support functions: Matti Alahuhta (mobile phones), Sari Baldauf (networks), Olli-Pekka Kallasvuo (finance), Veli Sundbäck (trade policy), Hallstein Moerk (human resources), Ursula Ranin (legal affairs) and Lauri Kivinen (corporate communications).

In addition to his position as president of Nokia, Ala-Pietilä continued as head of Nokia Communications Products and was responsible for the Nokia Ventures Organization and Nokia Ventures Fund. Juhani Kuusi, head of the Nokia Research Center, and Mikko Kosonen, vice president of corporate strategy and information technology, also reported to Ala-Pietilä. At Board meetings, most matters would now be presented by Ala-Pietilä rather than Ollila.

Soon after his appointment, Ala-Pietilä moved to Silicon Valley in California for a few months to focus on future customer needs, technologies and the Internet-based businesses.

The appointment of Ala-Pietilä was not, however, an answer to the question of Ollila's succession. Ollila was still young, and the division of labor was not really affected at the top. The more likely reason for the change in titles was, as Ehrnrooth said, simply a way of rewarding Ollila for a job well done. More importantly the role of the chairman had become too demanding for a part-time position. Casimir Ehrnrooth had spent half of his working hours on it. There also seemed to be no other suitable candidate in Finland to take the position.

The move should be seen as part of the gradual adaptation toward the American-style corporate governance practice as an increasing proportion of Nokia's shares were held there. The strength and independence of Nokia's two key business areas, mobile phones and networks, meant that their respective heads, Alahuhta and Baldauf, had at least as strong a claim to Nokia's de facto No. 2 spot as Ala-Pietilä, who held the nominal position.

While the top management team continued in their old roles, a bigger change took place on the Board where 'owners' stepped down, and the roles changed. The traditional checks and balances between the Board and management were removed and replaced by feedback from the stock market.

Global IP Mobility

● Nokia had become a giant on the strength of its knowhow in mobile communications. In parallel, the Internet grew exponentially and in the late 1990s Nokia had to reassess its strategic architecture within this new environment.

In September 1999, Pekka Ala-Pietilä, who was in charge of new business development and implementation, and now also served as president of the Nokia Group, presented the outline strategy to the Board of Directors.

Called Global IP Mobility, it was a strategy under which Nokia would 'take a leading, brand-recognized role in creating the Mobile Information Society'. This would be achieved by 'combining mobility and the Internet and stimulating the creation of new services'.

The new environment brought about a range of new challenges. For example, the customer base was now much more fragmented and unknown whereas in the past Nokia knew its customers and their requirements rather well. As Ala-Pietilä underlined, it was vitally important to find and create new markets. Likewise, Nokia faced an entirely new competitive environment that required mastering new industrial and other partnerships. In short, Nokia needed to find a new way to conduct business.

Ala-Pietilä believed there were three key elements in Nokia's strategy: enhancing the company's position in mobile phones, shaping and leading the digital convergence market, and steering the markets toward the mobile Internet. It was too early to assess the success of the strategy at the time of writing (early 2002). But the outline described above explains why Nokia has invested massively in new customers, distribution channels, technologies and knowhow.

As outlined by Ala-Pietilä, the cornerstones of the Internet strategy were: orchestration for new markets, application-driven solutions, fully embracing IP Mobility and personal mobile terminals.

Renewal of the organization: products and processes

● The new strategy led to yet another reorganization. The concept of 'platform' has played an important role at Nokia throughout the 1990s. The platform approach allows unification of the technical solutions and components that form the basis for evolving product lines.

In October 1999 Nokia set up Technology and Platform Management with the aim of ensuring the efficient development of mobile phones and 'convergence products'.

Mikko Kosonen recalls that Nokia sharpened its e-business strategy in the autumn of 1999. According to the new outline, the group would aim to integrate economies of scale with agility by developing new, increasingly modular business processes. These would enable:

- Customer-oriented processes; tailoring product and service configurations across organizational borders
- Flexibility in organizational changes and in networking
- Fast inventory cycle through transparency in logistics

Implementation of the processes became the responsibility of the company's information technology and process development organization as well as the e-business program. The two were later merged into the Nokia Business Infrastructure organization. The centralized structure produced economies of scale by developing the required processes and systems once

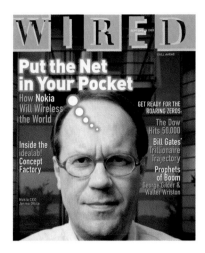

CEO Jorma Ollila on the cover of Wired *in September 1999.*

and adapting them to other applications and business models. Benefits are created by recycling brainpower while agility is derived from reorganizing processes and modules that have already been developed.

Nokia's main business processes are delivery, product creation and support and management functions for business operations.

In the summer of 1999, Nokia refocussed its e-business strategy by making 'mobile e-business' an integral part of its 'Mobile Information Society' vision. A new task force reporting directly to Ollila was established. It comprised the so-called 'owners of the e-business model'. The task force turned the tables by taking the customer's view on how best to deal with and develop new ways to cooperate with Nokia. Mikko Kosonen, one of the key members of the task force, cited Cisco as one example for the model.

The organizational structure was built on a modular process library. Business was divided into processes and their parts. Generally, a business would comprise five processes: procurement, manufacturing, sales, planning and management/supervision.

One of the major issues in mobile phone production is the tension between different standards and customer groups. Traditionally mobile phones had been produced for the existing frequencies and standards, such as NMT and GSM. As the mobile phones became mass consumer product, customers' special requirements became more important than technology. Product categories based on users' needs became more important than standards. So Nokia aimed to move from standards-oriented thinking to production-oriented thinking.

The first designs for the corporate head office at Keilaniemi, Espoo, some 10 kilometers west of Helsinki, were drawn in 1982. The architectural competition was won by the proposal called 'Crystal', by architects Pekka Helin and Tuomo Siitonen of Finland. After numerous delays the final decision on the head office was not made until 1994. The first stage was completed in 1997 and the second stage in 2001. Interior design was by Iiris Ulin of Finland. Nokia's worldwide real estate in 1999 amounted to some 2–2.5 million square meters, including about one million square meters in Finland of which one-half was located in the metropolitan area of Helsinki.

The Nokia Global IP Mobility concept included three areas: personal use, office and home. This gave rise to a new unit, Home Communications.

A major change took place also at the group level when Hallstein Moerk of Norway was appointed senior vice president for human resources. His task was to take a tighter grip on the previously decentralized personnel policy. One element was to create common procedures or 'platforms', similar to the common procedures that were adopted in production.

CHAPTER 19

Convergence of the digital world

A s we have seen, throughout its long history Nokia has been forced again and again to adapt to rapidly a changing marketplace. But as it was emerging as a major company on the global business scene in the 1990s, Nokia would also come to play an important role in shaping the world to come.

The nature of change came in various forms. Telecom operators remained the most important players. They bought the fixed and mobile phone networks and the bulk of the handsets. Alongside them, the Internet world was developing in a decentralized, almost anarchic way with no guiding hand. The third force was standards of telecommunications represented by international organizations and negotiation mechanisms. In this area, equipment suppliers and operators wielded the most influence.

In a 1998 report to the Board, Matti Alahuhta had this to say about the characteristics of the telecommunications industry in the 1990s:

> There are three to five global mega-operators in the world. They are involved in about half of all telecommunications systems procurement in the world. The Internet service providers create a new customer group, currently numbering thousands.

Nokia's Telecommunications division developed rapidly in the early 1990s through international expansion. In June 1997 the group set goals that emphasized support for the development of mobile phone operations and operators' systems, integration of systems and the importance of large operators. The goals would be achieved through quality, operational efficiency and employee and customer satisfaction. Key concepts included 'total mobility', 'integrated services' and 'all digital'.

From the equipment manufacturers' perspective, the nature of telecommunications had changed dramatically. Alahuhta described the change in more detail:

> In the telecommunications value chain, equipment manufacturers will increasingly need to focus on marketing, customer service, systems integration and other functions close to the customer. On the other hand the functions at the front end of the chain can increasingly be outsourced to specialized industry.

Changes in Nokia's customer base originated in deregulation, and the changes have continued. Liberalization gave birth to new operators, followed in the 1990s by more consolidation – the large operators bought up the smaller ones. In addition, new service providers emerged.

The character of Nokia as a company was changing at the same time. Traditionally a hardware manufacturer, Nokia now focussed more on the intangibles. This was evident in the patents, acquisitions and the nature of its partners and projects. In February 2000, Chairman and Chief Executive Ollila told an interviewer:

> While the physical side of Nokia's business in wireless and Internet products is a key driver for the company, the virtual aspect of its business – digital services and e-commerce capabilities – is becoming increasingly important ... Nokia will build bridges between the physical and virtual worlds.

The big battle over the birth of the 3G standard

● International standards usually create the biggest changes in the operating environment of a telecommunications company. The change from analog networks and handsets to digital ones paved the way for Nokia's growth since the late 1980s. The next decade was spent in the preparation for the 3G mobile phone standard. Its technical solutions, timetable and particularly the technological multimedia innovations will have a great impact on Nokia's future. More precisely, what would follow the second-generation digital mobile phone standard in which Nokia had been so successful?

Nokia had established Future Watch groups to analyze technical and market developments. A broad-based and high-level watch group prepared a memorandum on Spectrum Allocation in Mobile Communication at 2GHz in September 1997. The group saw that allocation of spectrum would be the subject of increasing global competition.

Nokia's basic principle was to support technologies that would allow global roaming. The use of frequencies was highly fragmented in different areas, and hence Nokia supported recommendations by the International

TRANSFORMATION PROCESS DRIVING THE 1990s

Nokia's unifying management processes in the 1990s included the deep crisis that touched every employee, followed by the building of common values and by creation of common finance, information and human resources management systems.

Telecommunications Union (ITU). The memorandum also warned against delays in the development process, which could be caused by auctions of frequencies or other factors.

Nokia has consistently contributed to the development of standards since the 1980s. In the 1990s its role increased as its stature in the industry grew. Key aspects in development and cooperation included building bridges between the largest equipment manufacturers, and between manufacturers and operators.

As the mobile phone industry became increasingly global, the aim was to create worldwide standards. The second-generation mobile phone standards were still predominantly regional. Europe had GSM, the United States had the IS-41 standard and the Japanese operated their own Personal Digital Communications (PDC) standard.

Nokia played a key role in the improvement of voice quality in the digital mobile phone networks. In 1996 the European Telecommunications Standards Institute (ETSI) chose Nokia's Enhanced Full-Rate (EFR) voice coding system as the new standard in the GSM- and DCS systems. The American IS-136 Time Division Multiple Access (TDMA) system is based on the same solution. Nokia also played a part in the selection of the voice coding method for the IS-95 Code Division Multiple Access (CDMA) system.

Nokia has helped develop standards for the European GSM and DCS

THE GLOBAL DRIVE TOWARDS 3G

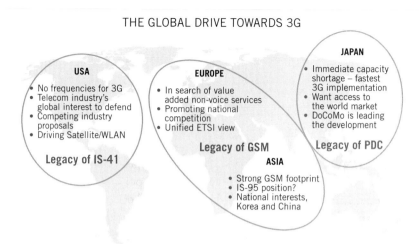

JAPAN
- Immediate capacity shortage – fastest 3G implementation
- Want access to the world market
- DoCoMo is leading the development

USA
- No frequencies for 3G
- Telecom industry's global interest to defend
- Competing industry proposals
- Driving Satellite/WLAN

Legacy of IS-41

EUROPE
- In search of value added non-voice services
- Promoting national competition
- Unified ETSI view

Legacy of GSM

Legacy of PDC

ASIA
- Strong GSM footprint
- IS-95 position?
- National interests, Korea and China

The global drive toward 3G has involved the untangling of web of interests in Europe, the United States and Japan. Based on a slide by Heikki Ahava in 1997.

systems, the American AMPS (Advanced Mobile Phone System), TDMA and CDMA systems, as well as the Japanese PDC systems. In the third-generation wireless systems Nokia took part in the development of the UMTS/FPLMTS (Universal Mobile Telecommunications System/Future Public Land Mobile Telecommunications System) standard.

In 1992 the World Administrative Radio Conference (WARC) decided on the new global frequency 1,900–2,100 MHz, initially dubbed the FPLMTS and later named IMT-2000. The United States had wanted to reserve the frequency for satellite communications but later auctioned parts of it to second-generation mobile phone systems.

The decision formed the basis for the development of the third-generation system. Here, Japan took the lead. Foreign companies such as Nokia were also involved but with a low profile in the early years. The European Union had its own project called FRAMES (Future Wideband Multiple Access System), which was initially driven by Nokia and Siemens. Ericsson joined the project somewhat later. FRAMES was one of the largest telecommunications research projects financed by the EU. The aim was to make a joint proposal to ETSI on the future UMTS system. Although FRAMES failed to reach its ultimate goal, it provided ETSI with most of the technical solutions in the selection process. FRAMES also provided a discussion forum for competing equipment manufacturers.

The dialog between Nokia, Siemens and Ericsson was carried on in a positive atmosphere until July 1997. In August, Siemens surprised the other two by announcing that it had joined forces with Alcatel and Nortel to support the TD-CDMA system. Motorola, Sony, Bosch and several other companies later joined this consortium.

This created battle lines, pitting Nokia and Ericsson against the others. Among larger equipment manufacturers, Lucent and Qualcomm remained neutral. TIM, the Italian operator supported Nokia and Ericsson, and so did NTT DoCoMo, the big Japanese operator. However, Japanese equipment manufacturers supported the opposition.

Discussion of technical aspects quickly turned political, and the battle over operators' votes at ETSI heated up. At the end of November and the beginning of December 1997 operators announced that they would back the solution proposed by Nokia and Ericsson. The vital element was the support by British operators, which had global repercussions.

Nokia knew that its proposal was backed by a majority of votes just prior to the ETSI meeting in Madrid, but not the required majority of 71 percent. Although the issue was a European system, participants aimed to influence the outcome through the United States and Japan. Nokia and Ericsson were accused of opening 'Fortress Europe' to Japanese competition. The two companies called the claim old-fashioned thinking, not compatible with the global competition, which they felt was inevitable.

As neither camp won a required majority and ETSI failed to make a choice, the parties negotiated a compromise solution that was approved the following day. Nokia and Ericsson interpreted the result as a victory.

The solution opened a global battle. American companies started preparations for a counter-strike. Americans wielded a host of weapons including Intellectual Property Rights and the US Congress. The confrontation between the United States and the European Union put a lot of pressure on Japan.

The choice of the 3G standard was not easy in Europe, either. Fixed line operators tried to slow the process, but eventually gave up their resistance. Following complicated global negotiations, a compromise was struck in the autumn of 1998. As a result, a new organization called 3GPP commenced operations in December 1988 with the aim of creating common standards for third-generation radio communications.

Unlike other innovations such as computer software where the sky – or brainpower – is the limit, radio frequencies are strictly limited by nature. They are scarce and vulnerable to disturbance. Hence allocation and standardization of those frequencies cannot be left to market forces alone; international authorities must take control.

Nokia has made it a point to participate actively in the activities of 3GPP. First, development of a common standard is clearly in Nokia's interest, and secondly Nokia has pushed its own technical solutions as part of the standards. A good example is the 3GPP voice codec test in Osaka in October 2000, which Nokia won hands-down (See Chapter 5).

The second stage of focussing: more outsourcing in production and distribution

● At the end of the 1990s Nokia had one foot still firmly in the world of mobile communications while the other was planted amid new Internet solutions, most of which were still blurred ideas on the horizon. Nokia faced the crucial challenge of connecting the two worlds – wireless communications and the Internet – and in a way that would secure its own future in the process.

Although Nokia was the undisputed leader in mobile phones, the company felt an increasing need for cooperation with various kinds of partners. This was starting to happen on two levels. Traditionally Nokia cooperated with subcontractors who supplied parts or components. Later the company outsourced parts of the production chain to other manufacturers. The second form of cooperation entailed creation of new markets. Nokia had engaged in cooperative deals with its biggest competitors, including Motorola and Ericsson, to promote the proliferation of wireless and other technical standards. The potential growth of the whole industry was seen as more important than pushing one's own narrow interests. All parties, however competitive, understood that a company can only prosper in growing markets.

Creation of new markets required close cooperation with companies and with regulators. Nokia announced that it would seek a broad range of cooperation. Some of the partnerships hardly managed to leave the starting blocks while others have developed into extensive and complex cooperative ventures.

Nokia took a new approach in building alliances and partnerships. The aim in its core businesses, mobile phones and networks, was to rationalize and increase efficiency. Its resources were focussed on areas and operations that would add most value. Already a world leader, Nokia aimed to continue being a pioneer and to make the markets.

Outsourcing in mobile phone production differs considerably from outsourcing in the network industry. In mobile phones, product cycles are short and volumes large. In networks, cycles are considerably longer but volumes are smaller. Nokia began outsourcing in networks in the early 1990s. But in mobile phones, production efficiency and quality control are of paramount importance, and hence Nokia has kept most of the production, over 80 percent, in its own hands.

Nokia started to develop systematically network production towards larger entities. In network production, it started to outsource ever larger entities – even complete base stations. Previously it had subcontracted only parts or modules. The logic behind this stemmed from the so-called 'core vs. context' thinking. Nokia made a distinction between operations deemed too important to outsource, and the rest. The latter would be outsourced as efficiently as possible. Reasons for keeping production at Nokia could include patents or other intellectual property rights (IPR), higher than average margins, speed, or the possibility of controlling some larger business.

Nokia's business partnerships at the end of the 1990s

- Nokia and Intel, integration of the Internet and digital television
- Nokia and IBM, e-business in the mobile Internet; enterprise WAP-solutions
- Symbian: the joint venture formed by Nokia, Ericsson and Motorola with Psion PLC of Britain, Symbian aims to develop an operating system.
- Bluetooth (Bluetooth Special Interest Group). Grew in two years to a group whose core partners in addition to Nokia include 3Com, Ericsson, Intel, IBM, Lucent, Microsoft, Motorola and Toshiba. Some 1,200 companies had joined as adopters.
- 3Com, Aironet, Intersil, Lucent Technologies, Nokia and Symbol Technologies formed an alliance to promote the compatibility of the wireless LAN systems in different operating environments.
- Nokia and Visa, payment solutions for mobile e-commerce.
- Ericsson, Nokia and RTS Wireless, mobile Internet with AOL Europe.
- Nokia and Fuji Photo Film, Bluetooth wireless digital photo transmission solutions.
- Nokia and Motorola, standardization for 1XTREME technology.
- Ericsson, Matsushita, Motorola, Nokia and Siemens join in the MeT, initiative to secure mobile electronic transactions.
- Nokia joined MasterCard's payment system project.
- Nokia and Cable & Wireless to develop global mobile Internet platform.
- Alcatel, Ericsson, Nokia and Siemens, Wireless World Research Forum (WWRF).

In base stations, for instance, Nokia would make the first version it-self. In this case 'core' would include learning, speed, IPR and full control. After that it would outsource the production of the various versions for different countries and frequencies. Here the term 'context' would mean more efficient use of own resources and production efficiency. Nokia aimed for a 'win-win' situation whereby the partner company was offered a contract that would help its business prosper while also supporting Nokia. For example, in base stations Nokia has offered partners not only production but also maintenance business.

Matti Alahuhta says that in Telecommunications some 60 percent of the production of high-volume base stations was outsourced in 1998. The figure was considerably lower in Fixed Access Systems (FAS). The same year Nokia sold one of its production plants in Oulu to SCI Systems of the United States. Alahuhta explained his reasons for the deal:

> This arrangement brought the world's leading contract manufacturer practically next door to our main plants (base station plant in Oulu and transmission system plant in Haukipudas). This creates a good basis for further outsourcing of production in future. It also improves both the cost efficiency of our production as well as flexibility.

Flexible production control and logistics became increasingly important. A telling example is that for 2002 the difference between the lowest and highest estimates in mobile phone production was as wide as the total production in 1999. Nokia aimed to increase production without building new production plants or adding employees. To achieve the goal, Nokia designed products for greater ease of manufacture, improved processes, made automation more flexible and outsourced operations.

Outsourcing was gradually extended to new levels to increase production efficiency. By 1999, some 13 percent of the company's mobile phone production operations were outsourced, and the figure was rising. Meanwhile, fixed production costs and direct personnel costs accounted for only 7–9 percent of mobile phone's net retail price.

As mobile phones were increasingly packed with new features, Nokia began to work more closely with content producers, game designers and the entertainment industry.

Convergence – of information technology and telecommunications – has been one of the main issues in Nokia since the 1980s. One example is the aim to integrate the television set and computer terminal. This never quite caught on, although it could still happen in the coming era of digital television. Nokia made some inroads into this area at the end of the 1990s. As part of the convergence process distinctions between equipment

The Nokia logistics center was built in Fort Worth, Texas in 1994. From left: Ross Perot Jr., Todd Hertzberg of Nokia, Deborah Kastrin of Texas Instruments, Kay Granger, Kari-Pekka Wilska, Anssi Räty and John Robinson. Wilska has worked with Nokia Mobile Phones since the beginning of the 1970s. He was involved in the establishment of Mobira, the joint venture between Nokia and Salora. He has spearheaded Nokia's operations in the United States since the late 1980s, and he is president of Nokia Americas Inc.

manufacturers and software producers became blurred. In the spring of 1999 Nokia concluded that telecommunications, data networks and IT players will integrate in order to establish a leading position in future markets.

Alahuhta, head of Mobile Phones, told the Board there was 'chaos in product categories and uncertainty about the winner'. He was referring to the multitude of roles and uses of voice and data, the field composed of multiservice telephones, palm-top computers, cameras and recorders, where new combinations of digitalization, mobility and software were constantly merging and morphing throughout the world.

Technologies and business operations were evolving rapidly. Baldauf estimated that successful companies received some 20–30 percent of their income from partnership products. Nokia focussed strongly on the mobility of home and office, in other words, bringing wireless and convergence-promoting telecommunications solutions to everybody.

The huge changes brought about another important challenge for the Nokia managers: how to keep a giant company together as a cohesive entity. Decentralized decision-making and freedom without a clear,

In the spring of 2002 Nokia introduced model 7650 that has an integrated digital camera. It can send and receive pictures, audio and text by MMS and e-mail. It has a color display, graphical user interface and a joystick with 5-way navigation.

Nokia developed the WAP 1.1 browser for its Nokia 7100 mobile phone, adding a mobile dimension to the Internet.

unifying strategy can lead to disintegration. Cohesion was severely tested in the early 1990s when the company went through a financial and management crisis.

Following the crisis, Nokia management started building corporate-wide values more systematically. They were developed and maintained by a cascading dialog, from top management down to functions, business areas and regions.

In the second half of the 1990s, top management strengthened the role of corporate support functions, including finance, information and human resources. The crisis at Mobile Phones had created more pressure and eventually brought about the unification of group control mechanisms. The next step was taken at the information systems level, which created a common corporate-wide system. The basis for a new process-oriented organization was now taking shape.

For example, Nokia's competitive edge in the fast-growing mobile phone markets is partly based on continuous innovation and new products. At the PT/Expo-Comm Fair in Beijing in October 1998, Nokia launched its High Capacity solution for the GSM network. This multiplied the capacity and performance of the GSM network ten-fold. Base station capacity doubled to 400,000 subscribers. At the same time investment costs declined markedly. This was achieved through better products such as the GSM station switchboard, home location register, base station, base station controller as well as new service concepts in education, network design and communication.

WWW.Nokia.com users	
	Million hits
1995	0.1
1996	0.5
1997	1.5
1998	7.0
1999	47.0

Nokia's Internet home page became an increasingly important tool for communication in the late 1990s. The Internet and e-mail have provided new avenues for contacting users. The open, Internet-based Forum Nokia was established in 1995. It allows the general public to take part in the development of services and solutions for Nokia's products. In 2001, Forum Nokia consisted of some 500,000 program developers around the world.

Nokia expects a large number of multimedia messaging services (MMS) messages over mobile phones. In the spring of 2002, Nokia introduced model 7650 that has an integrated digital camera. It can send and receive pictures, audios and text by MMS and e-mail. It has a color display, graphical user interface and a joystick with 5-way navigation.

Conglomeration or narrower business focus?

● At the conclusion of this saga, it might be worth reflecting on the pros and cons of the conglomerate structure versus the sharper focus of a corporation – the eternal dilemma of every large and dynamic company, including Nokia.

Like many other conglomerates, Nokia's history contains major changes as the company oscillated between diversified decision-making and more centrally controlled management. It is impossible to say which of the two models would have performed better historically. Each must be judged against its historical context and, above all, against operational results.

The chosen model in the early decades of the informal Nokia

grouping, from the beginning of the 1920s until 1966, was decentralization. The first step toward more centralized management was taken at
the beginning of 1967 with the formation of Oy Nokia Ab. This resulted
in a more uniform approach to personnel management, research and development, and corporate culture. But most of all it became evident in
finance: all major investments were decided at group level.

Nokia clearly benefited from the centralized approach in trade with
the centrally controlled Soviet economy. Nokia's cable exports had established the company's brand in Moscow, paving the way for electronics
exports. The pendulum of central control reached full swing in the mid-
1980s when the leading executives at the head office became an internal
Board of Directors and got involved in operational issues at the level of
business areas – sometimes sidelining the heads of those businesses.

Nokia in 2002

- Sales office
- Research and development
- Production, incl. joint ventures

The mid-1980s also saw a marked change in the spirit of the times when the closed economies of the Cold War era began to crumble. In the new atmosphere, decentralized management would perhaps have proved more appropriate. At the same time the proliferation of computers and data networks resulted in more decentralized information systems.

Nokia streamlined its corporate structure at the beginning of the 1990s by selling old, non-core businesses. The remaining business areas, telecommunications (Telecommunications, later Nokia Networks) and Nokia Mobile Phones, were given a larger measure of independence. Following a logistics crisis at Mobile Phones in the mid-1990s, corporate management assumed a larger role in coordinating procedures in information systems, financial control and personnel management.

Conglomerates were defended on the classic grounds: when one

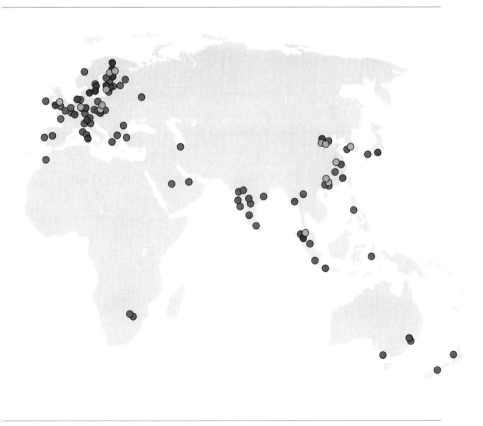

industry suffers a downturn, better performance at another industry may compensate. The traditional defense for the more focussed company was that competitive edge can be sharpened by concentration of resources on familiar businesses. There is no simple way to prove one superior to the other. But no theory of corporate structure can override the knowledge in the specific logic of each business area and the requirements for profitable growth.

I would summarize the Nokia success factors as they eventually emerged in these terms: the creation of a clear and straightforward business strategy, consistent execution of strategy, creation of an inspirational work atmosphere and the recruitment of talented personnel. Perhaps even more important was the identification of high-growth business areas, first the cellular networks, then the handsets. All of these factors came together in the later 1990s to put Nokia on the map as a leading global corporation.

Nokia facts and figures, 1987–2001

Deflated to 2000 values

	Group Sales, mill eur	Group Operating Profit, IAS, mill eur	NMP Operating Profit, mill eur	NET Operating Profit, mill eur	Group Personnel	Percentage of NMP Sales of the Group
1987	3,367	295			29,300	
1988	4,991	249			44,600	5
1989	4,869	129			41,300	8
1990	4,466	144			37,300	10
1991	2,990	-19	14	7	29,100	16
1992	3,453	55	83	81	26,770	20
1993	4,384	271	176	182	25,801	26
1994	5,532	659	320	312	28,043	35
1995	6,686	910	318	494	31,948	43
1996	7,076	768	258	537	31,766	54
1997	9,380	1,507	684	723	35,490	51
1998	13,992	2,489	1,617	1,008	41,091	60
1999	20,365	4,025	3,192	1,114	51,177	66
2000	30,376	5,776	4,879	1,358	58,708	72
2001	31,191	3,362	4,521	-73	57,716	74

Market value of all stocks at years end, mill eur	Percentage of Personnel in Finland	NMP production, millions of units	NMP production, yearly growth %	NMP world market share %	R&D, mill eur
1,928					140
1,632	48				239
1,152					246
677		0.5	72		235
714	50	0.8	57		191
1,000	51	1.6	97		212
3,493	54	2.5	59	18	272
9,103	53	5	119	20	355
8,850	56	11	92	24	460
13,595	57	15	42	22	632
19,613	54	21	42	19	813
61,590	47	41	92	24	1,208
215,652	42	79	92	28	1,755
222,876	40	128	62	32	2,584
137,163	41	140	9	37	2,985

Index